"This isn't your typical UFC [ ] and takes a hard look at each c[ ]t she can uncover. She presents the pros and cons [ ]aders make up their own minds. All of this makes for one of the best UFO books I have read recently."
   —Alejandro Rojas, UFO Researcher and Journalist, Emcee
      for the International UFO Congress

"I read *Montana UFO's and Extraterrestrials* twice before I picked up another book. Joan Bird made me. She writes engagingly and convincingly about a topic that has invited too many lesser efforts."
   —Tom Harpole, award-winning writer and journalist,
      frequent contributor to *Smithsonian* and other national
      magazines.

"Joan Bird writes with clarity and ease as readers are gently pulled into the nexus of her research, only to discover that her velvet hammer has shattered what they once believed could not possibly be true. Please, read this book."
   —Rebecca Hardcastle Wright, PhD, author, *Exoconsciousness:
      Your 21st Century Mind*

"I am very impressed with this book. It provides a great deal of information leading to the rational conclusion that there have been visits to Montana and elsewhere by intelligently controlled alien craft. Bird has dug much more deeply than most investigators."
   —Stan Friedman, Nuclear physicist, Lecturer, Author

"Highly recommended—for Montana and beyond."
   —John Hart, Ph.D., Professor of Christian Ethics, Boston
      University School of Theology; author of *Cosmic Commons:
      Spirit, Science, and Space*

"Bird's copious research and personal interviews result in a judicious hypothesis that ETs should not be feared, but embraced as a part of our history, culture, and consciousness. This book is a must-read for skeptics and believers and even those Not-So-Sure!"
—Dr. Ardy Sixkiller Clarke, author of *Encounters with Star People: Untold Stories of American Indians*

"It's probably one of the best books on UFOs that I've read during the past 10 years. Good research. Beautifully documented. All explained very clearly. Good work!"
—Chris Rutkowski, Astronomer, UFO Researcher, Science Writer and Educator

"I congratulate Joan Bird for her dedication and persistence in composing this book about a subject which unfortunately remains out-of-bounds for many, but which will prove to be of immense importance in the scientific, social, and spiritual evolution of the human race."
—Richard K. O'Connor, M.D., Founder of the Jesse A. Marcel Memorial UFO Library

"Joan Bird's book is impressive. It certainly stands head and shoulders above the vast majority of works published in the UFO field."
—Warren Aston, Australian UFO Researcher and Author

"If you had seen what Tom Schmidt, his brother Jerry, their dog, and I saw at dusk at the sandlot ball field in 1959 [in Great Falls, Montana], you would already be reading this book. We witnessed a round, glowing disk, maybe 100 yards directly above our heads, which appeared three separate times in rapid succession before vanishing. The dog went crazy and we all ran for the house! Tom and I were 6th-grade, first-team, all-city Little Leaguers. We could hit any of the pitchers: We had good eyes…."
—Hal Harper, Former Speaker of the House, Montana Legislature

# MONTANA UFOs
## AND EXTRATERRESTRIALS

### JOAN BIRD

RIVERBEND
PUBLISHING

*Montana UFOs and Extraterrestrials*
© 2013 Joan Bird

ISBN 13: 978-1-60639-057-3

Printed in the United States of America.

6 7 8 9 MG 24 23 22

Cover design by Sarah E. Grant
Text design by Barbara Fifer
Cover photo of Heaven's Peak, Glacier National Park, Montana, by Christopher Cauble
Spaceship image by iStock Photo

Riverbend Publishing
P.O. Box 5833
Helena, MT 59604
1-866-787-2363
www.riverbendpublishing.com

# Contents

INTRODUCTION .. . .. . .. .. .. .. .. .. .. .. . 11

1
NICK MARIANA'S "MONTANA MOVIE" .. . .. . .. . .. . 15

2
UFOs AND THE MINUTEMAN MISSILES.. . .. . .. . .. .. 77

3
CEREAL MYSTERY: CROP CIRCLES IN MONTANA . .. . .. ..119

4
THE CANYON FERRY SIGHTING — OR SOCORRO COPYCAT?.. . ..147

5
THE LEO DWORSHAK CONTACT CASE . .. . .. .. . .. . ..161

6
THE UDO WARTENA CONTACT CASE . .. . .. .. . .. .. . ..187

AFTERWORD. .. . .. . .. . .. .. . .. .. .. . .213

BIBLIOGRAPHY .. . . .. . .. .. . .. . .. . .. . 222

INDEX . .. . .. .. . .. . .. .. .. .. .. . ..227

*To the people of Montana, that these pieces of our history
may not be lost.*

*And to the witnesses, whether you have spoken or not. May you
someday be free from fear of ridicule and persecution,
and lay claim to the validity of
your own perceptions and experiences.*

# ACKNOWLEDGMENTS

The writing and publication of this book would never have been possible without the Herculean efforts of the UFO researchers who came before me, and the assistance, support and encouragement of numerous friends, family members and colleagues. If I have forgotten anyone, please forgive me. At my age, that likelihood grows daily.

For granting permissions, interviews, inspiration and otherwise contributing to my research, I would like to thank the following people, some now in spirit:

Gil Alexander, Colin Andrews, Warren Aston, Jon Axline, Bill Bahny, Robert Barrow, Louise Bowman, Bob Brown, Mary Castner, Jerome Clark, Sandra Corcoran, Tom Cottle, Lynda Croonquist Cowan, Tom Danenhower, Thom Davis, Robert Dean, John Dell, Jim Doerter, Monte Dolack, Richard Dolan, Leo and Ryniene Dworshak, Richard Ecke, Joel and Kelly Flynn, Timothy Good, Jeff Goodrich, Barry Greenwood, Fran Hankinson, Terry Hansen, Paola Harris, John Hart, Robert Hastings, Jimi and Dana Hughes, Linda Moulton Howe, Beth Ihle, Michael Jamison, Shannon Kelly, Clynt King, Herb Koenig, Ed Komarek, Martin Kidston and the *Independent Record*, Jim Klotz, Ann Kreilkamp, Dave Krogstad, Barbara Lamb, Tom Lawrence, Robert Lelieuvre, Ted Loman, Wayne MacLean, John Mack, Luis Fernando Mustajo Maertens, Jesse Marcel, Jr., Nick Mariana, Jr., and Michele Mariana, Karen and Ken McLean, Judy Mickelson, Edgar Mitchell, Barbara Mittal and the *Great Falls Tribune*, Emma Doig Morrison, Randolph Morsette, Dick O'Connor, Jerry Puffer, Barry Potter, Dean Radin, Daniel Reeves, Francis Ridge and the archivists at NICAP, Jim Robbins, Mark Rodeghier and the CUFOS contributors and supporters, Peter Russell, Robert Salas, Michael Salla, Leon Secatero, Marcia Shafer, Robert & Shirley

Short, Brian Shovers and all the staff at the Montana Historical Society Library, Freddy Silva, Rod Skenandore, Ray Stanford, Jennifer Stein, Wendelle and Cece Stevens, Raland Strom, Curt Synness, Judy Swanson, Nancy Talbott and the BLT Research Team, Dana Thelin, Jeffrey W. Thomas and the Ohio Congressional Archives, Veronica Vertes, Treva Voreyer, Donald Ware, Scott Wartena, Melody (Mega) Watts, Jeffrey Wilson, Keith Wolverton, and Rebecca Hardcastle Wright.

For help with proofreading and cheerleading, special thanks to Julia Cougill, Phyllis Lefohn, and Jo Smith.

For tech support and encouragement, Jim Lubek.

For friendship, sharing your stories and general moral support to affirm my sanity and help me stay the course, my appreciation to friends in body and spirit:

Bunny Albers, Jill Alexander, Marilyn Alexander, Barda Allen, Susan Allred, Jami Anesi, Suzy Metcalf Baldwin, Andrea Bateen, Sandy Bellingham, Virginia Bird (Aunt Ginny), Stella Bennett, Tahdi Blackstone, Lynn Bowman, Mary Bradshaw, Nancy Briggs, Susan Burns, Marta Bush, Cate Clark, Marla Clark, Nancy Cobble, Sylvia Connick, Deb Corcoran, Bruce Day, Christy Dodson, Jay Dufrechou, Candace Durran, Sharon Elliott, Julia Evans, Judy Fay, Marilyn Fitzgerald, Beverly Fox, Liz Gans, Lynn Gardner, Marta Royo Gelabert, Mitzi Grover, Florence Guest, Brenda Lindlief Hall, Keith Hamilton, Sarah Hannah, Hal Harper, Linda Hassler, Susan Hemion, Charlotte Henson, Whit Hibbard, Joy Holloway, Ella & Nick Hungria, Alice Hutchinson, Lynn James, Star and Brian Jameson, Cathy Jenkins, Terri John, Kathryn Kelley, Maureen Kiely, Diana King, Linda King, Chuck Kinney, Adelle Klungland, Leah Lambert, Mary Lansing, JoEllen Legg, Jeannette Leimel, Patti Linnell, Orlinda Lusher, Beverly Magley, Charles Mann, Patrick Marsolek, Kathy Martinka, Pam Mavrolas, Brenda McClellan, Suzanna McDougal, Dwayne McNeil, Will Michael, Lillian Michalsky, Sheryl Mooney, Terry Mills, Lois

Neal, Rick Newby, Christine Neilson, Connie O'Conner, James O'Dea, Sharon O'Hara, Donna Porter, George Prudden, Marvie Redmond, Peter and Judith Reynolds, Generessa Rose, Bill & Julie Ryder, Lynda Saul, Marc Scow, Mary Sexton, Sharon Schell, Sandra Smiley, Mariahn Smith, Pam Sommer, Baker Stocking, Alexandra Swaney, Paula Tarvid, Cherryl Taylor, Gwin Taylor, Donna Therkelson, Valann Valdason, Sharon Valentine, Julia Vincent, Jim West, Jeannette Whitney Williams, Ann Wilsnack, Wilbur and Elizabeth Wood and Mary Yeshe.

My deep gratitude also to:

Everyone on my "UFO List," for your contributions, your comments, and your willingness to learn and explore.

My deceased parents, Daniel K. and Mary Ella Howell Bird, for their many gifts, of which critical thinking, a passion for learning and compassion for the world have been especially valuable.

My huge, wonderful family, and especially my brother Mike and his wife Mirka, my sister Mary Kay and her husband David, my aunt Jean Kay McClelland and my son, Amory Genter, who loved and supported me even when this was not their thing.

Janet Spencer, Chris Cauble and everyone at Riverbend Publishing for marrying me to this task, careful reading and questioning of the manuscript, and all the myriad details that go into publishing a book.

And finally my dear life partner, Maxwell Milton, who has been an unfailing source of support, encouragement, and stability, and without whom this book could never have been written.

# INTRODUCTION

Congratulations, dear reader. By picking up this book, you have demonstrated your capability to push through the "ridicule barrier" in our culture and question what the dominant culture has told you is true. Because humans are highly social animals, this is not an easy step for most people to take.

How do we humans come to know what we know? Believe what we believe? The answer is not simple. Life experience is important, and so is our family of origin, the schools and community we grew up in, and the culture that surrounds us. By the time we reach adulthood, we like to think we've pretty much figured out most things. What we've learned and done so far has kept us alive, so we're not too keen on changing our understanding of the world and our role in it, our beliefs about "what it's all about."

Nevertheless, it's clear we've not all arrived in the same place in our "worldviews." Consensus reality seems to be a thing of the past, if it ever existed. Here at the dawn of the Third Millennium, we may have more "worldviews" to choose from than at any time in history, and they are colliding. This is both unsettling and liberating.

If security is very important to us, then we may resist information that "rocks" our understanding of the way things are. But if truth is important to us, we will be more open to that which challenges our worldview. This book is not for those ruled by the need for security. It is for those secure enough within themselves to be open to new information, and humble enough to know they might not have all the answers.

I invite you to accompany me on a journey that has not been easy, but it has been gratifying and wondrous. To introduce myself, your prospective guide, let me tell you a little about my background. I came to Montana in 1973 to pursue graduate work in zoology at the University of Montana. I was twenty-four. Over the next ten years I was thoroughly steeped in evolutionary biology and scientific methodology. I studied inter-island variation in West Indian finches and eventually completed my Ph.D. in zoology and animal behavior.

My family of origin valued education, especially in science. My father left his family wheat farm and earned one of the first aeronautical engineering degrees in 1948 in Wichita, Kansas, "Air Capital of the World." My mother's family, like many others in the Great Depression, struggled to make ends meet, but she was able to complete a college degree with a scholarship she received as valedictorian of her high school graduating class. My older brother became a planetary scientist. One of his career achievements was an experiment on board the Cassini-Huygens Mission to Titan, Saturn's largest moon. My younger sister earned an M.S. in Library Science and was Collection Manager for the Wichita Public Library until her retirement in 2011. We are all lifelong learners, with a heavy bent toward rationalism and critical thinking.

There is another piece important to my background. In 1963 my mother had to undergo closed heart surgery, a dangerous operation on a beating heart with a fifty percent mortality risk. A few hours after surgery, my mother's heart arrested, and she was technically dead for several minutes. She was revived and eventually recovered, though never to her previous strength. During that period of no heartbeat, my mother had what is now known as a "near-death experience." Years later, books came out about the astounding similarities in these experiences and their after-effects on people's lives.

My mother's case was a classic example. She had complete memory of that time, including meeting her own mother who had died six months earlier and other wondrous experiences she struggled to find words for, while tears welled in her eyes during the telling. I remember especially her saying she had never felt so surrounded in love. My mother had always been a staunch Methodist and a deeply moral person, but this experience had a truly profound effect on her life. Among other things, she entirely lost her fear of death. Her near-death experience is part of my heritage.

So I have a critical mind with a great respect for knowledge and scientific method. And I am comfortable with the fact that there are some things that science just can't explain, at least not yet. Perhaps that is why I have always had an interest in those pieces of information that don't quite fit into the dominant worldview. This is how I ended up studying what we in the trade call "ufology."

Like many Americans living in the mainstream scientific materialist world, the subject of UFOs was out-of-bounds for me for the first forty-nine years of my life. I worked predominantly in the science-based fields of ecology and conservation. As I moved into writing, a series of circumstances led me through a door I had not previously opened. In fact, I did not even know the door was there.

Although curious about the topic of extraterrestrial life, I was basically convinced it was highly unlikely that extraterrestrial spacecraft were visiting Earth. For the most part, I accepted the dominant viewpoint that people who had these sightings or spoke of contact were deluded and even laughable. However, once I walked through that wall of prevailing opinion, I was astonished to find a vast literature and a mass of evidence I had had no idea existed. Because this is such a huge field of study, I chose to begin right here in my own backyard. It has been an amazing journey of discovery. In this book, I invite you to accompany me as I retrace those first footsteps and introduce you to some of that evidence.

I was surprised to learn that some of the most famous UFO cases happened in Montana. Those of us who live in Montana share a certain amount of regional pride and like to think we know something about the history of this place. I submit that here you will find some missing chapters. Some of these cases are so significant everyone in Montana ought to know about them. Yet their importance extends beyond the state's boundaries. They are key parts of the whole hidden history of unexplained flying objects on planet Earth.

It is my goal to use these well-documented events as a "UFOs 101" course with regional roots. By putting these local events into a larger context, whoever reads this book will have a good introduction to the study of UFOs and some of its most significant players.

Montana is known for its vast open spaces, sparsely populated landscapes, and legendary "Big Sky." Much of its original wild spirit remains. Maybe it's not only the humans who have been drawn here to imbibe it.

# 1

# NICK MARIANA'S "MONTANA MOVIE"

*…Mariana's was the one sighting of all time that did more
than any other single case to convince me
that there is something to the UFO Problem.*
David R. Saunders, Ph.D.
Condon Committee investigator

Not many people owned movie cameras in 1950. Nick Mariana, a graduate of the University of Montana School of Journalism, once caught a train wreck on film that made the nightly news.[1] Ever after, Mariana kept his 16mm Revere movie camera[2] at the ready in the glove box of his car. His preparedness paid off. On August 15, 1950, Mariana captured the first known movie of "flying saucers" anywhere in the country. He filmed them from the parking lot of the Legion Ballpark in Great Falls, Montana.

Mariana's fifteen-second film is famous in UFO history. Its impact includes the conversion of many UFO skeptics, and it is interwoven with the long, tangled history of government investigations and policies regarding UFOs. Following its circuitous trail, this chapter is a short course in the history of American ufology, and an introduction to many of its major players. The literature about this film is fraught with discrepancies, even in recent historical accounts, so I've made an effort to locate primary sources and untangle the threads, wherever possible.

Capt. Edward J. Ruppelt, head of the U.S. Air Force Project Blue Book responsible for investigating UFOs from 1952 to 1953, called it the "Montana Movie." It is widely considered to be what Mariana always said it was: footage of two, silvery, flying "discs" not resembling anything known to exist then or now. Among other roles, the film was featured in the first feature-length UFO documentary, *U.F.O.: Unidentified Flying Objects* (1956).[3] The section of the documentary with the clip of Mariana's original scratchy footage is easily found on the Internet, often accompanied by footage of Mariana telling the story of his sighting and filming. Here is a transcription of Mariana's narrative from the documentary:

> My name is Nick Mariana. For the past 6 years I've been the general manager of a minor league baseball club called the Electrics.[4] We play out of Great Falls, Montana, and are a farm club of the Brooklyn Dodgers.
>
> On August 15,[5] 1950, at Legion Ball Park in Great Falls, Montana, after a couple of hours in the clubhouse office, I went up into the grandstand to call the groundskeeper. As I reached the top of the stairway, I glanced northward to the tall Anaconda Company smokestack to check the direction of the wind from the white smoke. Force of habit, I suppose because our outfielders use it as an indicator on defensive play. As I looked up I saw two silvery objects moving swiftly out of the northwest. They appeared to be moving directly south. The objects were very bright and about 10,000 feet in the air. They appeared to be of a bright shiny metal, like polished silver. Both were the same size and were traveling at the same rate of speed, which was much slower than the

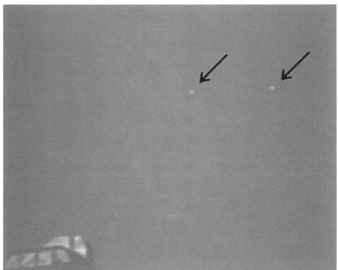

*Above: Mariana's slightly blurry, color movie film translates poorly to printing in black and white, but the two silvery objects can be seen approaching the water tower near the baseball field. Below: The UFOs are closer to passing behind the water tower. Mariana and others said the Air Force confiscated an earlier portion of the film that showed the objects closer and hovering.*

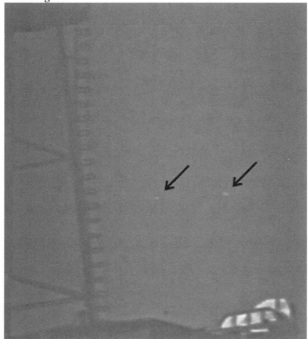

jets which shot by shortly after I filmed the discs. Suddenly they stopped. It was then I remembered the camera in the glove compartment of my car. I raced downstairs, yelling for my secretary, Miss Virginia Raunig. The distance from the top of the stairway to my car is about 60 feet, and I must have made that in about six jumps. I asked my secretary if she saw anything, and she said, "Yes, two silvery spheres." I unlocked the glove compartment of my car, took out the camera, turned the telephoto lens on the turret into position, set the camera at F-22, picked up the objects in the viewfinder and pressed the trigger.

The discs appeared to be spinning like a top, and were about 50 feet across and about 50 yards apart. I could not see any exhaust, wings, or any kind of fuselage. There was no cabin, no odor, no sound, except I thought I heard a whooshing sound when I first saw them. As the film clicked through the camera, I could see the objects moving southeast behind the General Mills grain building, and the black water tank directly south of the ballpark. I filmed the objects until they disappeared into the blue sky, behind the water tank.

Nick Mariana was born in Miles City, Montana, on August 20, 1913, to Italian immigrant parents. Although his father never learned to speak English, Nick adapted easily to American culture. He augmented the family income with a newspaper route, even selling papers to famed western artist Charlie Russell during Russell's final years in Miles City.[6] This early newspaper experience may have given Mariana the journalism bug. While still a teen, Mariana made a name for himself as a pitcher in American Legion Junior League baseball.[7] According to his daughter, he was offered a full contract with the Brooklyn Dodgers right out of high school, but he had set his sights on college.[8]

In 1937, Mariana earned a B.A. from the highly regarded Journalism School at the University of Montana. In 1939, he married Claretta Dunn, a theater major from Great Falls College who hailed from Irish immigrant stock in Butte, Montana. From June 19, 1943, until October 26, 1945, Mariana served in the Army Air Corps as editor of a newspaper, *The Northern Dispatch*, published on the East Air Base in Great Falls. He attained the rank of corporal before his honorable discharge.[9] This experience undoubtedly gave Mariana some familiarity with the world of military aircraft.

Mariana had a great love for sports, especially baseball. He was at one time the youngest referee in the Montana Officials Association. Although he turned down a career as a major league player, he scouted and managed farm clubs for both the Brooklyn Dodgers and Minnesota Twins. From 1948 until 1953, he was the general manager of the Great Falls Electrics (Selectrics) baseball team in the Class C Pioneer League.[10]

In 1950, Mariana was thirty-eight years old, had a two-year-old daughter, and was something of a public figure in Great Falls, at least in the sports world. Besides his job as general manager of the Selectrics, Mariana officiated high school football and basketball games, occasionally did play-by-play radio broadcasting for those games, and frequently contributed to the lo-

*Nick Mariana, the year before he filmed UFOs .*

# Mariana Reports Flying Discs

Could it be that even baseballs now come home to roost?

Nick Mariana, general manager of the Selectrics, was asking himself that question this morning. Two objects—for all the world like the "long gone" ball slugged out of the Twin Falls ball park last night by Lou Briganti and Joe Nally—sailed across the sky at Legion park this morning.

At least so the troubled Brewers' general manager reported today—even while admitting he could have been seeing things. Only he hopes to have photographic proof for skeptics.

It all happened at 11:30 a. m. while Mariana was out taking a look around the reserved seat section at Legion park—and there sailing smoothly above the smelter stack at the ACM plant were two spherical silvery objects at a height he estimated at 5,000 feet. After a quick double take and a minute lost while he brushed the cobwebs from his eyes he called his secretary as a witness.

Very opportunely he remembered his movie camera and shot the movies he hopes will verify what he hopes isn't failing eyesight.

No report is available on possible weather balloons floating in the atmosphere today—but it is feared that the high-flying baseball version may be more acceptable to Great Falls residents than "flying saucers."

*The* Great Falls Leader, *August 15, 1950, played Mariana's first report of the UFOs on page 1—along with news of the United Kingdom's new princess, troubles in the Soviet bloc ("satellite") nations, and from the battlefront in Korea.*

cal newspapers' sports columns. He had a popular syndicated radio program, later a weekly half-hour television program, called *Nick's Picks*, where he predicted the outcomes of college football, basketball, and baseball games. At that time, Great Falls was the largest city in Montana,[11] and Mariana's radio show enjoyed a wide listening audience.

Soon after he filmed the flying disks, Mariana notified the Great Falls newspapers about what he had seen. The *Great Falls Leader*, an afternoon daily, published a front-page story on it that day.[12] Mariana sent the film to Eastman Kodak in Chicago for processing, and when it came back, he showed it to local community groups, including the Central Roundtable Athletic Club[13] and the Lions Club. Mariana told how his colleagues in the Lions Club used the occasion for mischief. As he took the floor in the meeting room of the Rainbow Hotel, the room erupted in a flurry of flying paper plates. A few (planted) china plates sailed into the stone fireplace, making quite a crash. The officials at the head table weren't in on the joke, so they dove for cover under the table. "But you know these Lions' Clubs—they're really wild," Mariana said. When the commotion died down and Mariana showed the film, he said "you could hear a pin drop." He estimated there were 175 people at that meeting alone.[14]

*Leader* reporter Clifton Sullivan suggested Mariana send the film to the Air Force for analysis. With Mariana's permission, he sent a letter dated September 13 to the Commanding General of the Air Materiel Command at Wright-Patterson Air Force Base in Dayton, Ohio, informing him of the sighting and movie footage.[15]

## GOVERNMENT INVESTIGATIONS

### *Project Sign*

The United States Air Force conducted a succession of UFO investigations after World War II. The first study began in 1947, the year of the widely reported Kenneth Arnold sighting of "flying saucers" near Mt. Rainier in Washington state, and the Roswell crash. "Project Sign" (identified to the public as "Project Saucer") was a direct result of a classified letter from the commander of the Air Materiel Command (AMC), Lt. Gen. Nathan F. Twining, to the commanding general of the Army Air Forces.[16] The letter, dated September 23, 1947, was not revealed to the public or confirmed by the Air Force for twenty years, but it described unknown aircraft as metallic or light-reflecting, disc or elliptic-shaped, usually soundless, and highly maneuverable.[17] Twining concluded:

> The phenomenon reported is something real and not visionary or fictitious. It is recommended that…Headquarters, Army Air Forces issue a directive assigning a priority, security classification and Code Name for a detailed study of this matter.[18]

Project Sign was set up in the Air Materiel Command at Wright Field, which became Wright-Patterson Air Force Base. Project Sign's director, Capt. Robert R. Sneider, became convinced the reported objects were beyond present human technologies and must be extraterrestrial. In the fall of 1948 he presented his best evidence and conclusions in a Top Secret "Estimate of the Situation" (EOTS) report, which reportedly rattled the chain of command.[19] No copy of this document has ever surfaced, but Ed Ruppelt, chief of the Air Force's later UFO investigation named Project Blue Book, saw it and reported that its conclusion was interplanetary visitation.[20]

Sneider's EOTS was rejected by Air Force Chief of Staff Gen. Hoyt Vandenberg, the Air Force's top official. According to Ruppelt, the report was declassified and, for whatever reasons, all but a few copies were burned. This is evidently not standard procedure, and perhaps Ruppelt was wrong about the declassification.[21]

For years, the Air Force denied the existence of the report, though Major Dewey Fournet, who worked on later UFO investigations, signed an affidavit in the late 1950s confirming its existence.[22] Fournet believed there was a copy in the USAF Intelligence Files. Many files from this time period at the Air Force Directorate of Intelligence and Air Technical Intelligence Center (ATIC) were declassified in 1987, but Jan Aldrich, a UFO researcher who searched these files at the National Archives II facility at College Park, Maryland, was unable to find Sneider's EOTS.[23] He estimated at least 40 percent of the UFO files were withdrawn from declassification. "Everyone had a say on withdrawal, CIA, DOD, USN, British Government, etc.," Aldrich said.[24] Even now, more than sixty years later, much is still kept hidden from public view.

Early on, there was a schism in the Air Force between those who believed the ET hypothesis and those who didn't, as well as sharp conflict over what to tell the public and what to keep secret. These conflicting views resulted in years of flip-flopping between open scientific investigation and superficial window-dressing, between transparency and obfuscation. After Vandenburg's rejection of the EOTS, believers in the ET hypothesis fell out of favor. The Air Force produced a separate report later in 1948, "Top Secret Analysis of Flying Object Incidents in the U.S.," Study #100-203-79.[25] While admitting the existence of unidentified flying objects, this report carefully avoided considering an extraterrestrial explanation. Instead, it suggested the UFOs were foreign aircraft of some unknown kind.

On April 27, 1949, the Air Force released a 22-page "Memorandum to the Press" summarizing "Project Saucers" findings. The memorandum concluded with the following paragraphs.[26]

> The "saucers" are not a joke. Neither are they a cause
> for alarm to the population. Many of the incidents already
> have answers, Meteors, Balloons, Falling stars. Birds in

flight. Testing devices, etc. Some of them still end in question marks.

It is the mission of the AMC Technical Intelligence Division's Project "Saucer" to supply the periods.

At the same time, a dismissive article appeared in the *Saturday Evening Post*. Written by well-known journalist Sydney Shallett, the article "What You Can Believe About Flying Saucers" appeared on April 30, 1949. Less well known was the Air Force's active role in shaping Shallett's story.[27]

### *Project Grudge and the First Analysis (1950)*

Project Sign became Project Grudge in 1949, a curiously appropriate name given that the personnel in charge held the preconceived opinion that all UFO reports could be explained as misidentification of conventional objects, intentional hoaxes, or forms of mental illnesses in the witnesses. Capt. Ruppelt, the last director of Grudge and the head of its successor, Project Blue Book, called Project Grudge the "Dark Ages" of the Air Force's UFO studies.[28]

Officially, Project Grudge was short-lived, beginning February 11, 1949, and ending December 27, 1949. The final report was written in August 1949 and released to the public in December.

The report's release happened to occur about the same time another national magazine published a pro-UFO article. In December 1949, a retired U.S. Marine published an article in *True* magazine entitled "The Flying Saucers are Real." Donald Keyhoe came out of WWII as a major in the Marines and had written aviation articles for *True*. Ken Purdy, *True*'s editor, was suspicious of the government influence on Shallett's article in the *Saturday Evening Post* and solicited Keyhoe to investigate UFOs for an article in *True*.[29] Keyhoe began his investigation as a skeptic, but his many insider contacts convinced him the government knew the flying saucers were extraterrestrial and were covering it up.[30] He went on to write several UFO books and became a civilian UFO investigator with the National Investigations Committee on Aerial Phenomena (NICAP). Keyhoe was an advocate for serious government UFO investigations and a frequent critic of what he felt were flawed efforts. His *True* article was a bombshell. It sold more copies of the magazine than any issue *True* had ever published. Readers besieged the Air Force with calls and letters.[31]

The Air Force felt it needed to counter the Keyhoe article and, according to Ruppelt, came up with a plan.

> It called for a general officer to hold a short press conference, flash his stars, and speak the magic words 'hoaxes, hallucinations, and the misidentification of known objects.'[32]

The Air Force also touted the 600-page Project Grudge Report, basically debunking the extraterrestrial hypothesis. However, if a reader goes beyond the Air Force conclusions and actually reads the appendices, one learns that of 237 UFO reports the project examined, 23 percent were declared "unknown." In other words, they could not be explained. In addition, many UFO researchers, including Ruppelt, found some of the explanations for the "known" to be untenable.[33] Included in the summary was the phrase:

> Evaluation of reports of unidentified flying objects constitute no direct threat to the national security of the United States.[34]

This phrase has reverberated through many government communications regarding UFOs over the years. It's interesting because it does not actually deny their reality, only their potential threat, which would be the military's prime concern.

In one appendix of the Grudge Report, Air Force psychologists said:

> There are sufficient psychological explanations for the reports of unidentified objects to provide plausible explanations for reports not otherwise explainable.[35]

Thus the character or sanity of UFO witnesses became the final catchall to explain away all sightings.

The report recommended that Project Grudge be reduced in scope, in effect saying that further investigation was a waste of time. Although the Air Force publicly announced the closure of Project Grudge on December 27, 1949, Ruppelt later learned Project Grudge was not actually disbanded. Its special project status ended, but its functions were transferred to intelligence channels.[36]

While the Air Force was no longer officially investigating UFOs, a de facto Project Grudge was in charge of UFO reports when Mariana's sighting occurred in August 1950. All UFO reports were filtered through Air Force Intelligence. There was a significant wave of UFO events earlier in 1950, and many branches of the U.S. government were doing their own investigations, including the Navy, the Army, the Federal Bureau of Investigation (FBI) and the Central Intelligence Agency (CIA).[37]

On October 4, Air Force Captain John P. Brynildsen visited Mariana and his secretary. Brynildsen was commander of the Great Falls District of the Air Force Office of Special Investigations (AFOSI), the intelligence wing of the Air Force. Brynildsen was dispatched by Lt. Colonel James O'Connell at Wright-Patterson Air Force Base in a letter dated September 26 to obtain the films in Mariana's possession. Brynildsen was instructed quite specifically:

> In approaching Mr. Mariana for the films, you are requested to exercise every caution so as not to unduly excite his curiosity or interest or in anywise have him conclude

that the Air Force may have reversed its policy from that previously announced with regard to the existence or non-existence of such unconventional objects. In this connection, you should avoid any detailed discussion, advising simply that the Air Force is always interested in any item that will contribute to the fund of technical intelligence. It is requested that the films be obtained and transmitted to the Intelligence Department at Air Materiel Command.[38]

Brynildsen listened to Mariana's and Raunig's story, which included their observation of two jets flying over the baseball park shortly after filming the silvery discs. Mariana had questions for Brynildsen and was frustrated by the officer's stonewall refusal to engage in discussion.[39] Nonetheless, Mariana did hand over his film to be sent to Air Materiel Command at Wright-Patterson AFB for analysis.[40]

On October 6 Brynildsen told a reporter that he picked up about eight feet of film from Mariana. However, in his official letter of transmittal to the District Commander of AFOSI at Wright-Patterson written that same day, Brynildsen said he was sending "approximately fifteen feet of moving picture film." This discrepancy has never been explained and raises questions about what happened to the film after Brynildsen received it from Mariana.[41] Brynildsen did say in his report that Mariana "enjoys an excellent reputation in the local community and is regarded as a reliable, trustworthy and honest individual."[42]

After Mariana gave the film to the Air Force, publicity about the film and the sighting escalated. Mariana started receiving calls at all times of day and night, from reporters as far away as the *London Daily Herald*.[43] Mariana soon wearied of all the publicity and turned down an invitation to go on the air for a national radio network based out of Chicago. The local press said, "Mariana is wishing he never took the pictures."[44]

In addition to O'Connell's instructions to Brynildsen, other recently declassified documents from Project Grudge tell us more about the UFO "climate" in the Air Force at the time. In fact, several documents outlining security procedures regarding UFO reports were dated just before or soon after Sullivan's Sept. 13 letter notifying them of the existence of Mariana's film, as well as during the time the film was in their possession.[45]

On September 8, 1950, the Air Force Director of Intelligence circulated a letter to all commanding generals and air commands, "Reporting of Information on Unconventional Aircraft," with detailed instructions and requirements, including:

> 2g. Any physical evidence of the sighting will be forwarded by most expeditious means to Commanding General, Air Materiel Command, Attn: MCIS, under cover of a letter identifying the shipment with the report of the sighting. Mention of the method and time of shipping of this evidence will be included in written report of the sighting. It is desired that no publicity be given this reporting or analysis activity.

Brynildsen's report thoroughly followed the detailed instructions, including an estimate of the reliability and experience of the observer(s) and witnesses (2.d.(5)). Given the number of local people who had seen the film, and the interest of local and national media, he and the Air Materiel Command at Wright Patterson had little success trying to dodge the press.

On September 25, a letter from "Dept of the Air Force Hqs U.S. Air Force" was evidently circulated under the subject line: "Destruction of Air Intelligence Report Number 100-203-79."

> It is requested that action be taken to destroy all copies of Top Secret Air Intelligence Report Number 100-203-79,

subject, "Analysis of Flying Object Incidents in the U.S.,"
dtd 10 Dec 1948.

The report, referred to briefly above, was prepared coopera-
tively by the USAF Directorate of Intelligence (DI) and the Office of Naval Intelligence (ONI). It includes accounts of some
of Project Sign's best-documented UFO reports and photos of
unusual "flying wing" aircraft either in development by the U.S.
or the U.S.S.R. This report concludes there are two possible explanations for UFOs: domestic or foreign. The wording of the
conclusions in this report carefully avoids naming a potential extraterrestrial explanation:

CONCLUSIONS

11. SINCE the Air Force is responsible for control of
the air in the defense of the U.S., it is imperative that all
other agencies cooperate in confirming or denying the
possibility that these objects have a domestic origin. Otherwise, if it is firmly indicated that there is no domestic explanation, the objects are a threat and warrant more active
efforts of identification and interception.

12. IT MUST be accepted that some type of flying
objects have been observed, although their identification
and origin are not discernable. In the interest of national
defense it would be unwise to overlook the possibility that
some of these objects may be of foreign origin.

The concern of a foreign threat (mainly from the Soviet Union)
seems to overshadow any other possibilities in the report. Whether
there is significance to the report being destroyed is unknown. Perhaps the Air Force was just housecleaning, given that the Grudge
Report followed one year later. (The Grudge Report does not include
photos of known or suspected experimental aircraft.) A few copies of

the Air Intelligence Report were archived. It was declassified in 1985 and is currently accessible.[46] So while this report omitting any reference to an ET hypothesis is declassified, the existence of the Project Sign EOTS report supporting the ET hypothesis is still denied, despite testimony that such a report was made.

On October 2, 1950, two days before Brynildsen obtained the Mariana film, instructions were sent to Air Force public information officers:

> Queries from the press as to USAF interest in any air technical subject to include so-called "flying saucers", may be answered to the effect that the USAF has a continuing interest in all air technical and scientific information and therefore has a normal interest in any report which may appear to be pertinent to this category of information. The foregoing should be used only in response to queries; not to initiate press statements.[47]

Shortly after the arrival of the film at Wright Patterson AFB, an Air Force spokesperson told a reporter from the *Dayton Daily News* (October 10, 1950) that, "The film is too dark to distinguish any recognizable objects." This statement was in spite of the fact that the film was taken at 11:30 A.M. on a clear, sunny day and that anyone who sees it would not call it dark. The Dayton article was carried in numerous U.S. and Canadian papers, with a diversity of "slant" in the headlines.[48] The film was returned to Mariana on October 18 with a letter asserting "Our photoanalysts were unable to find on it anything identifiable of an unusual nature."[49]

Two Project Grudge documents (declassified in 2011) from October 1950 appear to pertain specifically to the Mariana film and the Air Force statements to the press.[50] The statements about the Mariana film conform to the instructions in these documents for wording to use in press releases:

~~CONFIDENTIAL~~

Col Harris/aws/52466
Wrtn 11 Oct 50

OCT 18 1950

AFOIV-TC

SUBJECT: (Restricted) Releasing Results of Analysis and Evaluation of "Unidentified Aerial Objects" Reports

TO: Commanding General
Air Materiel Command
Wright-Patterson Air Force Base
Dayton, Ohio
ATTENTION: Chief, Intelligence Dept

1. This headquarters is cognizant of press interests in the so-called "flying saucers" reports, referred to by this headquarters as "unidentified aerial objects." Your headquarters has previously been advised as to the release of information concerning Air Force interest in this subject. Your attention is invited to USAF PIO release of 6 September 1950 and Hq USAF letter, subject "Reporting of Information on Unconventional Aircraft," dated 8 September 1950.

2. In a recent telephone conversation between Colonel Watson, Hq AMC and Colonel Harris, this headquarters, Colonel Watson requested guidance in the matter of releasing results of investigation, analysis, and evaluation of incidents brought to his attention. This headquarters believes that release of details of analysis and evaluation of incidents is inadvisable, and desires that, in lieu thereof, releases conform to the policy and spirit of the following:

"We have investigated and evaluated _____ incident and have found nothing of value and nothing which would change our previous estimates on this subject."

3. Results of analysis and evaluation of incidents possessing any intelligence value will be forwarded to this headquarters for information and for any action relative to possible press releases.

BY COMMAND OF THE CHIEF OF STAFF:

S/ MOORE
Brig. Gen., USAF
Assistant for Production
Directorate of Intelligence

*One of the previously classified Project Grudge documents instructing the military not to reveal "details of analysis and evaluation" of UFO incidents but to issue a "nothing of value" conclusion to the public.*

We had investigated and evaluated _____ incident and have found nothing of value and nothing which would change our previous estimates on this subject.

Though the official press statement said the film was "too dark to distinguish any objects," Project Grudge concluded the images were "the reflections from two F-94 jet fighters that were in the area."[51]

When the film was returned to Mariana, he immediately noticed that the first part of the film was missing. The missing footage showed the clearest views of the two spinning metallic discs, each featuring a notch or band along their outer edges, hovering to the left of the tall smokestack at the Anaconda Mining Company's copper smelter in Great Falls. Mariana viewed the returned film in the back of the Allsport Supply Store with his friend and colleague, Tony Dalich, owner of the store. When interviewed some years later, Dalich said they both noticed a splice in the film that was made differently than what Mariana usually made, and Dalich confirmed Mariana's claim, "There was a lot missing."[52]

Other witnesses who had viewed the film before it was handed over to the Air Force concurred that the best footage was gone. Mariana thought it was missing about 35 frames. The Air Force denied it had tampered with the film,[53] but Ruppelt's comments on Project Grudge raised doubts about the denial:

> To one who is intimately familiar with UFO history it is clear that Project Grudge had a two-phase program of UFO annihilation. The first phase consisted of explaining every UFO report. The second phase was to tell the public how the Air Force had solved all the sightings. This, Project Grudge reasoned, would put an end to UFO reports.[54]

There are other important cases where witnesses claim that film in the hands of the Air Force disappeared. On July 2, 1952, Navy Warrant Officer and Photographer Delbert Newhouse filmed a formation of disc-shaped objects in Tremonton, Utah, a film which is nearly as famous as the Mariana film. Newhouse also turned over his original film to the Air Force, which later returned only a shorter, inferior copy of the film. Newhouse reported that 10 to 20 feet from the first and best part of his 60-

foot film was missing.[55] The objects on his film were eventually dismissed as "seagulls," although both the photo reconnaissance laboratory at Wright Patterson AFB and the Navy photography laboratory in Anacostia, Maryland, rejected the "bird explanation." In fact, the Navy laboratory went so far as to say that Newhouse's UFOs were "unknown objects under intelligent control."[56]

Pilot Kenneth Arnold, credited with starting the "flying saucer" era in June 1947, also had problems with altered film in the hands of the Air Force. Besides his legendary sighting of nine flying saucers in formation over the Cascade Mountains in Washington State, he had several more sightings in his lifetime, including one he caught on film. He also submitted his film to the Air Force. According to his daughter,

> The military cut the photos out of the film, sent it back to him, and said there was nothing there. He was really upset about that.[57]

These incidents look like a pattern. While none of these allegations are provable at this time, all three of the witnesses were highly competent and widely respected individuals. UFO researchers Michael David Hall and Wendy Connors attest to similar correspondence in Air Force files from other cases where people make the very same complaint—missing film or negatives after possession by the Air Force.[58] If the films were not destroyed but instead buried deeply in classified files, perhaps they may surface one day.

Certainly in the case of the Mariana film, footage of large objects *hovering* would have nullified the explanation that the discs were reflections of F-94 military jets, as well as the statement that the film showed "nothing of an unusual nature." The October 12, 1950, Memorandum (section 5) makes it clear that if the results of analyses contained information of technical intelligence value, the results should *not be released* but instead should be sent to the Director-ate of Intelligence at Air Force Headquarters in Washington, D.C. One would assume that hovering silver discs would have significant technical intelligence value. Could the Air Force memorandum have resulted in Mariana's (and others') best footage being "censured"?

## COSMOPOLITAN MAGAZINE ARTICLE (1951)

> The Disgraceful Flying Saucer Hoax:
> It has cost millions of dollars and some lives. Our dreams have been haunted by little men from nowhere. Here is the truth about the most wild-eyed fake of our time.[59]

As already shown, the popular press was a major player in shap-ing public opinion on UFOs. Reporter Bob Considine wrote a series of UFO articles in 1950 for the International News Service. He reported the Mariana sighting in his third article, published in the Hearst Corporation's New York newspaper, the *Journal-American*, on November 21.[60] In January 1951, he published a UFO-bashing piece in *Cosmopolitan*, a magazine also owned by the Hearst media conglomerate. The article, entitled "The Dis-graceful Flying Saucer Hoax," debased UFO witnesses, whom he characterized as "screwballs" and "true believers."[61]

Considine was a prolific writer, legendary among journalists at the time, though with a mixed reputation.[62] *Time* magazine described him as "no great writer, but he is the Hearstling who gets there first with the most words on almost any subject."[63] Cu-riously, even though Air Force officials had first said the objects in Mariana's film were too dark to make out, and the Grudge report concluded they were reflections from two F-94 jets, Considine wrote that the Air Force told him the "bright discs" on the film were sun reflections from the water tower.

Considine later told Hearst Publications that his source for all his information not otherwise attributed was the Air Materiel Command. One researcher pointed out, "It is a matter of extreme interest…that the Air Force acknowledged to Considine that the film showed discs and that these discs could be identified."[64] Changing official explanations for UFO sightings is not unusual. Over the years, the explanation for the famous Roswell crash has changed several times, disregarding testimony from highly regarded military and civilian witnesses.[65]

Mariana was outraged by the *Cosmopolitan* article. In David vs. Goliath fashion, he filed a $25,000 libel suit against Bob Considine and Hearst Magazines, Inc., hiring attorneys in both Great Falls and New York. He maintained Considine's article was "false, libelous, and defamatory" and caused readers to believe "that the plaintiff was a liar, prankster, halfwit, crank, publicity hound and fanatic." Mariana claimed the article accused him of "maliciously fabricating the story concerning objects in flight to play upon the gullibility and war apprehensions of the average citizen, and that he needlessly caused the U.S. Air Force to expend time, money and effort to investigate a 'flying saucer' delusion."[66] The bad publicity resulted in decisions by nine of fourteen radio stations carrying Mariana's sports show to cancel it, resulting in a significant financial hit to him. It was nine months before these stations resubscribed to "Nick's Picks."[67]

While Mariana may have had biblical courage, he did not prevail against the corporate giant and eventually dropped his lawsuit in September 1955.[68] However, in a crucial hearing in 1954, Judge David N. Edelstein, of the Southern District Court of New York, wrote that the language in the article was "libelous on its face…The problem, then, is whether the article can be fairly read as applying the force of its barb to the plaintiff." Judge Edelstein decided not, partly because Considine did write, three paragraphs before the Mariana section, "There can, of course, be honest mistakes."[69]

It is worth noting the political context at the time. The U.S.

was in the height of Senator Joe McCarthy's communist witch-
hunts, and the military and citizenry felt terribly threatened by
the power and aggression of communist countries. Just weeks before Mariana's sighting, the Korean War had started. Given the
gravity of war and the nuclear arms race, it's not surprising there
was concern about UFOs as a distraction, or potential competi-
tion, for stretched military resources.

However, it is also the case that the CIA was becoming increasingly powerful. Historian Richard Dolan asserts that by the early
1950s, the CIA had "cozy relationships with most major media
executives in America," including Hearst newspapers.[70]

The Considine article illustrates the controversy surrounding
UFOs that was prevalent at the time and that continues today. It
is also an example of the shame and ridicule often unleashed on
UFO witnesses who have gone public, a chilling response that
probably seals the lips of many witnesses. And as Mariana found
out, reporting UFOs could seriously endanger one's livelihood.

However, Project Grudge's dismissive conclusions were challenged in subsequent civilian and military investigations. In fact,
Mariana's "Montana Movie" went on to play a starring role in
both Project Blue Book and the Condon Committee investigations.

## PROJECT BLUE BOOK
## AND THE SECOND ANALYSIS (1952)

Captain Edward J. Ruppelt took over Project Grudge in October 1951, putting together a staff which had no firm opinions
about the UFO phenomenon. ("I had to let three people go for
being too pro or too con."[71]) Ruppelt is generally credited with
replacing the misleading term "flying saucers" with "unidentified
flying objects," or "UFOs," in military reports.[72] By March 1952,
the Air Force upgraded Grudge to a new organization and gave it
the name Project Blue Book.

In July 1952, a UFO event of epic proportion shocked the military and much of the nation. Mass sightings and radar trackings of as many as 14 UFOs occurred over Washington, D.C. Military jets were scrambled and reported seeing bright lights performing impossible maneuvers. Although some government reports and journalists have tried to dismiss the event as temperature inversions (which may sometimes leave faint radar traces), official investigations and reports refuted that explanation. The event was widely reported in the press.[73] As a result of that showstopper, General John A. Samford, director of Air Force intelligence, ordered Project Blue Book to take a new look at the evidence.

Ruppelt reopened the Mariana case. He found an officer at the Great Falls AFB whom Mariana knew and trusted, Lt. Peter Marquez, and Marquez conducted three or four interviews with Mariana. The report summarizing Marquez's interviews contained a few additional details of the sighting, including the statement that the objects were still hovering next to the smokestack when Mariana began filming them.[74] Marquez's summary of "Mr. Mariana's version of the incident" includes the following passage:

> The two objects were again motionless, but at a point to the left of the smoke stack. It was at this point that I first filmed these two objects. I repeat, they were not covering any distance; that is they were motionless, but an occasional vibration seemed to momentarily tilt them, after which they would instantly correct their level plane to its seemingly balanced position. The two objects made an abrupt flight in an arc motion at very high speeds. I approximate the speed to have been over 400 MPH. At all times the altitude was definitely in the 5,000 ft. to 10,000 ft. above the terrain bracket. The end frames of the movie reel show the object to be in line with a high water tower, which is approximately 130 ft. high. I approximate a 30° angle to

have been formed by the level ground and a straight line from the objects to the spot where I was standing. At the point above the water tower, the objects hovered motionless for two or three minutes and then flew out of sight. The clearest films of the reel were removed by the Air Force when I first lent them the movie. The only ones which remain in my possession are those which show the objects at a considerable distance. I believe the objects were at all times within 2 or $2^1/_2$ miles of me. Total time that the objects were in view: approximately $3^1/_2$ minutes.

Unfortunately, in one paragraph Marquez also introduced a number of errors in the Mariana story that have plagued the literature ever since:

On about the 5th or 15th of August 1950, I, as manager of the Electrics, a local baseball team, walked to the grandstand of the local stadium here in Great Falls, Montana. It was approximately 11:30 AM and my purpose was to check the direction of the wind in preparation for the afternoon's game.[75]

It's been suggested that Marquez could not read his own notes regarding the date because newspaper accounts confirm the event occurred August 15. The name of the baseball team was the "Selectrics" in 1950, but it was changed to the "Electrics" in 1951, explaining that discrepancy. There was no baseball game in Great Falls that afternoon, so either Marquez made incorrect assumptions, or Mariana's memory was faulty. In earlier interviews, Mariana mentions looking at the smokestack out of habit, since it provided wind information useful during a game, but he does not say there was a game that day. Regardless of these discrepancies, Marquez concludes by speaking highly of Mariana's character and accountability:

Mr. Mariana is well-known as a pleasant, friendly, cour-
teous and competent individual. There seem to be no ulte-
rior motives involved.

Marquez was able to convince Mariana to let the Air Force take
the film again, for a more detailed analysis. Mariana reluctantly
agreed, and only on the condition that the Air Force sign an agreement not to remove any frames of the film.[76]

## THE ROBERTSON PANEL

In January 1953, Ruppelt assembled his best UFO evidence
for a review by a CIA-sponsored panel of highly credentialed scientists. The panel was known officially as the Scientific Advisory
Panel on Unidentified Flying Objects, but unofficially as the Robertson Panel, since it was chaired by California Institute of Technology physicist H.P. Robertson. Robertson was also head of the
Defense Department's Weapons System Evaluation Group and a
CIA employee. In fact, according to UFO historian Jerome Clark,
all members of the panel had extensive backgrounds in classified
government research, and all were skeptical if not hostile to UFO
reports.[77]

Project Blue Book analyzed 1,593 reports out of 4,400 reports received. The results were summarized using three levels of
certainty in identification: "known, probable, or possible." The
categories of identification were: Balloons, Aircraft, Astronomical Bodies, Other (includes such things as birds, blowing paper,
clouds, air inversions, reflections, etc.), and Unknown. In spite
of the fact that "possible" identifications were considered just as
conclusive as "known" and "probable" identifications, the project
still came up with 23 percent of analyzed reports having "Insuf-
ficient data" and 27 percent being "Unknowns." In other words,
an astonishing 50 percent of the analyzed UFO reports remained
"unidentified."[78]

The Robertson Panel was purportedly charged to review the evidence provided by Project Blue Book and to come up with one of three possible verdicts:

1) All UFO reports are explainable as known objects or natural phenomenon, and the project should be discontinued.

2) The reports do not contain enough data on which to base a conclusion, therefore the project should continue in hopes of more conclusive data.

3) The UFOs are interplanetary spacecraft.

For the first two days, Ruppelt reviewed Project Blue Book's entire body of findings. The question and answer period went on for another full day. Then Ruppelt spent another day and a half reviewing their top 50 "Unknown" cases. Ruppelt's final presentation to the Robertson panel was a controversial analysis of UFO movement to determine if UFOs were intelligently controlled. Though they sifted through several hundred of the most detailed UFO reports, only 10 or 20 of the best cases were used for this analysis. Ruppelt brought in retired Air Force Intelligence officer Major Dewey J. Fournet Jr., to present their results, since he worked closely with the group that prepared the report and was highly credentialed.

Fournet told the panel that the movement analysis proved beyond a doubt that UFOs were intelligently controlled by persons with brains equal to or far surpassing human brains. He further concluded that the controllers were not "earthlings" and therefore must be spacemen.[79] Ruppelt was not sure how the panel would react to that conclusion, but based on their questions, he felt they at least took it seriously.

The final presentations, indeed Ruppelt called them the "feature attractions," were the "Montana Movie" and Newhouse's

Tremonton, Utah, movie (later called the "Utah Movie"). Here is Ruppelt's report on the role of the Montana Movie in this historic summit:

> On Friday morning we presented the feature attractions of the session, the Tremonton Movie and the Montana Movie. These two bits of evidence represented the best photos of UFO's that Project Blue Book had to offer. The scientists knew about them, especially the Tremonton Movie, because since late July they had been the subject of many closed door conferences. Generals, admirals, and GS-16's had seen them at "command performances," and they had been flown to Kelly AFB in Texas to be shown to a conference of intelligence officers from all over the world. Two of the country's best military photo laboratories, the Air Force lab at Wright Field and the Navy's lab at Anacostia, Maryland, had spent many hours trying to prove that the UFO's were balloons, airplanes, or stray light reflections, but they failed—the UFO's were true unknowns. The possibility that the movie had been faked was considered but quickly rejected because only a Hollywood studio with elaborate equipment could do such a job and the people who filmed the movies didn't have this kind of equipment.
>
> When the photo lab got the [Montana] movie, they had a little something to work with because the two UFO's had passed behind a reference point, the water tower. Their calculations quickly confirmed that the objects were not birds, balloons, or meteors. Balloons drift with the wind and the wind was not blowing in the direction that the two UFO's were traveling. No exact speeds could be measured, but the lab could determine that the lights were traveling too fast to be birds and too slow to be meteors.

This left airplanes as the only answer. The intelligence officer at Great Falls had dug through huge stacks of files and found that only two airplanes, two F-94's, were near the city during the sighting and that they had landed about two minutes afterwards. Both Mariana and his secretary, who had also seen the UFO's, had said that the two jets had appeared in another part of the sky only a minute or two after the two UFO's had disappeared in the southeast. This in itself would eliminate the jets as candidates for the UFO's, but we wanted to double check. The two circular lights didn't look like F-94's, but anyone who has done any flying can tell you that an airplane so far away that it can't be seen can suddenly catch the sun's rays and make a brilliant flash.

First we studied the flight paths of the two F-94's. We knew the landing pattern that was being used on the day of the sighting, and we knew when the two F-94's landed. The two jets just weren't anywhere close to where the two UFO's had been. Next we studied each individual light and both appeared to be too steady to be reflections. We drew a blank on the Montana Movie—it was an unknown.[80]

Despite Ruppelt's conclusion that jet aircraft could be eliminated as an explanation, the Robertson Panel obstinately clung to that explanation for the Mariana movie. The panel dismissed the Project Blue Book researchers' conclusions and the testimony of Mariana and his secretary that the jets appeared after the silvery discs disappeared. And, despite Fournet's testimony that the evidence supported the extraterrestrial hypothesis, the panel decided there wasn't enough data to make that conclusion. Their overall conclusion was:

> …The reports do not contain enough data on which to

base a conclusion, therefore the project should continue in hopes of more conclusive data.

Some observers doubted whether the panel could have concluded that UFOs were extraterrestrial spacecraft no matter what the evidence showed. Panel member Dr. Thornton Page made a statement in 1992 that belied any notion of objectivity:

> H.P. Robertson told us in the first private (no outsiders) session that our job was to reduce public concern, and show that UFO reports could be explained by conventional reasoning.[81]

Dr. J. Allen Hynek was an associate member of the Robertson Panel and probably its youngest member. Relatively new to ufology at the time, Hynek was an astrophysicist/astronomer who had been a consultant for Project Grudge and then Project Blue Book. Hynek was initially a skeptic, but by the time he left Blue Book in 1969, he was convinced of the extraterrestrial hypothesis. In 1974, he made the following comments about Newhouse's Tremonton film and the Robertson Panel:

> Now the Navy, on the basis of their detailed analysis, they had concluded that the objects shown on the films could not be birds, balloons, aircraft and so forth but indeed that they were self-luminous unidentified objects. Despite this conclusion, the panel rejected it, and concluded that the objects were birds. They couldn't be unidentified; therefore they had to be birds.
>
> I came away from the meeting and from the room with the distinct feeling however, that the panel had deliberately moved to debunk the whole subject, and not to give it the serious scientific attention which it deserved.[82]

In 1952, a year before the Robertson Panel's conclusions, Hynek conducted a poll among his professional colleagues and found that 5 percent of 44 astronomers had seen UFOs but were deeply fearful of letting that be known for fear of ruining their careers.[83] Since most funding for academic scientific research comes from government sources, it's important for scientists to know which way the policy wind is blowing.

The fact that Robertson was employed by the CIA and that the other four members of the panel had all been involved with military defense projects is important in interpreting their conclusions.[84] While the panel recommended that the American public should be told every detail of every phase of the UFO investigation, they had a specific agenda in mind:

> ...the Air Force should de-emphasize the subject of UFOs and embark on a "debunking" campaign that would result in reduction in public interest in flying saucers...
> This education could be accomplished by *mass media, and scientists, psychologists, amateur astronomers, and celebrities should be brought into the effort to show that even puzzling sightings were potentially explainable.* The Air Force UFO project should be expanded slightly and temporarily so that it could educate and debunk effectively. Moreover, civilian UFO groups should be watched because of their potentially great influence on mass thinking...The apparent irresponsibility and the possible use of such groups for subversive purposes should be kept in mind.[85] [emphasis added]

Project Blue Book continued with reduced staff and morphed from a credible research project into a spin machine. According to Major Fournet,

Captain Ruppelt confided to me that he could see the negativism developing following the report by the CIA Scientific Panel [Robertson Panel] in early 1953, and this was the main reason for his request to be reassigned from the project.[86]

Ruppelt's statement to Donald Keyhoe was more candid:

We're ordered to hide sightings when possible, but if a strong report does get out we have to publish a fast explanation—make up something to kill the report in a hurry, and also ridicule the witness, especially if we can't figure out a plausible answer. We even have to ridicule our own pilots. It's a raw deal, but we can't buck the CIA. The whole thing makes me sick—I'm thinking of putting [in] for inactive.[87]

Another troubling fact arose from the Robertson Panel report. The official text stated the panel examined more than 1,900 UFO reports in 1952, yet Blue Book only shows 1,503 reports for that year. This begs the question, where did the rest of the reports come from?[88] According to Richard Dolan's extensive research on UFOs and government secrecy, Joint Army-Navy-Air-Publication "JANAP 146 (B)," first issued in 1949 and reissued in 1953, made it clear that the most important UFO reports did not go to Project Grudge or Blue Book, but instead went to the Air Defense Command, the Secretary of Defense, the CIA, and "other appropriate agencies."[89]

In August 1953, the Air Force issued regulations (AFR 200-2) instructing air base officers how to handle UFO reports. All UFO reports were now to be sent first to Air Intelligence Service Squadron (AISS) 4602, part of Air Defense Command (ADC) at Ent AFB in Colorado Springs.[90] Sightings could be discussed only with authorized personnel, and only solved reports could be discussed publicly. All unsolved reports were classified.

In December 1953, the Joint Chiefs of Staff installed another airlock on UFO secrecy. JANAP 146 made any public release of UFO reports a crime punishable by one to ten years in prison or a $10,000 fine under the Espionage Act. It applied not only to everyone in the military but also to commercial airline pilots.[91] (In 1958, 450 airline pilots signed a petition protesting the official policy of debunking sightings. Fifty of them had reported UFO sightings and been told they were mistaken. The Air Force reminded them that they could face up to ten years in prison if they divulged details of any UFO sightings to the media.[92])

In 1955 the Air Technical Intelligence Center told the commander of Project Blue Book to minimize the number of unsolved cases. "Probable" and "Possible" categories of identification were discontinued and now lumped into "Known Identification." The investigative staff were "encouraged" to find conventional explanations for as many reports as possible. By the end of 1956, the number of unsolved cases was whittled down to 0.4 percent.[93] The Mariana case was again dismissed as "aircraft" in the Blue Book files. According to Ruppelt, a number of spectators who had observed the UFO's "trial" felt the members of the Robertson Panel were prejudiced and fearful of sticking their necks out.[94]

Nonetheless, many who participated in the Air Force investigation were convinced that UFOs were interplanetary vehicles.[95] They did not forget what they had learned and were key players in producing a documentary a few years later, when Mariana's "Montana Movie" once again played a leading role.

## THE FIRST UFO DOCUMENTARY (1956)

Shortly after the mass UFO sightings over Washington, D.C. in July 1952, movie producer Clarence Greene had a UFO sighting outside his home in Los Angeles. A friend called his attention to a "sphere of light" in the sky. They both watched for five minutes as the object made multiples stops and turns before disappearing over the horizon. Greene said it made an "indelible impression" on him. As he began to share his experience, he learned there were hundreds of other sightings, but people were afraid to talk about it for fear of ridicule.

> I was at a complete loss to understand why there seemed to be such a determined effort to suppress all news of UFOs by what seemed to be a planned campaign of skepticism and scoffing.[96]

Greene decided the public needed to know the facts about "flying saucers" and began to "delve into the UFO enigma."[97] He discovered that Albert M. Chop, once the Pentagon's Press Information Specialist handling UFO news, lived nearby on the West Coast.[98]

Greene's UFO experience and his opportune meeting with Al Chop eventually led to the filming of "Unidentified Flying Objects" in 1956. The astonishing background story of this largely forgotten film was not revealed until twenty years later, when UFO researcher Robert Barrow penned a detailed "behind-the-scenes" article on the movie, interviewing some of the people who collaborated in its production. Barrow calls the 1956 film "the Granddaddy of all UFO Films."[99]

The 92-minute documentary presented the Montana Movie and the Utah Movie to the public for the first time. It included interviews with several pilots who had UFO encounters and concluded with a dramatic re-enactment of the 1952 mass sighting of multiple UFOs over Washington D.C. Perhaps the most amazing aspect of this documentary was that it was a collaborative effort between Greene and key people from the Air Force's Project Blue Book investigation. Following are some excerpts of Barrow's 1975 interview with Clarence Greene:[100]

Chop was reluctant to talk at first. But when he realized I was dead serious about the unidentified flying object business, he gave me a breakdown on Project Blue Book, code name for the investigation of UFOs.

Greene reported that Chop and certain newsmen were able to arrange a meeting between himself and Capt. Edward Ruppelt, the former director of Project Blue Book now with the USAF Reserve. Greene recalled,

Together, we went into a lengthy and exhaustive study of reports, various documents and affidavits of UFO sightings and reports from radar experts which, with some heretofore top secret motion pictures, in color, of flying saucers, form the basis of the film. [Referring to the Montana and Utah movies.]

When "Unidentified Flying Objects" was released in 1956, Project Blue Book still existed, though much changed from Ruppelt's days. Capt. George T. Gregory became head of Project Blue Book in April 1956. He was a UFO debunker and "kept a file of all the movie's reviews, notifications, and advertisements, carefully underlining every statement that might cause problems for the Air Force or generate interest in UFOs."[101]

Despite what went on behind closed doors, Greene reported there was no official opposition to his plans to make the movie, nor any from his colleagues. He had no trouble negotiating to use the Montana and Utah films, which had only recently been declassified and made available publicly.

Barrow also did some background research on Al Chop and was able to contact him for his 1976 article about the movie. Chop was a journalist hired in 1950 by the Air Force to write press releases and answer queries. He was initially with the Press Section at the

Air Materiel Command (AMC) at Wright-Patterson Air Force Base. (Perhaps he was there when the Mariana film arrived.) Chop's opinion about UFOs at the time was: "this whole saucer business is pure, unadulterated bunk."[102] He was a confirmed skeptic. However, his opinion began to change after he became Chief of the Press Section in AMC. Shortly thereafter, he was transferred to the Pentagon and assigned to UFO investigation. He told Barrow,

> You must remember that I was privy to the project files. These contained hundreds of official reports of UFO encounters made by military personnel from all branches of the service. They were all classified with a high degree of security classification. Almost all of these made pretty scary reading from the verbatim descriptions of the pilots concerned.[103]

By the time Chop viewed the famous Montana and Utah films two years later, his observation of them "merely strengthened my personal beliefs and theories on the subject of UFOs. I leaned heavily toward the extraterrestrial theory prior to viewing the Montana and Newhouse films."[104]

Drawing again on his own experiences with official UFO investigations, Al Chop commented on changes he observed in experts as they were exposed to more information:

> It was interesting to observe from the sidelines how Dr. Robert L. Baker changed 180 degrees from a disbeliever to one embracing the extraterrestrial theory as a result of his study of the Montana and Newhouse [Utah] films. In similar fashion, it was interesting to observe the change in Allen Hynek. I met him many years ago when his primary mission in the project seemed to be that of casting discredit on all those who reported UFO encounters.[105]

## The Baker analysis

In 1953, when Chop was contacted about the documentary film, he was working for Douglas Aircraft. Greene wanted an independent scientific analysis of the two UFO movies, so he approached Douglas Aircraft. They assigned the job to Robert L. Baker, a scientist employed by Douglas Aircraft who had expertise in computers and engineering. He completed his first analysis of the Montana and Utah films in early 1956. Al Chop interviewed Mariana again about the sighting, providing a few additional details for Baker's analysis.

> All of the soft-data [eye witness reports of Mr. Mariana and his secretary] indicated that the objects were silvery in appearance with a notch or band at one point on their periphery and could be seen to rotate in unison, hover, and then...with a swishing sound, floated away to the left (SW). According to Mariana, 35 of the earlier frames, allegedly lost by the Air Force, showed a larger image, complete with a "rotating notch."[106]

This detail of the notch and synchronized rotation is intriguing. There are other records within the UFO literature of disc-shaped craft with notches, most notably a UFO seen from the NASA STS-75 Space Shuttle Mission, February 22, 1996.[107]

Baker's initial report on the Montana film concluded that the F-94 jet explanation given by the Robertson Panel was "quite strained."[108] Years later, in 1968, Baker published an article in the *Journal of Astronautical Sciences*, concluding,

> On the basis of the photographic evidence, the images cannot be explained by any presently known natural phenomenon.

Baker concluded that the speed of the UFOs was far beyond the capability of F-94s at the distance from the camera the objects had to be to produce such an undefined image.[109]

On July 29, 1968, Baker spoke at the first ever congressionally held "symposium" on UFOs, a hearing requested by the House Committee on Science and Astronautics. Baker reported on his analysis of the Montana movie and told the Committee that the F-94 explanation was "devoid of merit."[110] His technical paper, complete with photos from Mariana's footage, was included in his report to the Congressional Committee. Baker's definitive analysis is still the best and last word on the authenticity of Mariana's UFOs.

Major Dewey Fournet from Project Blue Book was another key player in the production of the UFO documentary who was interviewed by Barrow. Fournet had concluded that UFOs were piloted by non-human intelligence. In 1952, Fournet convinced his superiors that all non-sensitive UFO information should be made available to the public. Al Chop was the public information officer at the time, so Chop was "a privileged recipient of considerable information." Regarding those times, Fournet told Barrow,

> This was the only "open" period that I know of in the entire existence of the UFO project.

Barrow asked Fournet in 1975 whether important UFO information was being censored by government agencies.

> To the best of my knowledge there has never been any censoring per se, with the exception of deleting names of witnesses and any data pertaining to radar or intercept procedures. On the other hand, I'm positive that the public was frequently fed misleading statistics and examples of reports that were atypical, intended only to make the subject appear to be entirely asinine.

(Evidently, from a military perspective, the classification and ban on discussion of unsolved UFO cases and the manipulation of statistics and examples is not censorship. I am not sure the American public would agree.)

Clarence Greene and co-producer Russell Rouse took great pains to make sure the film was as factual as possible. Every document backing up the film was placed in the custody of a Los Angeles insurance company and made available for inspection. This included the weather report from the dates of the 1952 mass UFO sightings over Washington D.C., proving the radar signals were not due to a temperature inversion. It also included signed testimony from Al Chop, Ed Ruppelt, and Dewey Fournet swearing to the authenticity of the facts and incidents portrayed in the film.[111] The very fact that the movie was produced and released without government interference was astounding and perhaps more an example of bureaucratic inconsistency than approval.

The same year Capt. Ruppelt published his landmark book, *The Report on Unidentified Flying Objects*.[112] J. Allen Hynek suggested that Ruppelt's "book should be required reading for anyone seriously interested in the history of this subject."[113] His final sentences read, *"Maybe the earth is being visited by interplanetary spaceships. Only time will tell."* (For reasons that are not clear, Ruppelt added three chapters in a 1960 edition of his book essentially echoing the Air Force's dismissive stance on an extraterrestrial hypothesis, though changing nothing in the original 17 chapters. He died of a heart attack that same year at the early age of 37. There is some circumstantial evidence that Ruppelt was coerced into revising his book, and this stress may have contributed to his untimely death.[114])

Greene and Rouse's UFO documentary generated at least some favorable publicity upon its release on April 23, 1956.[115] Louella Parsons, who was actually America's first newspaper movie columnist, wrote a glowing review:

> Hollywood is talking about the incredible interest expressed by fans and those in the industry over the flying saucer film made by Clarence Greene and Russell Rouse with our government's knowledge. It actually shows pictures of the saucers and is attracting front page and editorial attention although what the saucers are is still a mystery.

And the entertainment industry's trade magazine *Variety* said: "An authentic beat! Interesting, informing and important! Gripping climax! Should register well!"

Nonetheless, the film was not a box office success. In fact, it lost more than $100,000. Was it true, as some assert, that the public is just not all that interested? Or had the campaign to "reduce public interest in flying saucers" been incredibly effective?

Chop left the press desk at the Pentagon in 1953 shortly after the Robertson Panel report "because it was apparent the lid was back on the project and I don't believe in working in a vacuum." From there, he went to the job at Douglas Aircraft.

In his 1976 interview, Chop told Barrow,

> One wonders what it will take to get people on Earth vitally interested. I wince when I think of the cost of the University of Colorado's "Condon Study." It is so damn obvious to anyone involved in the project that the "findings" are nothing but a calculated farce. But why? Somewhere, there's a reasoned motive I will never understand.[116]

## THE UNIVERSITY OF COLORADO UFO PROJECT: CONDON COMMITTEE

By the late 1950s, Project Blue Book had fallen into disregard by serious UFO researchers. Even certain Congressmen were unhappy with its transparent agenda to find or fabricate conventional explanations for UFO reports. Washington D.C.–based National

Investigations Committee on Aerial Phenomena (NICAP), a private UFO research organization under the direction of Ret. Major Donald Keyhoe, was critical of Blue Book and lobbied Congress for hearings. For its part, the Air Force just wanted out of the UFO investigation business.

In 1965, a major wave of UFO sightings swept the country, and Prof. J. Allen Hynek of Northwestern University, then Blue Book's chief scientific consultant, urged the Air Force to assemble a panel of civilian scientists to review the issue and offer direction for Project Blue Book. A series of multiwitness sightings in Michigan on March 21-22, 1966, resulted in Hynek's ludicrous "swamp gas" comment to the press. Though Hynek had already turned the corner on his skepticism, he found himself in a press conference shortly after his arrival in Michigan and before he was able to conduct much of an investigation.[11/] Though Hynek regretted his hasty off-the-cuff comment, the press had a heyday with it, making a laughing stock of government UFO investigators. As a result, in April the House Armed Services Committee hauled in Air Force officials for hearings. The Congressional committee endorsed Hynek's idea of a civilian, expert-scientist review.

The Air Force had difficulty finding a university willing to host this panel, a problem not surprising given the CIA's and Air Force's UFO debunking campaigns. In July 1966, they approached Professor Edward U. Condon at the University of Colorado. Condon had a lengthy, distinguished career as a physical scientist in government, business, and academia. During World War II, he had been part of the ultra-secret Manhattan Project that produced the atomic bomb, and he had held many powerful posts, including president of the American Association for the Advancement of Science (AAAS). He was reluctant, but the university was facing budgetary shortfalls and the panel's government funding would help. Assistant Dean of Graduate Studies Robert Low explored the option with prominent scientists and was told "Even to consider the *possibility* that UFOs may exist was not 'respectable'."[118] Low wrote a memo to the dean of the graduate school and the vice president of the University, later referred to as the "trick" memo. [119]

> Our study would be conducted almost exclusively by nonbelievers who, although they couldn't possibly prove a negative result, could and probably would add an impressive body of evidence that there is no reality to the observations. The *trick* would be, I think, to describe the project so that, to the public, it would appear a totally objective study but, to the scientific community, would present the image of a group of nonbelievers trying their best to be objective but having an almost zero expectation of finding a saucer. One way to do this would be to stress investigation, not of the physical phenomena, but rather of the people who do the observing—the psychology and sociology of persons and groups who report seeing UFO's. If the emphasis were put here, rather than on examination of the old question of the physical reality of the saucer, I think the scientific community would quickly get the message. [emphasis added]

The University of Colorado signed the contract October 6, 1966, and assembled a team of physical scientists and psychologists. Condon was the project's chief scientist. Low was the Project Director and became the liaison between Condon and the rest of the team. The members of the team were apparently unaware of Low's "trick" memo, and at least some took their task seriously. However, Condon had difficulty concealing his skepticism and did not participate in any of the data collection or analysis. James McDonald, a highly respected atmospheric physicist from the University of Arizona and a serious UFO researcher, was a likely candidate for the research team, but he was not invited. Disgusted with the poor science evidenced by

Project Blue Book, McDonald hoped the Condon Committee would be different. He tried to assist by sending them what he thought were the best cases he had encountered. In the end he and other UFO researchers were bitterly disappointed by the debacle that unfolded.

The saga of the Condon Committee has been told at length by many authors.[120] Members of the committee became increasingly disenchanted with Condon's and Low's leadership, yet slogged on under the co-principal investigator, psychologist and statistician, David R. Saunders. Saunders and Roy Craig, a physical scientist hired the following May, reinvestigated Mariana's Montana Movie, with very different conclusions.

Craig did not believe Mariana's claim that the Air Force had taken the first thirty-five frames. When he interviewed Virginia Raunig, Mariana's ex-secretary, seventeen years after the fact, her hesitant comment was, "What you have to remember in all this is…that Nick Mariana is a promoter." He included that comment in his 1995 book about his experience on the Condon Committee but failed to mention that Raunig finished her statement by affirming that Mariana was not dishonest.[121]

Nevertheless, Craig said that was enough for him to end the conversation. Together with the misinformation in the Marquez report, Craig found the case too flawed to take seriously. Oddly, Craig also reports that Ms. Raunig recalled only seeing one object.[122] Given that the film clearly shows two objects, one can only assume she never saw the actual film, either before or after it went to the Air Force.

Craig also interviewed three witnesses who viewed the film before it went to the Air Force, and they all backed up Mariana's claim of missing footage after the film came back. These included John Wuerthner, Mariana's attorney; E.P. Furlong, managing editor of the *Great Falls Tribune*; and Tony Dalich, mentioned earlier.[123] Wuerthner reported that the missing footage showed the discs directly overhead, and that he could see the disc's spinning movement (not discernible in the remaining footage). Furlong reported that it seemed "considerably shorter" to him when he saw it again after the Air Force returned it, and he thought two or three feet had been removed. Dalich reported the two objects were closer and clearer in the missing footage, shaped like peppermint wafers and definitely spinning. For whatever reasons, Craig did not mention those interviews or witnesses in his book on the Condon Committee. He seemed to have selectively focused on Ms. Raunig's comments.[124] But in the actual Condon Report, Craig at least mentioned the existence of these other witnesses:

> Others who had seen it both before and after it was lent to the Air Force firmly believed that not all the original film was returned by the Air Force. This claim was generally accepted as true by Great Falls Residents.[125]

Ironically, Craig used the Mariana case to demonstrate the use of out-of-context quotes by the Air Force to support their jet aircraft explanation of the movie while, as he pointed out, the Baker report decisively rejects that explanation. Craig wrote,

> Whether or not either Air Force or Dr. Baker's conclusions were correct, the tactic is that of the propagandist. Our desires and illusions continue to determine what we see in the world around us and what we believe of the testimony.[126]

How true, and Craig was equally guilty.

Craig also focused on Mariana's inability to find a letter from the Air Force admitting that part of the film was lost.[127] In his interview with Mariana in October 1967, Craig asked Mariana about the letter.[128] There was some confusion in the literature about the existence of such a letter.[129] When Project Blue Book requested to have the films again in 1952, Mariana wanted a guarantee that his film not be tampered with. On October 29, 1952, he accepted a receipt specifying it be returned intact within a month. Evidently the film was worn from repeated showings, and the Air Force sought specific permission to make a splice that would destroy one frame. Mariana agreed, but the Air Force figured out another way to solve the problem.[130]

Two weeks later Mariana received a letter dated November 14, 1952, from Colonel William Adams, chief of the Topical Division of the Directorate of Intelligence, reporting on the analysis. Adams mentioned the "torn" film and that instead of splicing it they repaired it with cellulose tape to avoid the loss of any frames. He cautioned Mariana not to run the film until it was permanently spliced.[131] Saunders, the other Condon Committee investigator, suggested this was the letter Mariana thought Craig was asking about during his visit in 1967.[132] Craig used the Mariana case as an illustration of the problems of investigating "Old UFO Cases" because of the "failures of memory and because of a tendency to crystallization of the story upon repeated retelling."[133] This is a legitimate investigative problem, and Mariana admitted that his memory of the event seventeen years before was "fuzzy." Oddly, he didn't remember the jets seen after the UFOs, though they were mentioned in all his early accounts. However, this is hardly enough reason to dismiss the case.

Saunders, on the other hand, found the "Great Falls, Montana" case compelling. He focused on the analysis of the existing film, rather than trying to find or document the missing footage. In his book about the Condon Committee investigation, Saunders devoted two chapters to a detailed review of the case and included extensive sections of Baker's scientific analysis. He called it the "one sighting of all time that did more than any other to convince me that there is something to the UFO problem," and that, "for my money, subsequent investigation has proved it to be airtight."[134] Saunders went on to say that not only did this case prove to him the existence of UFOs, but it also added considerable evidence to the hypothesis that there was a government conspiracy to conceal the truth about UFOs from the public.[135]

Problems on the Condon Committee erupted when the staff learned of Low's "trick" memo. Two late-coming researchers, including Roy Craig, were hired in May of 1967. Low gave them a background file on the project, probably unaware it contained the "trick" memo. Here was a document belying any intention of objectivity from the get-go. Craig shared it with the rest of the staff. (Craig maintained his faith in the scientific integrity of Ed Condon, in spite of Low's breach of scientific ethics, and continued with the project.)

Later that year, as most of the staff became increasingly concerned about Condon's and Low's objectivity, several staff members shared the memo with NICAP and Professor McDonald. In January 1968, Low called McDonald to request information. On January 31, 1968, McDonald used that opening to write a seven-page letter to Low, first complaining about Condon—his many negative comments to the press regarding UFOs, his obsession with UFO "crackpots," his non-involvement in field investigations, his distance from staff, and his failure to focus on truly anomalous, scientifically interesting cases.[136] He then quoted Low's memo, saying, "I am rather puzzled by the viewpoints expressed there."

Low was mortified and furious that this memo had surfaced and been leaked to McDonald. He showed the letter to Condon, who was likewise enraged, though he insisted he had not before been aware of the memo. Scientists on the staff were threatened with the ruination of their careers, and those involved in passing the memo to outsiders, including Saunders, were fired. Condon didn't stop there but tried to wreak vengeance on everyone involved in this exposure because it obviously raised doubts about the scientific integrity of the project and himself as the director.

He threatened lawsuits and used his considerable power to at-tempt to damage his detractors.

Within two weeks of the "trick" memo revelation, Mary Lou Armstrong, Bob Low's administrative assistant for the project, re-signed, saying, "there is an almost unanimous 'lack of confidence' in Low as project coordinator and in his exercise of the power of that position." Condon and Low were unable to keep the scandal from the press. *Look* magazine, with a circulation of eight million, featured an article calling the Condon Committee a "fiasco" and a "$500,000 trick."[137] Highly esteemed *Science* magazine reported problems with the research project, and Condon promptly can-celed his membership with the AAAS, the magazine's publisher, despite his past presidency of the prestigious organization. More tales of frustration by scientists on the staff and sabotage of valid research emerged the following year, when Saunders published a book with his own version of what happened.[138]

### Congressional UFO Symposium

The *Look* magazine article caught the attention of Indiana Con-gressman J. Edward Roush, who questioned the project's scientific integrity on the floor of the House.[139] He was already acquainted with Dr. McDonald, and together with the efforts of the private organization NICAP (where Donald Keyhoe was still the direc-tor), they hoped to launch a Congressional investigation. Their ef-forts resulted in a "UFO Symposium" presented before the House Science and Astronautics Committee on July 29, 1968.[140]

Five scientists presented their research and opinions on the subject, including McDonald, J. Allen Hynek, James A. Hard-er, Carl Sagan, and Robert M.L. Baker, whose testimony high-lighted his rigorous analysis of the Mariana film that had been published in the January/February 1968 issue of *Journal of As-tronautical Sciences*. According to UFO historian Jerome Clark, it was James McDonald who made the greatest impression, addressing those present and the scientific community at large:

> I have become convinced that the scientific community,
> not only in this country but throughout the world, has
> been casually ignoring as nonsense a matter of extraordi-
> nary scientific importance...
>
> [My] position is that UFOs are entirely real and we do
> not know what they are, because we have laughed them out
> of court....My own present opinion, based on two years of
> careful study, is that UFOs are probably extraterrestrial de-
> vices engaged in something that might very tentatively be
> termed "surveillance["]...
>
> I believe no other problem within your jurisdiction is of
> comparable scientific and national importance. These are
> strong words, and I intend them to be.

Some criticized the Congressional symposium for being too
"pro-UFO," and indeed, McDonald, the atmosphere scientist,
dissected and dismissed meteorological explanations given for
UFOs by two of the most vociferous UFO debunkers: Donald H.
Menzel, Harvard astronomer, and Philip J. Klass, Senior Editor
of *Aviation Week*.[141] However, the presenters were not allowed to
comment on the Condon Committee itself, even though credibility issues with that project led to the symposium.

In spite of excellent testimony from some of the greatest minds
studying UFOs at the time, and their urgent requests for more research (presumably beyond what the Condon Committee was doing), Congress took no action. The Condon Committee was allowed
to continue without any Congressional intervention or oversight.

### Publication of the Condon Report

Despite the project's implosion of credibility and staffing,
Condon and Low carried on, hiring a new recruit to write the

committee's report. In November, what was left of the Condon Committee handed over its report to the National Academy of Science (NAS), which happened to be headed by Condon's old friend and former student, Frederick Seitz. The report was approved by NAS, and shortly afterwards the *New York Times* heralded its conclusion: "U.F.O. Finding: No Visits from Afar." The science writer who wrote the *Times* article also had been hired to write the introduction to the official book on the committee's work, essentially a revisionist history of the committee that portrayed Condon and Low as victims of insubordination.[142]

The media focused on Condon's opening summary:

> Our general conclusion is that nothing has come from the study of UFOs in the past 21 years that has added to scientific knowledge. Careful consideration of the record as it is available to us leads us to conclude that further extensive study of UFOs probably cannot be justified in the expectation that science will be advanced thereby.[143]

Condon concludes by urging teachers to discourage student interest in UFOs:

> [W]e strongly recommend that teachers refrain from giving students credit for school work based on their reading of the presently available UFO books and magazine articles.

Publication of the Condon Report inspired widespread gloating among UFO skeptics and derision of anyone expressing interest in UFOs. I personally recall reading the newspaper coverage of the Condon Report as a college student and accepting its conclusions, totally oblivious to the underlying controversy. The media stories certainly dampened my interest in reading the report, and I'm sure many minds were sealed against further interest or investigation into the subject.

However, very few people ever saw the comments by highly credentialed critics of the report. As Hynek noted in the *Bulletin of Atomic Scientists*, a whopping 30 of the 91 cases investigated could not be explained, a higher percentage than in the Air Force investigations. What if the newspaper headlines had proclaimed, "Condon Report: One Third of UFO Cases Defy Explanation!" It is sobering to realize how much influence (and responsibility) the press carries.

Stanford University astrophysicist Peter Sturrock said Condon's summaries of the investigations were inaccurate, misleading, or false, and wondered how NAS had approved it. A subcommittee of the American Institute for Aeronautics and Astronautics (AIAA) concluded that "a careful reading of the report would lead to a conclusion precisely opposite to Condon's. Far from discouraging further scientific inquiry into the UFO phenomenon, the report should encourage it."[144] Obviously, a cautionary message about government studies would be to ignore the conclusions but look closely at the data.

### Hartmann's Conclusions

Astronomer William K. Hartmann wrote the Condon Report chapter on photographic case studies. Only two cases were not dismissed as fabrications, misidentifications, poor image quality, or clear images lacking sufficient information for analysis. These were a set of still photos from McMinnville, Oregon, and the ever-unsinkable Montana Movie. Regarding Mariana's illustrious footage, the report concludes:

> The case remains unexplained. Analysis indicates that the images on the film are difficult to reconcile with aircraft or other known phenomena, although aircraft cannot

be entirely ruled out…While such a hypothesis (the F-94 explanation) is tenable, it conflicts with some of the soft data. It is judged reasonable only to regard this object as unidentified. At the same time, the data are inconclusive and cannot be said to give probative support for the existence of extraordinary aircraft, or "flying saucers."

An analysis of the report by UFO researcher Michael Swords showed that eleven of the sixteen project members believed in the value of UFO research. Sadly the two project leaders, Condon and Low, believed UFO research was a waste of time.[145]

J. Allen Hynek called the Condon Report the "Blue Book End Game" and "the *coup de grâce* to the UFO era."[146] The report's overall effect was to end any official acknowledgment of the importance of possible extraterrestrial visitation. The Condon Committee may have been the *Titanic* of UFO research, but the Mariana film remained afloat.

## AFTER THE CONDON REPORT

### Barry Greenwood's Analysis

Veteran UFO researcher Barry Greenwood obtained an actual film copy of the National Archives copy of Mariana's film around 1975. Examining this copy, Greenwood could see that the first frame was diagonally cut. It included a small corner of a previous frame showing power lines across the lower right hand corner that matched the same corner in the first frame. This indicated at least one additional frame in the sequence had been cut.

Mariana told Craig in 1967 he knew the film had been cut because his film splices were always horizontal, not diagonal.[147] Greenwood measured the total length of the UFO footage at just over six feet. Adding the blank leader and blank end of the film made a total of about fourteen feet. If Brynildsen did pick up eight feet of UFO footage from Mariana, then two feet of UFO footage was missing, which matches what Mariana and other witnesses estimated was missing.[148] Greenwood also presented evidence that more frames were removed between the time of the Baker analysis and when he obtained a copy of the film and suggested it be called "The Incredible Shrinking Film."[149]

Greenwood also unearthed additional files and witness testimony in the Edward Uhler Condon Papers at the American Philosophical Society, which were not included in the Condon Report. These included transcripts of Roy Craig's interviews with Mariana and other witnesses, as well as Craig's correspondence on the Mariana case.

### The Rumor of a Bribe

Another paper published in the MUFON Journal suggested that Mariana may have taken a bribe from the Air Force to "lose interest in UFOs." The author claimed (based on a third-hand report) that a friend of Mariana's overheard such a conversation in Mariana's Great Falls home between Mariana and two Air Force personnel. To be sure, in the first newspaper accounts of Mariana surrendering the film to the Air Force, Mariana said he was told not to release any further information about the films.[150]

However, many of the "facts" related by this alleged witness regarding what happened after this purported conversation are demonstrably wrong.[151] Furthermore, Mariana's enthusiastic participation in the 1956 UFO documentary flies in the face of any "hush" bribe. Both of Mariana's children as well as Great Falls resident Jerry Puffer remember him appearing on the national television program, "I've Got a Secret," where he stumped the celebrity panel and most certainly announced his story to the world.[152] Finally, to put all doubt to rest, Mariana wrote a letter to the *Great Falls Tribune* in October 1966, sixteen years after the event, which included the following statements:

When anyone asks me now if I believe in flying saucers…I do …where before I was somewhat leery about
being so positive…Like other Montanans, I suspect the
USAF is censoring stuff; I have absolute proof… The film
I showed to men like Bill Zadick, Ed Furlong and C.T.
Sullivan of the Leader, and the late O.S. Warden, Bob
Warden and others of the Tribune staff at a closed meeting was sharp and clear; however, when I got the film back
and showed it to them again the opening portion of the
objects hovering just west and almost over the ball park
was missing…I tried for years to get back the portion the
Air Force cut out and never did receive it. I believe it is still
somewhere in the Pentagon. My portion of the film which
was returned showed only the objects in flight. The hovering portion which was included in the showings in Great
Falls to the Lions Club and Booster Club was spectacular
and breathtaking. Some of these days I expect a return visit
so I carry my camera with me, loaded at all times.[153]

Mariana was working for the federal government in Portland,
Oregon, at the time of this letter (for the USDI Bureau of Sports
and Wildlife, later the Fish & Wildlife Service), but he had certainly not lost interest in UFOs and was not afraid to tell his story
in public.[154] The bribe-taking rumor was spun on a few spindles
of truth but is nevertheless full of holes.

Although Mariana continued to speak publicly about his experiences, there are many witnesses to UFO events who describe being bribed and even threatened to maintain silence. The Roswell
case has many troubling examples.[155] Kenneth Arnold, according to his daughter, was told by a visiting stranger that speaking
publicly about his sightings could be dangerous. He and his wife
considered this a threat to their lives. As a result, he curtailed his
speaking plans and became something of a recluse.[156] Recently, a

witness to the famous Travis Walton (*Fire in the Sky*) case reported that renowned UFO debunker Philip Klass offered him $10,000 if he would say the whole affair was a hoax.[157] Whether Mariana was actually offered a bribe will probably never be known, but if he was offered a bribe to stay silent, his actions indicated he rejected it.

## MARIANA MOVES ON

Mariana left his position as manager of the Electrics baseball team in 1953 and moved to Missoula, where he was instrumental in securing a Pioneer League baseball franchise for the Missoula Timberjacks. The Timberjacks never quite made it as a successful business venture, despite much effort and personal investment on Mariana's part, and the team only lasted from 1956 to 1960.[158] In 1962, Mariana moved his family to Portland, Oregon, and his job as State Conservation Coordinator for what became the U.S. Fish and Wildlife Service. When that position disappeared due to funding cuts, he moved to other jobs in both the public and private sector.

Throughout his life, Mariana was active in the community and the Catholic Church. Instead of retiring, he and his wife Claretta realized a dream of launching a Catholic radio station in Portland. This was no small effort, and one journalist described him as a "sweet-talking and charismatic fundraiser."[159] In 1976 Mariana was honored as the "Outstanding Man of the Year" by the Metropolitan Holy Name Union in Portland.[160]

Mariana's son, Nick Jr., remembers his father as a really great dad and larger-than-life character. He recalled that wherever his father worked, he was someone people sought out for advice and turned to with their troubles. Movie cameras were always a part of family holidays. His father put a camera in Nick Jr.'s hands at a very early age, and he remembers great fun making movies together. No wonder Nick Jr. developed a career as a videographer, with his company

"Mr. Video Productions." And his son, Nick Mariana III, having developed skills in his father's video shop, is now an art director in feature films. Nick Jr. believed the UFO film was a big event in his father's life and said his father felt bad about not making a copy of the film before turning it over to the Air Force.[161]

Mariana's daughter Michele also described her father with obvious affection and endearment, "a passionate Italian, kind and honest." She mentioned he'd once been named an honorary Blackfeet chief. She gave a glimpse of his openhearted and trusting nature when she said, "I was raised to believe everyone was family until proved otherwise. He was a lovely man."[162] Mariana died on his birthday, August 20, 1999, in Vancouver, Washington.

## THE VOYAGERS: A NEW ERA

On January 15, 2008, the Great Falls Baseball Club announced a name change: the Great Falls "White Sox" would henceforth be called the "Voyagers." While no doubt part of a trend away from using the name of the club's major league parent team, Great Falls team officials announced the new moniker with great fanfare and a multi-media presentation featuring the legendary Mariana film.[163] It may have been a marketing decision, but it reflected the city's ownership of this historic event, and possibly, in some quarters, a degree of pride.

The team's new mascot, a little green alien named "Orbit," has rocketed (what else) souvenir sales to record levels. The club's food stands feature

*Flag of the Great Falls Baseball Club's Voyagers, featuring team mascot "Orbit."*

"Orbit Burgers" and "Voyager Fries," and every game begins with Orbit circling the ballpark on a scooter to the triumphant theme music from the movie "Star Wars," his fans cheering.

Great Falls has surely had a lion's share of sightings and events, earning its place as "one of the UFO Capitals of the world."[164] Many sightings followed Mariana's, adding up to hundreds of reported sightings over the years, though unfortunately, there are no other known early films or photos. In today's world, video software has flooded the Internet with hoaxed UFO movies. But Great Falls was also the first area where military witnesses reported nuclear missile shutdowns while UFOs hovered overhead. These incidents may have fostered a more open attitude in the local press

*"Saucers Over the Big Stack"*

*Missoula artist Monte Dolack imagined the Great Falls incident this way, in his 1985 color painting that includes a bright red 1959 Plymouth Fury. In Mariana's film there were two discs, not three, and they hovered to the left of the "stack." Artwork used with permission of the artist, www. dolack.com.*

while the national media eschewed the subject. Great Falls continues to have many residents willing to report UFOs in recent times,[165] and an amateur Great Falls videographer has several years of extensive footage of a specific UFO that may pass the authenticity test. But I'll save that story for another volume.

## Notes

1. Roy Craig, interview of Nick Mariana, August 31, 1967, transcript, pp. 3-4, Edward Uhler Condon Papers, Series V, UFO Materials, "Mariana Case #47, Great Falls, Montana," American Philosophical Society, http://www.amphilsoc.org/mole/view?docId=ead/Mss.B.C752-ead.xml#d9964322e183176060207104/

2. National Investigations Committee on Aerial Phenomena Report, "The Nicholas Mariana UFO Color Film," http://www.nicap.org/montanadir.htm/

3. Robert Barrow, "UFO Revisited," *Official UFO Magazine*, February 1977; NICAP website http://www.nicap.org/ufochop1.htm/

4. Some articles report the name of the ball club at the time to be the "Selectrics." According to Wikipedia, it was called the "Selectrics" in 1949-1950, http://en.wikipedia.org/wiki/Great_Falls_Electrics/ At the time of Nick's 1953 interview for the movie, the team was again the "Electrics." Great Falls is known as the "Electric City" because of hydroelectric plants in the area.

5. Confusion about whether the date was August 5 or 15 apparently began with a report filed by Air Force Lieutenant Peter Marquez, who interviewed Mariana on January 7, 1953, at the behest of Major Ruppelt for Project Blue Book. This confusion was reported again by Roy Craig of the Condon Committee in 1967, and reiterated by other sources, including Richard Dolan, *UFOs and the National Security State* (Charlottesville, VA: Hampton Roads Publishing, 2002), and Wikipedia. Craig assumed the August 15 date had to be wrong, because the Selectrics played in Twin Falls, Idaho, that night. He was unable to access the newspaper article from August 15 to verify that date. Evidently the team's budget did not allow the business manager to travel with the team. Though there was no home game that night, Mariana was in the Great Falls ballpark on the 15th. Some researchers have suggested Marquez had trouble reading his interview notes.

6. Author phone interview with Nick Mariana Jr., September 13, 2011.

7. "Nick Mariana Gives Masterly Mound Exhibition," *Billings* [MT] *Gazette*, August 2, 1931.

8. Author telephone conversation with Michele Mariana, April 18, 2012.

9. Capt. John P. Brynildsen, "Unconventional Aircraft," October 7, 1950, Blue Book Archives, NARA PBB89, 409-416, http://bluebookarchive.org/ Brynildsen's 8-page report on the Mariana case went both to Director of Special Investigations in Washington, D.C., and to the District Commander of OSI at Wright Patterson AFB, Dayton, Ohio.

10. "Former Electrics official, announcer Mariana dies," *Great Falls* [MT] *Tribune*, August

25, 1999, 2M.

11. http://en.wikipedia.org/wiki/Great_Falls,_Montana/

12. "Mariana Reports Flying Discs," *Great Falls* [MT] *Leader*, August 15, 1950, 1. Two different sources report that the sighting was also printed in the *Great Falls Tribune* on August 16: Jerome Clark, *The UFO Book: Encyclopedia of the Extraterrestrial* (Detroit: Visible Ink Press, 1998), 489, and Saunders and Harkins, *UFOs? Yes: Where the Condon Committee Went Wrong* (New York: Signet Books/New American Library, 1968), 96-97. The author scoured microfilms of August 16–19, 1950, editions of the *Great Falls Tribune* at Montana Historical Society, Helena, and did not find it, so believes they are in error.

13. "Flying Saucer Movies To Be Shown Here," *Great Falls Tribune*, September 11, 1950. To my knowledge, this is the first time Mariana's sighting is reported in the *Tribune*.

14. Craig interview of Mariana, August 31, 1967, transcript, p. 12.

15. Sullivan's letter can be found in the Blue Book Archives, www.bluebook archive.org, MAXW-PBB8, 206.

16. Clark, 489.

17. Richard Dolan, *UFOs and the National Security State* (Charlottesville, VA: Hampton Roads Publishing, 2002), 43-44.

18. Clark, 489.

19. Clark, 489-91.

20. Captain Edward J. Ruppelt, *The Report on Unidentified Flying Objects* (1956; repr. 2011, Pacific Publishing Studio http://www.PacPS.com), 25.

21. Jan Aldrich, "1948 UFO Documents: Background: Early UFO Documents," n.d., http://www.project1947.com/fig/1948back.htm/

22. Dolan, 60-61.

23. Dolan, 60.

24. Aldrich, "1948 UFO Documents."

25. "Top Secret Analysis of Flying Object Incidents in the U.S.," Study #100-203-79, December 10, 1948, http://www.project1947.com/fig/1948air.htm/

26. Air Materiel Command, "Memorandum to the Press," April 29, 1949, http://www.project1947.com/fig/projsauc.htm/

27. Dolan, 69-70.

28. Ruppelt, 38.

29. Dolan, 69-70.

30. Donald E. Keyhoe, "Flying Saucers are Real," *True*, January 1950, 11-13, 83-87.

31. Dolan, 79.

32. Ruppelt, 41.

33. Ruppelt, 43-44.

34. Ruppelt, 43.

35. Ruppelt, 42.

36. Ruppelt, 44.

37. Dolan, 82-85.

38. Project Blue Book Roll 91, p. 80, NARA—PBB91, Document Code T1206-91, National Archives, Washington, DC, or at http://www.bluebookarchive.org/

39. Craig interview of Mariana, August 31, 1967, transcript, p. 2.

40. "'Flying Disc' Film Entangled In Federal 'Red Tape'," *Great Falls Tribune*, October 6, 1950, 8.

41. Clark, 397-98.

42. Project Blue Book Roll 89 (NARA—PBB89), 411-12, available through the National

Archives, or at www.bluebookarchive.org/

43. Craig interview of Mariana, August 31, 1967, transcript, p. 14.

44. "'Flying Disc' Film Entangled In Federal 'Red Tape'."

45. The Air Force Declassification Office announced the declassification of these Project Grudge documents on October 27, 2011, http://www.secretsdeclassified.af.mil/

46. "Top Secret Analysis of Flying Object Incidents in the U.S.," Study #100-203-79, 10 Dec., 1948, http://www.project1947.com/fig/1948air.htm/

47. "Dissemination of Publicity Policy on Reports of Unconventional Aircraft," Dated October 2, 1950, and signed by Col. H.J. Kieling, USAF Executive Directorate of Intelligence, http://www.secretsdeclassified.af.mil/news/story.asp?storyID=123277517/

48. "Pictures 'Show Nothing'," *Kingston* [N.Y.] *Daily Freeman*, October 11, 1950; "Air Force Seizes Mystery Photos," *Syracuse Herald-Journal*, October 11, 1950; "No One Will Ever Know of Results," *The Ada* [OK] *News*, October 11, 1950; "Saucer Pictures Too Dark for Air Force," *Austin* [TX] *Statesman*, October 11, 1950; "Maybe Mariana Should Stick to Baseball Snaps," [Walla Walla, WA] *Union Bulletin*, October 11, 1950; "Saucer Photos Are Confiscated," *Reno* [Nevada] *Evening Gazette*, October 12, 1950; "'Flying Saucer' Pictures Veiled By Air Force, *Portsmouth* [NH] *Herald*, October 11, 1950; "Flying Saucer Film Too Dark," *Mansfield* [OH] *News-Journal*, October 11, 1950; "No Flying Saucers," *The Lethbridge* [Alberta] *Herald*, October 11, 1950; "AF Couldn't See 'Saucers' In Pics," [Oak Ridge, TN] *Oak Ridger*, October 12, 1950.

49. Saunders and Harkins, 96-97. The letter was signed by Lt. Col. Ray Ward Taylor as Deputy Chief, Public Information Office, Air Materiel Command.

50. "(Restricted) [sic] Releasing Results of Analysis and Evaluation of 'Unidentified Aerial Objects' Reports," October 11, 1950, and "Memorandum for Record," October 12, 1950, Project Grudge Documents, http://www.secretsdeclassified.af.mil/shared/media/document/AFD-110719-005.pdf.

51. Ruppelt, *Report*, 138.

52. Roy Craig, "Mariana Movie—Memo for File: Notes from October 18-21 trip to Great Falls, Montana," 1967, p. 3, Series V, UFO Materials, "Mariana Case #47, Great Falls, Montana," Edward Uhler Condon Papers, American Philosophical Society, http://www.amphilsoc.org/mole/view?docId=ead/Mss.B.C752-ead.xml#d9964322e183176060207104/

53. In the Blue Book archives, a letter dated May 1, 1956 from Brigadier General Harold E. Watson to the Vice-President of Public Relations at Douglas Aircraft officially denies Mariana's statement quoted in the Baker report that the Air Force removed a number of frames. He says that official Air Force files say the film arrived in damaged condition and the AF asked to repair it, noting that might result in the loss of 1 or 2 frames. They say Mariana was notified and wired permission to repair the film. It is unclear, since the documents are not provided, whether they are referring to the first time the Air Force had the film in 1950, or the second time in 1952, NARA-Maxwell Collection of Project Blue Book, Roll 8, pp. 234-35, http://bluebookarchive.org/page.aspx?PageCode=MAXW-PBB8-234/ Many of the microfilmed documents in the PBB Mariana file are illegible in the online archives, so the author can't tell whether other Air Force documents address the missing film, or know if better copies are available for inspection (Mariana File in Roll 8, pp. 196-301).

54. Ruppelt, 38.

55. Letter from Dr. James E. McDonald, May 4, 1970, to Mr. Arthur C. Lundahl, head of the Navy photography lab that analyzed the original Newhouse film, after the Air Force completed their analysis; NICAP (National Investigations Committee On Aerial

Phenomena) File: The Tremonton, Utah/Newhouse Color Film, http://www.nicap. org/reports/utah4.htm/

56. Dolan, 103.

57. Paola Harris, "An Interview with Kim Arnold: Daughter to the 1947 UFO Wave Witness," *Open Minds Magazine* 13 (April/May 2012), 58-65.

58. Wendy Connors and Michael David Hall, "The Montana Film: An Update From Newly Found Records," NICAP Case Directory (Category 8, Photographic Evidence), http://www.nicap.org/reports/montana3.htm/

59. Bob Considine, "The Disgraceful Flying Saucer Hoax," *Cosmopolitan* (130:1), January 1951, 32-33, 100-102.

60. Saunders and Harkins, 97.

61. Clark, 488.

62. "Bob Considine," http://en.wikipedia.org/wiki/Bob_Considine/

63. "The Press: Ghost at Work," *Time*, January 24, 1949.

64. Saunders and Harkins, 58.

65. See Jesse Marcel, Jr., Linda Marcel and Stanton Friedman, *The Roswell Legacy: The Untold Story of the First Military Officer at the 1947 Crash Site* (Franklin Lakes, NJ: Career Press, 2009); Col. Philip Corso, *The Day After Roswell* (New York: Pocket Books, 1997); Thomas J. Carey, et al., *Witness to Roswell: Unmasking the Government's Biggest Cover-up (Revised and Expanded Edition)* (Pompton Plains, NJ, New Page Books, 2009).

66. "Mariana Sues Magazine Firm for Alleged Libel," *Great Falls Tribune*, May 8, 1951.

67. "Project Blue Book," January 9, 1953, "Report on Marquez interview with Mariana," Blue Book Archives (MAXW—PBB8: 232) http://bluebookarchive.org/

68. Clark, 398.

69. Sanders and Harkins, 98-99.

70. Dolan, xxvi.

71. Clark, 488.

72. Ruppelt, 4.

73. See "Radar and the Saucers," *Washington Post*, July 25, 1952; "Blips on the Scopes," *Time*, August 4, 1952: 40, 45; "Washington's Blips," *Life*, August 4, 1952, 39-40.

74. "Project Blue Book," January 9, 1953, "Report on Marquez interview," 231-33, Notes on the memo say it was declassified after 12 years.

75. Ibid.

76. Saunders and Harkins, 100.

77. Clark, 513-15.

78. Ruppelt, 132-33.

79. Ruppelt, 137.

80. Ruppelt, 137-38.

81. Thornton Page to James L. Klotz (October 3, 1992), http://www.cufon.com/tp_corres.htm/

82. J. Allen Hynek, interview in 1974 film moderated by Rod Serling, http://www.hyper. net/ufo/video-footage.html

83. "Josef Allen Hynek"in Clark, 305.

84. "Robertson Panel" in Clark, 514.

85. Ibid.

86. Barrow, "UFO Revisited," Part 2.

87. Dolan, 129.

88. Dolan, 125.

89. Dolan, 93, 142.
90. Dolan, 128, 136, 142.
91. Dolan, 142.
92. Timothy Good, *Above Top Secret: The Worldwide UFO Cover-up* (New York: William Morrow & Co., 1988), 80.
93. "Project Blue Book," in Clark, 468.
94. Ruppelt, 141.
95. Ruppelt, 37-141.
96. Barrow, "UFO Revisited," Part 1.
97. Barrow, Part 1.
98. Barrow, Part 1.
99. Barrow, Part 1.
100. Barrow, Part 1.
101. David Michael Jacobs, *The UFO Controversy in America* (Bloomington: Indiana University Press, 1975).
102. Barrow, Part 1.
103. Barrow, Part 1.
104. Barrow, Part 1.
105. Barrow, Part 1.
106. Robert M.L. Baker Jr., "Observational Evidence of Anomalistic Phenomena," in *Journal of the Astronautical Sciences* 15 (January/February 1968), 31-36.
107. Martyn Stubbs' award-winning film, "The Secret NASA Transmissions: The Smoking Gun," released in 2000, featured footage of notched UFOs. As with all UFO video footage, there are competing interpretations. The official NASA explanation and that offered by UFO debunker James Oberg is that the notched discs are space debris or ice particles. However, a number of researchers believe that explanation is untenable, and that the NASA photos comprise some of the best available evidence for spacecraft. See Ronald Nussbeck, UFO: NASA STS 75 Shuttle Tether Science Mission, posted December 13, 2008, http://www.ufodigest.com/news/1208/tether.html/
108. Robert M.L. Baker Jr., *Photogrammetric Analysis of the "Montana Film" Tracking Two UFOs* (Santa Monica, CA: Douglas Aircraft Company, 1956). This paper also can be found at the Blue Book Archives website, MAXW-PBB8, pp. 255-83, http://www.bluebookarchive.org/page.aspx?PageCode=MAXW-PBB8-255/
109. Baker, "Observational Evidence of Anomalistic Phenomena," 31-36.
110. U.S. Congress, House Committee on Science and Astronautics, Symposium on Unidentified Flying Objects, Hearings, Ninetieth Congress, Second Session, July 29, 1968 (Washington, DC: Government Printing Office, 1968.)
111. Barrow, Part II.
112. Ruppelt, *Report.*
113. J. Allen Hynek, *The UFO Experience: A Scientific Inquiry* (Chicago: Henry Regnery Company, 1972).
114. Dolan, 234-37.
115. Barrow, Part II.
116. Barrow, Part I.
117. Dolan, 299-300.
118. "University of Colorado UFO Project," in Clark, 594.
119. Ibid., 601.
120. See Clark, 592-607; Dolan 308-70; Saunders and Harkins; Michael Swords, "The

University of Colorado UFO Project: The 'Scientific Study of UFOs'," *The Journal of UFO Studies*, n.s., 6 (1995/96), 149-84.

121. Craig, "Mariana Movie—Memo for File," 1.

122. Roy Craig, *UFOs: An Insider's View of the Official Quest for Evidence* (Denton: University of North Texas Press, 1995), 231.

123. Craig, "Mariana Movie—Memo for File," 3.

124. Craig, *UFOs: An Insider's View*, 158, 162, 195-96, 230-31.

125. Roy Craig, "Field Studies," in Section III of *Scientific Study of Unidentified Flying Objects*, Daniel S. Gillmor, ed. (New York: E.P. Dutton & Co, Inc., 1969), 53.

126. Craig, *UFOs: An Insider's View*, p. 133

127. Craig, "Field Studies," 53.

128. Craig interview of Mariana, August 31, 1967, transcript, p. 13.

129. The first reference the author can find to an Air Force "admission of removal" letter, was in Baker's 1956 *Photogrammatic Analysis of the "Montana Film" Tracking Two UFOs* (cited above). Baker writes: "The film as returned by the Air Force, according to Mr. Mariana, had had the first 35 frames removed, and only the remainder of the film was returned. He says he has a letter in his files admitting this removal and that the clipped off part was lost.", Project Blue Book Mariana case file, MAXW-PBB8, p. 255. http://www.bluebookarchive.org/page.aspx?PageCode=MAXW-PBB8-255/ The Air Force letter responding to this statement and denying Mariana's allegations as stated in Baker's report is also in the Project Blue Book Mariana case files, pp. 234-35, http://www.bluebookarchive.org/page.aspx?PageCode=MAXW-PBB8-234/

130. Saunders and Harkins, 100.

131. Barry Greenwood, "On the Question of Tampering with the 1950 Great Falls UFO Film," *U.F.O. Historical Review*, #7 (September 2000), 4, available at: http://www.greenwoodufoarchive.com/

132. Saunders and Harkins, 96-97.

133. Craig, "Field Studies," 52-53.

134. Saunders and Harkins, 83, 85.

135. Saunders and Harkins, 91-92.

136. "University of Colorado UFO Project," in Clark, 594.

137. John G. Fuller, "Flying Saucer Fiasco: The Half-million Dollar Cover-up on Whether UFOs Really Exist," *Look* (May 14, 1968).

138. Saunders and Harkins.

139. "James Edward McDonald," in Clark, 368.

140. Symposium on Unidentified Flying Objects: Hearings Before the Committee on Science and Aeronautics, U.S. House of Representatives, Ninetieth Congress, Second Session, July 29, 1968 [No. 7]. U.S. Government Printing Office, Washington: 1968.

141. The story of James E. McDonald is one of the great tragedies in ufology. After relentless hounding by Philip Klass in particular, and rejection by many of his peers as a fanatic, McDonald's otherwise distinguished career and his marriage suffered. He committed suicide in 1971. See "James Edward McDonald," in Clark, 363-72.

142. Edward U. Condon, *Final Report of the Scientific Study of Unidentified Flying Objects Conducted by the University of Colorado Under Contract to the United States Air Force* (New York: Bantam Books, 1969).

143. Edward U. Condon, "Conclusion and Recommendations" in *Scientific Study of Unidentified Flying Objects*, Daniel S. Gillmor, ed. (New York: E.P. Dutton & Co, Inc., 1969), 1-6.

144. See "University of Colorado UFO Project," in Clark, 604; and Sutrrock, Peter A. *Evaluation of the Condon Report on the Colorado UFO Project: SUIPR Report #599*, Stanford, CA: Institute for Plasma Research, Stanford University, 1974.

145. Michael. D. Swords, "The USAF-Sponsored Colorado Project for the Scientific Study of UFOs," in Walter H. Andrus Jr., ed., *MUFON 1995 International UFO Symposium Proceedings* (Seguin, TX: Mutual UFO Network, 1995), 149-63.

146. Dr. J. Allen Hynek, *The Hynek UFO Report* (New York: Dell Publishing Co., 1977), 279, 287.

147. Craig interview of Mariana, August 31, 1967, transcript, p. 6.

148. Greenwood, "On the Question of Tampering," 7.

149. Ibid.

150. "'Flying Disc' Film Entangled in 'Red Tape'."

151. James R. Leming, "The Montana Movie," *MUFON Journal* 223 (November 1986): 10-11, 17-18. The alleged witness claimed that Mariana received a paid relocation to another city, a job on government payroll and a purported lump sum of $10,000. In fact, Mariana stayed in Great Falls until 1953 before moving to Missoula, where he managed another minor league team.

152. Author telephone conversation with Michele Mariana, April 8, 2012; e-mail communication, September 12, 2011 from Jerry Puffer (currently a program radio host for KSEN Radio, Shelby, MT) to author. See also Richard Ecke, "Mariana's Film One of the Best produced," *Great Falls Tribune*, May 8, 2006, 1-2M; Ecke interview of Nick Mariana Jr., http://www.ufocasebook.com/marianafilm.html/

153. Carla Beck, "'Flying Saucer' Sighter Becomes More Positive," *Great Falls Tribune*, October 24, 1966: 8.

154. Craig interview of Nick Mariana, August 31, 1967, transcript, pp. 3-4.

155. See: Carey, et al., *Witness to Roswell.*

156. Paola Harris, 65.

157. Steve Pierce, one of the crewmembers who witnessed the spacecraft that took Travis Walton, shared this story when he joined Travis for his presentation, "Fire in the Sky Revisited," at the 2012 International UFO Congress.

158. Jack Herman, "Tales of the Timberjacks," *Missoulian,* July 11, 1999.

159. "Hail Marys, and Full of Grace," *Oregonian*, April 13, 2008, at http://blog.oregonlive.com/lifestories/2008/04/claretta_mariana.html/

160. "Religious Group Honors Former Great Falls Resident," *Great Falls Tribune*, February 7, 1976, 5.

161. Author telephone interview with Nick Mariana Jr., September 13, 2011.

162. Author telephone conversation with Michele Mariana, April 18, 2012.

163. George Geise, "The Voyagers Have Landed: 1950 Sighting at Ballpark Inspires New Name," *Great Falls Tribune*, January 16, 2008.

164. Jon Axline, "Montana's Flying Saucer Film (Or How the Great Falls Baseball Team Got its Name), *Montana Magazine*, May-June 2008, 29-30.

165. See Richard Ecke, "U.F.O. Sightings: Montanans Reveal Close Encounters," *Great Falls Tribune*, June 29, 1997, pp. 1-4P.

# 2

# UFOs and the Minuteman Missiles

*I, without reservation, accuse the U.S. Department of the
Air Force of blatant, pervasive and a continuing cover-up
of the facts, deception, distortion, and lying to the public
about the reality of the UFO phenomenon.*
Robert L. Salas
Captain, United States Air Force, Retired

The events detailed in this chapter seeded my first thoughts of
the need for this book. The extensive documentation of UFO
activity around nuclear weapons sites—and the convincing evidence that UFOs have deactivated nuclear missiles—is something
people need to know. It belongs in our Montana history texts, in
our American history texts, and in our world history texts. It is
that significant, and it is critical to our collective future. As citizens of the only country in the world that has used nuclear weapons in warfare, Americans particularly need to know about these
events. Frankly, I was outraged that information of this magnitude was being kept from the people.

When I first dipped my toe into the UFO literature, it was the testimony of retired military personnel that I found most compelling. There are hundreds of highly credentialed, former employees of military and intelligence agencies in the U.S. who have testified to the presence of extraterrestrial spacecraft and beings on Earth.[1] One of the most famous of these in UFO circles, and certainly in Montana, is Dr. Jesse Marcel Jr., the son of the first military officer at the 1947 Roswell, New Mexico, UFO crash site.

Dr. Marcel is a highly respected member of the Helena community and practiced medicine there for many years. A former sailor in the U.S. Navy, he joined the Montana Army National Guard in 1973, where he became a helicopter pilot and flight surgeon. While in the Guard, he was named State Surgeon for the state of Montana. Though he retired from the Guard in 1996, Marcel was called back to active duty in 2004 for the Iraq war. At the age of 68, Marcel flew 225 combat hours as a flight surgeon in the 189th Attack Helicopter Battalion. He was discharged to the Ready Reserve in December 2005.

After decades of telling his Roswell story whenever asked, Dr. Marcel finally wrote his own book about his and his father's first-hand experience with the Roswell crash, sometimes called the granddaddy of all UFO cases. His book is called *The Roswell Legacy*. The Roswell case is incredibly well documented. Although the UFO claim is still officially denied, the government's explanation of what happened at Roswell has changed at least four times.

On Sunday, July 6, 1947, Col. William Blanchard at the Roswell Army Air Field dispatched air intelligence officer Captain (later Major) Jesse Marcel Sr. to collect wreckage from the reported UFO crash site. Blanchard commanded the 509th Bomb Group, one of the nation's elite units and at that time the *only* military group in the world with atomic weapons.[2] Captain Marcel, along with Army Captain Sheridan Cavitt, were the first military personnel on the site. Marcel and Cavitt spent the day investigating the crash site and collecting crash debris. Late that night, Marcel started back to the base with his vehicle full of crash-site wreckage. Between 1 and 2 A.M. he stopped at his home, woke his wife and son, and showed them some of the unusual things he had found. His son Jesse specifically remembers a small metallic I-beam with purplish-violet symbols along the center section, and metal foil that spontaneously returned to its original smooth, unwrinkled shape after being crumpled.

On July 8, Col. Blanchard issued an earth-shattering press release saying that the Army had recovered a "flying disc." The press release was widely reported and is legendary in UFO history. Later that day, Captain Marcel flew to Fort Worth, Texas, where Brig. General Roger M. Ramey, commander of the Eighth Air Force, held a press conference retracting Blanchard's press release. Ramey had Marcel hold up a weather balloon radar reflector to support the Army's contention that the debris had been misidentified. At the press conference Marcel was ordered to keep silent and not make any comments to the civilian photographer. Thirty years later, in 1978, Marcel told UFO researcher Stan Friedman that he never believed what they found was a weather balloon, a device with which he and Col. Blanchard were quite familiar.[3]

How the abundance of highly credible testimony about UFOs can be ignored or dismissed as error or even lies by so many otherwise rational people astounds me. Over the years, I have come to understand there are many reasons why people have trouble accepting the evidence.

One reason is the effort the government has made to keep it secret. I have heard several people say they just don't believe our government is capable of keeping a secret of this magnitude. Perhaps they've never studied the history of the Manhattan Project, which developed nuclear weaponry in the U.S. But on another level they are correct. Some ufologists say that so much previously classified information is now available that disclosure has essentially already happened; the secret is out. However, there are millions of people, perhaps half of the people in the U.S., who still question the reality of extraterrestrial visitors. A 2007 poll of 400 Montanans conducted by Montana State University Billings said 35 percent of Montanans believe in the existence of UFOs, 15 percent are unsure, and 50 percent do not believe.[4] Perhaps the non-believers know, consciously or otherwise, that accepting extraterrestrial visitors as a real phenomenon means they also must accept a staggering level of government deception going back at least sixty-five years. For many, the existence of UFOs may be too challenging to what they believe, whether those beliefs concern religion, government, or the uniqueness of humans. In explaining entrenched skepticism, the deep commitment that humans have to their personal "worldviews" may be more powerful than government disinformation.

This chapter presents the best military witness testimony regarding UFOs and nuclear missiles in Montana, as well as an inside look at some ways this information was suppressed. As in Roswell, there is striking conflict between official reports and witness testimony.

While weapons technology grew exponentially since World War II, so did the science and technology of military "intelligence," which include many ways of obscuring the truth, both from our enemies and from our citizens. The increased understanding of psychology, and advanced techniques of "authoritative persuasion" have had a profound impact on the ability to influence human thinking and beliefs. That sentence bears reading twice. Humans like to believe they are rational and independent thinkers. I daresay many are largely unaware of the massive amounts of research on consumer marketing and on techniques for manipulation through unconscious fears, desires, and beliefs. Given the vast amount of contradictory information coming at us in these times, we need to develop ever greater powers of discernment.

To better understand the Montana UFO-missile events, it's

helpful to remember what was going on with nuclear weaponry leading up to and including the year 1967.

## Historical and Political Context

In 1967, Lyndon Baines Johnson was president of the United States. The nation was at the height of the Cold War with the Soviet Union while simultaneously hotly engaged in the Viet Nam War. Ten years prior, the Russian launch of the Sputnik satellite had caught the U.S. by surprise, and U.S. missile and satellite development vaulted to top priority, ushering in what we now call "the Space Age." In January 1958, less than four months after Sputnik, the U.S. launched its first satellite, Explorer I. From then until the mid-1970s, outer space became a new battlefield in the Cold War.

The space program fed the human drive for new frontiers and scientific advancement, but with it came a more sinister capacity: the ability to launch weapons of mass destruction to any location on the planet.

In 1961, based on pressure from Cuban refugees and advice from the military, President John F. Kennedy had given orders for a CIA invasion of Cuba, attempting to overthrow Fidel Castro's communist regime. The attempt at the Bay of Pigs failed, but it sent Castro looking for heavy backup. In October 1962, Soviet nuclear warheads designed for short- and intermediate-range missiles arrived in Cuba. The short-range missiles were to be used in Cuba against U.S. invasion forces. The intermediate-range missiles were aimed at the most vital targets in the U.S. Each intermediate-range warhead had twenty times the power of the Hiroshima nuclear bomb. Although the Cuban Missile Crisis was eventually defused (with the Soviet Union agreeing to remove the warheads and missiles in exchange for a promise that the U.S. would not invade Cuba), the event generated a tidal wave of paranoia and defense frenzy on American shores.

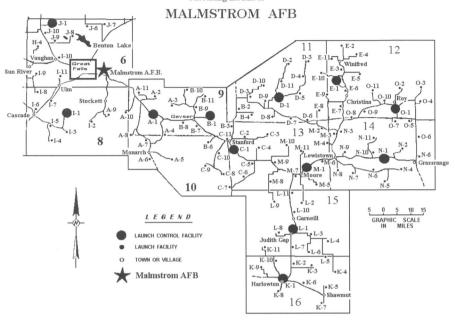

Minuteman Missile Installations
Surrounding and East of

# MALMSTROM AFB

*Above: Map of Minuteman missile sites controlled from Great Falls, Montana (from* Faded Giant, *by Salas and Klotz, used with permission); right: a Minuteman in its underground silo (from the Minuteman Missile National Historic Site/ National Park Service).*

*Above: Two Air Force officers spent long shifts below ground, awaiting launch orders, in this chamber—each at his own work station. To launch a ten-missile group, or "flight," of Minuteman missiles, their two separate keys would need to turn simultaneously in switches at the two well separated consoles. (M.M. NHS/NPS)*

*Control switch #1*

*Control switch #2*

U.S. Intercontinental Ballistic Missiles (ICBMs) had been in development since the 1950s, but the U.S. had nothing that could respond as quickly as was now needed. To have the ability to retaliate (and theoretically inhibit an attack), the U.S. needed missiles that could launch on a moment's notice and accurately hit Soviet targets more than 5,000 miles away. Perhaps the unspeakable horror of a nuclear event in the mass unconscious can explain the ensuing and irrational "overkill" in the arms race. By 1965, the Pentagon had developed and installed more than one thousand ICBMs near Air Force bases in Montana, Wyoming, North and South Dakota, Kansas, Missouri, and Arizona.[5] The U.S. goal was to be able to drop a nuclear bomb on every Soviet town and city *forty times over*.[6]

Malmstrom Air Force Base at Great Falls, Montana, was one of the bases to receive Minuteman missiles. Each Air Force Base (AFB) in the Minuteman Weapons System hosted one "Wing" of the ICBM force. A wing contained 150 missiles, organized into groups of 10 missiles called "flights." Each flight was given an alphabetical designation (e.g. Alpha, Bravo, Charlie, Delta, Echo, etc.). Each missile was placed in its own concrete and steel underground silo, or "Launch Facility" (LF), at least two miles from any other missile. The LF was connected via underground electrical cables to the central Launch Control Facility (LCF) for that flight. Each LCF was located behind ten-foot-tall security fences and under 24-hour armed guard.

At a LCF, a Launch Control Capsule (LCC) was buried 60 to 75 feet underground. The capsule was always staffed by a two-man team. These "Missile Launch Officers" (also called "Missile Combat Crew") were to ensure launch readiness at all times, and these were the men who, upon receiving the proper orders, would simultaneously turn two keys and launch the ten missiles in their flight toward designated targets in the Soviet Union. Each missile carried a one-megaton nuclear warhead, equivalent to the destructive power of *sixty* Hiroshima-type bombs. The design of the Minuteman weapon system specified that the missiles launch within thirty seconds of a launch command (beating by thirty seconds the American revolutionaries for whom they were named.)[7]

## THE 1967 MONTANA EVENT

In 1967, Lieutenant (later Captain) Robert Salas was the Deputy Missile Combat Crew Commander at Oscar Flight LCF based out of Malmstrom AFB. He and his commander, Lieutenant Fred Meiwald, shared 24-hour duty for the ten missiles in Oscar Flight. They took turns monitoring the electronic control panels to ensure all missile systems were in good order and in a "launch ready" state.

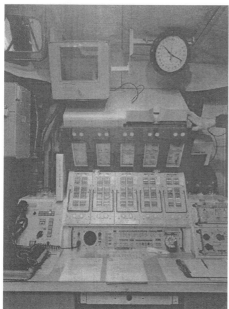

*Command console for the commander of a flight of ten missiles. Then-lieutenant Robert Salas would have sat at a similar station as he received the UFO reports on March 24, 1967. (M.M. NHS/NPS)*

In the early hours of March 24, Salas was on duty in the Launch Control Capsule. Before him were the monitoring panels that indicated the status of each missile, and they all showed the proper "ready" status. An airman above at ground level noticed what appeared to be a star zig-zagging across the sky. The airman called over to the guard station and asked the guard to take a look. Now closer, the lights streaked across the sky, changed directions at an impossible speed, and came back. The guard called Salas on the launch control's phone

*Minuteman missile trajectory over the North Pole. (M.M. NHS/NPS)*

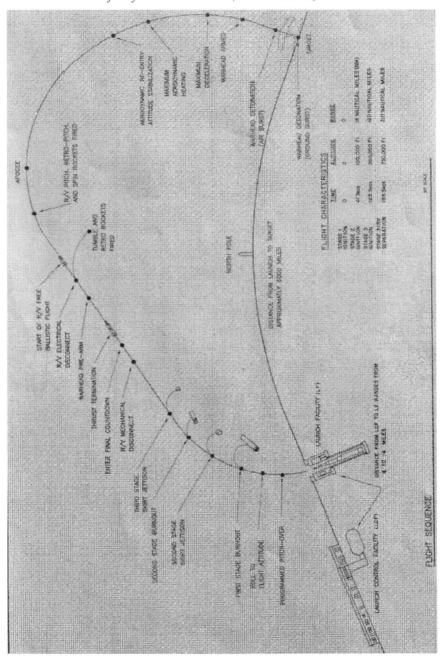

system and reported their strange sightings. After hearing a description of the lights, Salas asked, "You mean they're UFOs?"

Salas recalls the guard replying, "Well, something like that. All we can tell is they're not aircraft."

Though not a strong believer in UFOs, Salas had read some recent newspaper reports about sightings. He told the guard to keep watching and let him know if the lights came closer. Salas was taking college classes toward an engineering degree and often found time to study during the quiet duty shifts. He had returned to his books when he received a second call. Now the guard's voice was urgent. He sounded frightened, and he shouted his words:

> "SIR, THERE'S ONE HOVERING OUTSIDE THE FRONT GATE!"
>
> "*One what?*" Salas queried.
>
> "A UFO! IT'S JUST SITTING THERE. WE'RE ALL LOOKING AT IT. WHAT DO YOU WANT US TO DO?"
>
> "What? What does it look like?"
>
> "I CAN'T DESCRIBE IT. IT'S GLOWING RED. WHAT ARE WE SUPPOSED TO DO?"
>
> "Make sure the site is secure and I'll phone the Command Post."
>
> "Sir, I have to go now, one of the guys just got injured."[8]

Before he could learn more, the guard hung up. Salas went to awaken his superior officer, Lieutenant Meiwald, who was on a scheduled sleep period. Suddenly an alarm from a missile control panel sounded. The "No-Go" light and two red security lights lit up for that missile. As Meiwald tried to query the system, another missile's alarm went off, then two more simultaneously. Within seconds, all ten missiles in Oscar Flight were shut down.

While trying to determine the cause of the shutdowns, Meiwald called the Malmstrom Command Post to report the incident, and Salas dispatched a mobile security strike team to one of the deactivated missile sites.

The Oscar Flight Launch Control Facility was just south of the small community of Roy, about 100 miles east of Great Falls and Malmstrom AFB. The security team was dispatched to a missile silo about ten miles farther east, just east of State Highway 19. In Meiwald's recollections, the security team reported seeing a UFO while going to the missile silo. Unfortunately, no description of this UFO has been found.

No information or orders were offered by higher levels of command, so the security team was directed to return to the LCF. Ordered to maintain radio contact at all times, the team actually lost radio contact until their vehicle approached the LCF where Salas and Meiwald were still locked in the underground capsule. The two guards were clearly upset, and Mciwald later heard that one of them was so terrified by the incident that he had to be released from further duty as a security guard.[9]

Meiwald finished the procedural electronic query to determine the source of the problem. The Guidance and Control systems had malfunctioned, but for inexplicable reasons. There had been no interruption of electrical power. When Salas and Meiwald went off duty that morning (replaced as usual by another two-man team), Salas spoke with the guard that had called in the report. Here is the conversation as recalled by Salas.[10]

> "Were you telling me the truth about the UFO?"
>
> "It was no joke, sir. I swear, it was right out there, he replied, looking out toward the front gate."
>
> "What did it look like?"
>
> "It was like a big red-orange ball. It was so bright that it was hard to get a good look at it. But it was there for about a couple of minutes after we talked then it just took off."
>
> "What about the man that was injured?"

"It wasn't too bad. He cut his hand on the barbed wire fence."

Salas was never able to speak again with any of the guards about the incident, as he was soon forbidden to discuss the event with anyone. These unnamed witnesses have yet to come forward, if they are still living. Salas pointed out that the guards had no equipment that could have affected the functioning of the missiles.[11]

When Meiwald had called the Malmstrom Command Post to report their situation, he was told that Echo Flight also had experienced missile shutdowns, although Meiwald was not told when that incident happened. It was later revealed the Echo Flight incident took place several days earlier.

Captain Eric Carlson and Lieutenant Walt Figel were the Echo Flight Missile Launch Officers on March 16 when one of their missiles went off alert at 8:30 A.M.[12] Figel contacted a maintenance crew that was working on the missile, assuming the crew had failed to report they had placed the missile "off alert" to work on it. The crewmember reported they had not yet begun their maintenance work, and that a UFO had been hovering over the site. Figel thought the guard must have been drinking until he watched every missile in his flight shut down, one by one.[13]

Two security teams were dispatched to the two sites where the maintenance crews were working. The mobile security teams were not informed of the UFO sighting but upon arrival they reported that the security personnel and the two maintenance teams at the sites had seen UFOs. Figel recalls writing notes about the incident for his official log and his personal log. Maintenance crews worked on the missiles for the next twenty-four hours before they were restored to service. Later, the Air Force publicly reported the ten-missile shutdown at Echo Flight but dismissed the "rumors" of UFO sightings.[14]

Meanwhile, back at Oscar Flight one week after the Echo

Flight incident, Salas and Meiwald were flown by helicopter back to Malmstrom Air Force Base and taken to a debriefing room. In the room was their squadron commander, Colonel George Eldridge, and an agent from the Air Force Office of Special Investigations (AFOSI), the Air Force intelligence branch. Salas and Meiwald were questioned about the missile shutdowns, asked to sign nondisclosure statements, and told not to discuss the incident with anyone, including their wives and fellow crewmembers.

Salas later said he was dumbfounded they wanted him to sign a classified "Top Secret" nondisclosure statement. As a launch officer for Minuteman nuclear missiles, his position already required "Top Secret Sensitive" status, a classification far above "Top Secret," and he had already signed a non-disclosure statement for the higher classification. Salas said classification varies with the type of material, and that basically the government can keep documents classified as long as it wants.[15]

Salas recalled that the base was "abuzz" with talk about the UFO sightings. One of the guards from Oscar Flight called and practically begged Salas to come and talk to him and the other guards that had seen the UFO. They simply wanted some answers about what they had seen. Because of the nondisclosure statement, Salas had to tell the guard, reluctantly, that he could no longer speak about the incident. Salas later reflected that the best thing to do when you have access to classified information is to forget it. So that's what he did, for about twenty-seven years.

How this information made its way to light is a convoluted story that spans decades. In 1994, Salas read UFO researcher Timothy Good's first book, *Above Top Secret: The Worldwide U.F.O. Cover-Up*.[16] To his amazement, the book reported missile shutdowns in the presence of UFOs in Montana and in North Dakota in 1966 and 1967. Good's source was Ray Fowler's book, *Casebook of a UFO Investigator*.[17]

In the late 1960s, Fowler was working for the Sylvania Corporation, which had the private contract to build the Minuteman electrical monitoring systems. He heard talk about the coincident UFO sightings and shutdowns and found two Missile Launch Officers willing to verify the stories. After he heard about the Montana incidents from his contacts at Malmstrom AFB in 1967, Fowler contacted Dr. Roy Craig, an investigator for the government-funded University of Colorado UFO Project, also known as the Condon Committee. Fowler told Craig about the reports and gave him a list of witnesses to contact. Craig and the Condon Committee basically ignored Fowler's information, and the final Condon report was issued in 1969 without investigating the missile shutdowns. In fact, the Condon Committee was not granted access to a number of classified (and most probably some of the best documented) UFO cases.[18] As a result of what Fowler felt was a deliberate and irresponsible failure to conduct a fair investigation, he gave an interview about the UFO-missile events to the *Christian Science Monitor*. The interview appeared in the December 5, 1973, issue and produced quite a bit of "blowback" from the Air Force on Fowler and Sylvania, jeopardizing Fowler's job.

Privately, Fowler was also an investigator for the National Investigations Committee on Aerial Phenomena (NICAP), based in Washington, D.C. Through this volunteer sideline, he had become acquainted with Professor J. Allen Hynek, a highly respected astronomer and long-time consultant to the Air Force UFO investigations Project Grudge and Project Blue Book. Hynek had received unclassified reports during his investigations for Project Blue Book and had documented communications disruptions at missile silos associated with UFO sightings. He provided Fowler with material on the topic, essentially saving Fowler's bacon.[19] Fowler went on to become a highly respected UFO researcher with many books to his credit.

Reading these accounts emboldened Salas. He contacted the Mutual UFO Network (MUFON) to see if they would request documents from the Air Force about the missile shutdowns. He didn't

mention UFOs, but he did mention Good's book. MUFON put
him in touch with Jim Klotz, who began submitting Freedom of
Information Act (FOIA) requests to the Air Force. The Air Force did
declassify and send documents related to the Echo Flight incident.
Since the Oscar and Echo incidents happened at essentially the same
time, Salas felt he was free to speak about his experiences. In 1995
Salas told his Oscar Flight story for the first time on the television
show *Sightings*, with Jim Klotz. Don Crawford, a witness from Echo
Flight, also was on the show. In 1996, Salas was interviewed on Art
Bell's *Coast-to-Coast* radio program. Out of the shadowy underworld
of late-night radio, other witnesses emerged. One of the most important was Bob Kaminski, head of the Boeing team that investigated
the Echo Flight shutdowns.

## THE BOEING INVESTIGATION

Boeing was the principal support contractor for the Minuteman
Missile systems, and the company was asked to conduct an investigation of the missile shutdowns. Kaminksi was to coordinate Boeing's
response, and he sent out an investigation team of qualified engineers and technicians to survey the LCFs and the LFs. Following are
some of his recollections, from a letter to Salas and Klotz:

> At the outset, the team quickly noticed a lack of any-
> thing that would come close to explain why the event
> occurred. There were no significant failures, engineering
> data or findings that would explain how ten missiles were
> knocked off alert. This indeed turned out to be a rare event
> and not encountered before. The use of backup power sys-
> tems and other technical system circuit operational redun-
> dancy strongly suggests that this kind of event was *virtually
> impossible* once the system was up and running and on line
> with other LCF's and LF's interconnectivity.

The Boeing investigation continued for several months. Kaminski wrote:

> The team met with me to report their findings and
> it was decided that the final report would have nothing
> significant in it to explain what happened at E-flight. In
> other words, there was no technical explanation that could
> explain the event. The team went off to do the final re-
> port. Meanwhile, I was contacted by our representative at
> OOAMA (Ogden Air Material Command support facil-
> ity) (Don Peterson) and told by him that the incident was
> reported as being a UFO event—that a UFO was seen by
> some airmen over the LCF at the time E-flight went down.
> Subsequently, we were notified a few days later, that a stop
> work order was on the way from OOAMA to stop any fur-
> ther work on this project. We stopped. We were also told
> that we were not to submit the final engineering report.
> This was most unusual since all of our work required re-
> view by the customer and the submittal of a final Engineer-
> ing Report to OOAMA.[20]

It was highly unusual to stop work on an investigation without issuing a final report, especially in this case since Air Force
officials had stated in their telegrams to OOAMA that they had
"grave concern about the incidents." Past CIA Director Richard
Helms once said, "The first rule in keeping secrets is 'nothing on
paper'."[21] We see the Air Force practicing this maxim of secrecy in
their reluctance to even put the letters "UFO" or the words "unidentified flying object" in communications of any kind. Several
of the engineers on the team have come forward to verify Kaminski's recollection of the investigation.[22] Kaminski has written his
own book on the subject, *Lying Wonders*.[23]

## Additional Witnesses

Over the years, many additional witnesses have surfaced to corroborate the 1967 Echo and Oscar flights shutdowns, including maintenance and security personnel, radar technicians, and military officers. Some reports are from missile flights other than Echo and Oscar. UFO researcher Robert Hastings has done a commendable job of locating additional witnesses and providing pages of carefully researched documentation.[24]

There were also corroborating civilian sightings. A 1996 Great Falls newspaper article said central Montana was "awash with UFO reports" at that time.[25] One especially well-documented event was a multiple-witness sighting near the town of Belt, a few miles east of Great Falls, on the evening of March 24, 1967—the same day as the Oscar Flight event. Truck driver Kenneth C. Williams filed this report with the National Investigations Committee on Aerial Phenomena (NICAP) on April 7, 1967:

> Object was first observed approximately 5 miles southeast of Belt, Montana. I was traveling North on Highway 87 en route to Great Falls. Object was approximately one mile to my left and appeared to be five or six hundred yards in altitude. I would estimate its speed to vary from 40 to 50 mph. I am judging this speed by the speed I was traveling as object seemed to be running evenly with me. Its appearance was that of a large doomed [sic] shaped light or that of a giant headlight. Upon climbing up the Belt Hill in my truck, I looked to my left and about 1/2 mile up the gully I witnessed the object at about 200 yards in the air in a still position. I stopped my truck and the object dropped slowly to what appeared to me to be within a very few feet of the ground. It was at this time that I felt that something or someone was watching me. As a very bright

effecting light emerged from the object it momentarily
blinded me. This extreme bright light seemed to flare three
times, each time holding its brightness. By the third time
the light was so bright that it was nearly impossible to look
directly at it. It was at this time that I drove my truck onto
the top of the hill which was about another 1/2 mile. I
stopped a car and asked the people if they would stop at a
station at the foot of the hill and call the Highway patrol.
I went back down the hill and viewed the object for several
more minutes. It was while I was watching it the second
time that it rose and disappeared like a bolt of lightning. I
went back to the top of the hill where my truck was parked
and just as Highway Patrolman Bud Nader arrived, the object appeared once again about two miles away and traveling in a Northeast direction, whereas it stopped once again
and appeared to drop to the ground. There are several deep
gullies in the area where it appeared to drop out of sight.
This was my last sighting of the object. It was the following
day in the Great Falls newspaper that it was acknowledged
that the object was viewed again about 3:20 A.M. by two
Air Force missile men and the Air Force stated that an object appeared on the night of the 24th. Officers investigating the scene also stated that the area where I first viewed
the object, there were many freshly broken tree limbs and
branches.[26]

Montana Highway Patrolman Bud Nader was quoted in the
newspaper a day later saying he saw a light as he approached the
top of the hill where Williams had parked his truck, and that
the light went down and out of sight.[27] In the early hours of
March 25th, Airman Richard Moore plotted a UFO on radar
about five to ten miles northeast of Malmstrom AFB. This UFO
was also detected by Federal Aviation Administration (FAA) ra-

dar.[28] This matches the time and location of Kenneth Williams' sighting.

Two months later another group of witnesses saw a bright "zig-zagging" object in the sky near the Montana-Canada border northwest of Great Falls. It was precisely this motion that first caught the attention of the airman at Oscar Flight, so presumably this could have been the same or a similar object. On May 30, 1967, three recent high school graduates from Great Falls went camping at Waterton Lakes National Park in Canada, which borders Montana's Glacier National Park. The boys arrived in Cameron campground at Upper Waterton Lake about 11 P.M. One of the boys, Dave Krogstad, who later retired as a 21-year veteran of the Bozeman, Montana, police force, told me the following report of the sighting as he remembered it.[29]

The boys climbed into their sleeping bags about midnight but stayed awake "bullshitting" awhile longer. Krogstad said they weren't drunk, because they didn't drink. They were friends from a youth group at the Lutheran Church. About 1 A.M. they saw a "real bright white light" going across the sky in a zig-zag pattern.

> It went zip—fantastic, unbelievable speed and then just stop. Flat stop. Motionless. Right, left, right, left. When it was stopped it would be for one-thousand-one, one-thousand-two, then zip. Distance between the "zigs" and the "zags" were equal. But the speed! Oh my God. Unbelievable.

Krogstad figures they watched the object for at least four, maybe five minutes as it traversed a zig-zag pattern from west to east. It appeared to be flying along the U.S.-Canada border.

During my original interview, Krogstad thought the sighting was in August of 1968, but he kept a journal at the time and when he found it, he called me back to say the time was actually May-June 1967. He sent me a copy of the page from his journal. In hastily scribbled handwriting the entry for Friday, May 30, says, "got to Waterton about 11:00—camp at Cameron Lake—sat up at 1:00—saw UFO in skie [sic]." Krogstad recalls asking a friend named Paula Paun to ask her father if he'd seen anything that night. Paun's father was an air traffic controller at Malmstrom AFB. He told her they hadn't seen anything nor had the radar picked up anything unusual that night.

A zig-zag flight pattern of UFOs has been reported many times. According to Betty Hill's niece Kathleen Marden, Barney and Betty Hill reported the zig-zag flight on the night of their famous 1961 encounter.[30] Perhaps the quick zigs and zags followed by a sudden stop may be a way to "hide" from the rotating sweep of a radar beam or from targeting by ground-to-air or air-to-air weapons. The motion would make it difficult to plot a trajectory or predict future location.

Robert Salas found a witness who suggested there is a correlation between the zig-zag motion and altitude. Yuba City, California, resident John Mullican reported watching fighter planes chase UFOs near Beale Air Force Base, about forty miles north of Sacramento, in the late 1950s. The UFOs easily outran the fighters, and Mullican noticed they sometimes flew in a zig-zag motion, especially when they left earth's atmosphere. Mullican liked to watch the chases to the very end, and that is when the UFOs would most typically move in a zig-zag pattern. Mullican's mother signed an affidavit corroborating her son's UFO observations in those years.[31]

The motion could also potentially be an adaptation to atmospheric differences at high altitudes. At any rate, the sudden stops, starts, and turns would seem to create tremendous gravitational forces on physical bodies and are beyond the technical abilities of any known unclassified aircraft. Such motion is diagnostic of highly advanced technologies.

## An Interview with
## U.S. Air Force Capt. Robert Salas, Retd.

Robert Salas is a personal hero of mine, whom I credit with planting the seed for this book. His testimony in the 2001 Disclosure Project Press Conference was nothing less than shocking, and I am deeply grateful for his decision to bring this event to light. When I began writing, I wanted to visit Salas and personally thank him for his honesty and courage. When I called to ask if I could meet with him on my way through southern California, Salas graciously invited me to his home for tea. As I pulled up in front of his modest house in an older neighborhood in Ojai, I couldn't help but notice the prominently displayed Earth Flag, with the famous "Blue Marble" photo taken from the Apollo 17 spacecraft in 1972.

Salas took me into his small, elegant living room where we chatted about his life for the next couple of hours. I began by asking what made him decide to tell his missile story, much of which is summarized above. One item Salas does not usually reveal in his public appearances was the odd thing that happened after he first hung up the phone with the guard.

> The first thing I did was look at the board. I had the
> sensation I was being told "We're going to shut you down."

Salas told me a related story of a witness not yet willing to go public, though he has made a video of his testimony for release after his death. This witness was involved in retargeting the Echo Flight missiles after their deactivation. He also felt whoever was piloting the UFOs was somehow communicating with him. While working down in the silo, a guard shook the ladder and motioned for him to come up. Coming to the surface, the man saw a round, orange-glowing object not far from the silo. Though the guard was terrified, the witness reports he felt curiously calm, said "Interesting," to the guard, and went back down the ladder. He somehow felt that the occupants of the craft wanted him to go back down. He tried the start-up procedure again and again, and it would run into a glitch at the same point. During these attempts, he would go back up to observe the object and noticed that the glow would change to a "pulsation." He said he could feel an energy field coming down the shaft, like static electricity or something down there with him, though he did not feel threatened by it. His impression was that he was supposed to experience this, that they knew how the missile controls operated in exquisite detail, and were directing the pulse to the Guidance and Control system.

In retrospect, the witness said he found it strange that he was not frightened of the object, and he kept trying to run tests while it was there. He believes they wanted to demonstrate their familiarity with the retargeting process, and their ability to disable it. Salas knows this witness personally and believes he is telling the truth.

*Lieutenant Robert T. Salas in 1968.*

When I asked if Salas had ever been harassed by the military, he said he had not. He did mention one time in 1969, shortly after his transfer from Malmstrom AFB to Wright-Patterson AFB in Ohio, when he received a message to report to the base psychiatrist. When he arrived at the base hospital's mental health area, an orderly told him to go back and see the doctor. Salas asked what it was about, and the orderly told him the psychiatrist would tell him. Salas responded, "I'm not going to go unless you explain to me why I'm here." There was no response, so Salas walked out. Looking back, Salas believes that creating a mental health record may be a way to discredit witnesses. This was the closest he ever came to being harassed. He reported giving a talk to the MUFON chapter in Los Angeles and being congratulated afterwards by two men he had never met before. "They looked like military men. I can tell them in civilian clothing." Salas said he would welcome the military or Air Force trying to prosecute him on any of his statements. The official Air Force policy on UFOs states:

> No UFO reported, investigated and evaluated by the
> Air Force was ever an indication of threat to our national
> security.

According to Salas, this is clearly a false and misleading statement in view of his experience. He added the military have new ways of controlling witnesses. Salas said if you report anything in the missile field, it can affect your AFSC (Air Force Specialty Qualifications) and your career. (There is an example of this later in the chapter.)

I asked Salas what he thought was the purpose for the UFO deactivation of nuclear missiles. Was it an implied threat, demonstrating their technological superiority?

> I honestly think they were giving us a message. We need
> to get rid of our nuclear weapons. They really are no use to
> us. Not to (get rid of them) could result in the destruction
> of all life on the planet. We need to stop this love affair
> with nuclear weapons.

Salas reviewed some of the close calls we have already had: revelations by the Soviets of how close they came to firing in the Cuban missile crisis,[32] the collision between French and UK nuclear submarines in 2009,[33] the B-52 bomber that flew across the continental United States in 2008 not realizing it was carrying "hot" nuclear weapons.[34] Salas graduated from the U.S. Air Force Academy and says he knows the type of people who come out of there and become generals.

> Some are too "gung ho." I know there are people in the Pentagon who wouldn't even blink [to use a nuke] if they had the chance.

Chilling thought.

Salas said UFO visitors are undoubtedly more technically advanced, and they probably had to somehow make it through this same stage of nuclear weapons in their evolution. He admitted it was all speculation on his part, but he thinks they have been visiting us for a long time.

> I don't think they have ill intent. If they did, we would have seen it by now.

When I asked Salas how this event has affected his life and philosophy, he said,

> I am committed to the abolition of nuclear weapons and revealing the reality of the UFO phenomena. That's why I've come out. That's why I speak. I talk to my students about it. Most kids are ready to believe. Not too many are skeptical. I have no problem telling my story to anyone I meet. There is excessive secrecy in government, and a special group of people that have this information. God knows what they're going to do with it, in secret, without public input.

Salas said the Oscar Flight event opened his mind to extraterrestrial life. His commitment to revealing the truth keeps him on the road, speaking at UFO conferences and on radio and television. Salas is bilingual, so he spreads the information to Spanish-speaking countries as well as the U.S. and England.

## OTHER UFO-MISSILE SILO EVENTS, 1965-1966

### F.E. Warren AFB

The events around Malmstrom AFB in March 1967 were not isolated incidents. The Blue Book Files hold a 1965 case from F.E. Warren AFB near Cheyenne, Wyoming. On the night of August 1, multiple witnesses, including the base commander, telephoned Project Blue Book at Wright-Patterson Air Force Base. They reported several UFOs, as many as nine at one time, near the Minuteman Launch Control Facilities. Some hovered over base operations and at times the UFOs assembled into vertical "stacked" formations. Dr. J. Allen Hynek published the log entries of the witnesses in his 1972 book, *The UFO Experience: A Scientific Inquiry*. He once asked the project chief of the Blue Book Project, Major Hector Quintanilla, what was happening with the investigation of these reports. Quintanilla told him the sightings were stars. His answer offended Hynek:

> This is certainly tantamount to saying that our Strategic Air Command, responsible for the defense of our country against major attacks from the air, was staffed by a notable set of incompetents who mistook twinkling stars for strange craft.[35]

As UFO researcher Robert Hastings commented in his coverage of the Warren AFB event,

Regrettably, the "stars" answer offered by Major Quintanilla was a typical example of the innumerable dubious
rationalizations and wholly inadequate solutions publicly
offered by Project Blue Book.[36]

Starting in 1947, the U.S. Air Force investigated sightings
of unidentified flying objects in a series of projects named Sign,
Grudge, and Blue Book. The projects were headquartered at
Wright-Patterson AFB. Blue Book investigated more than 12,000
sighting reports, of which about 700 remain unidentified. Blue
Book ended in December, 1969, and the Air Force claimed to
be officially out of the UFO business.[37] In the book, *Project Blue
Book Exposed*, author and UFO Researcher Kevin Randle discuss-
es how Project Blue Book was, in many ways, a disinformation
tool.[38] Randle comments,

> In typical Blue Book fashion, objects sighted by differ-
> ent witnesses and detected by radar are separately explained
> away rather than the situation being analyzed as a whole.
> Some of these explanations do not seem reasonable.

### Minot AFB

There was another case of missile impairment on the night of
August 24-25, 1966, in Minot, North Dakota. The radio communications equipment between the Launch Control Facility and the individual Launch Facilities was disrupted by static while UFOs were
observed overhead. The equipment worked perfectly before and after the UFOs were present. Though the Air Force later claimed they
could find no reports of UFOs or malfunctions for that date and location, there are documents of the event in a Project Blue Book file.
Science consultant Dr. J. Allen Hynek wrote an article in the popular
press confirming those UFO reports based on his own interviews with
witnesses.[39]

Extensive details of the 1966 Minot event are covered in Salas' and Klotz' book, *Faded Giant*, and copies of the Blue Book files are included in the book's appendix.[40] In 2007 a new witness emerged with even more disturbing information about the Minot event. Former Missile Launch Officer David Schuur responded to a request for information that UFO researcher Robert Hastings published in the *Association of Air Force Missileers Newsletter*.[41] Schuur was a First Lieutenant and a Deputy Missile Combat Crew Commander in the 455th/91st strategic Missile wing at Minot AFB at that time. Astoundingly, Schuur reported that the missiles in his flight actually went into "launch mode."

> As this thing was passing over each missile site, we would start getting erratic indications on that particular missile…It was as if the object was scanning each missile, one by one….[O]n this particular night, we had to activate the "Inhibit" switch because we got "Launch in Progress" indicators!

When asked if this had ever happened on any other occasion that Schuur knew of, he replied, "No, never." Schuur explained that if the missile receives a launch signal and the Inhibit command is not given, the missile will wait for a specified time and then launch automatically. Schuur believed the UFO "scanning" activated the launch mode, as well as other erratic indicators, and that it was accidental.

When Schurr returned to the base the next day, he and his LCC commander were met by the base operations officer who said, "Nothing happened, nothing to discuss, goodbye." Schuur turned in logs and tapes of radio messages from the night, and they have never been released to the public. Schuur never heard anything more from anyone about the incident.[42]

This event makes it particularly hard to understand how the Air Force can continue to say that no reported UFO was ever a threat to U.S. national security. Were they truly that trusting of these intruders? Or were they trying to mollify the public? Or did they know something they weren't sharing? Maybe some day we'll know.

### Malmstrom AFB 1966

A former launch control officer at Malmstrom AFB told UFO researcher Ray Fowler about an event in early 1966, when all ten missiles in a flight were shut down, with a UFO seen in the vicinity. The specific flight was not identified, so this event is less well documented.[43] However, former Air Force Policeman David Hughes reports sightings that may support a 1966 event at Malmstrom:

> Many nights we observed a light in the sky between Choteau and Augusta, Montana. This light would move at incredible speeds, make right-angle moves, and continue for hours. And when seeking further info from wing command, we were often insulted when told it was a Telstar satellite.[44]

There is a detailed, single-witness report of shutdowns at Ellsworth Air Force Base in South Dakota in the summer of 1966. This event included the triggering of security alarms and an "object" landing on the ground inside the security fence next to the missile silo.[45] Clearly these UFO-missile events started before 1967.

### The 1975 Montana UFO Wave and Later Sightings

In 1975, another "wave" of UFO sightings occurred in Montana, well documented by Keith Wolverton and Roberta Donovan in their book, *Mystery Stalks the Prairie*.[46] Wolverton was a deputy sheriff and detective for Cascade County (Great Falls is the county seat). He was assigned to investigate cattle mutilations. Many of his reports included UFO sightings over missile silos. Early on October 19, Lloyd Stinebaugh, publisher of the *Shelby* (Montana) *Times* weekly newspaper, was awakened by the local police who were watching a UFO and wanted Stinebaugh to take pictures. The photo image is quite small, but Stinebaugh did get photos of a cigar-shaped UFO that he printed in the newspaper.[47] Shelby is located about 85 miles north of Great Falls; there were missile silos nearby.

On November 7, motion detectors triggered an alarm at Malmstrom missile site K-7. A security team was dispatched and reported a glowing disc as large as a football field hovering over the site. Though ordered to investigate, the team refused to go closer. F-106 intercept jets were scrambled to the scene, but NORAD radar staff watched the UFO climb to 200,000 feet and then disappear. Later it was discovered that the targeting programming for the K-7 missile had been changed. The same day, personnel from a total of five other launch facilities, including K and M flights, reported glowing objects over the missile silos; the objects glowed red to orange to yellow.[48]

## THE ROLE OF THE PRESS

More than 130 UFO sightings were reported in Montana in 1975.[49] Though the Montana press covered many of the sightings, the national media largely ignored them. Science journalist Terry Hansen studied this wave of sightings and the blackout in the national media.[50] His resulting book, *The Missing Times*, offers important insights into why the national media did not pick up the Montana news stories.

Actually, one story did go national. Not in the *Wall Street Journal* or the *New York Times* or the *Washington Post*, as Hansen dryly quips, but in the supermarket tabloid, the *National Enquirer*, and a tardy two years later (December 13, 1977).[51] As Hansen sleuthed in the intelligence underground, he discovered some surprising connections between the CIA and the publisher of the *National Enquirer*. He concluded that the CIA used the *National Enquirer* as an intentional part of the disinformation campaign. Just the appearance of an article in that magazine, no matter how newsworthy the topic, basically destroys the story's credibility. Who would have suspected that the *National Enquirer* played a significant role in CIA activities? While this is not welcome news for those of us who would like to believe in a free American press, Hansen's book provides many insights into why so many people still dismiss the existence of UFOs and ETs.

Perhaps Montana newspapers, and particularly the *Great Falls Tribune*, are more likely to fairly report events related to UFOs. One of the best articles in the nation reporting the September 27, 2010, National Press Conference on UFOs and Nukes was Ledyard King's detailed article and photo on the front page of the *Tribune*. A few other Montana papers picked up that article. It's possible that, at least in Montana, people are more open to hearing such news.

## Muzzling Military Personnel

UFO sightings over ICBM sites continued, both in Montana and elsewhere. Robert Hastings, in his book *UFOs and Nukes*, includes an extraordinary report from retired USAF Technical Sergeant John W. Mills III. Mills described a case in December 1978 or January 1979 at Ellsworth AFB in South Dakota where all the missiles of Echo Flight and part of the missiles at Delta Flight were disabled.[52] Mills was performing a targeting check with his team partner at Delta-3 when the guard at ground level started banging on the ladder into the silo and insisting the officers come up. They told him to stop, because the pounding was jarring the sensitive mechanisms, but the guard began screaming at them to come up. Frustrated with his behavior, they finally climbed the ladder. At the surface, Mills noticed a low hum that seemed to permeate his body and was incredibly loud. The guard looked up. He pointed out they could see stars in every direction except directly overhead. Shortly thereafter the site lost all power, even though there was a generator and battery back-up.

Mills said they were contacted by upset officers from both the Launch Control Facility and Job Control and ordered to immediately report back to the base, rather than to the next missile they were supposed to check. When they arrived at the base, all the targeting teams had been called in and it was teeming with officers querying each of the crews. Previously, Mills and his team partner had heard rumors that military personnel had been discharged for reporting UFOs, so they said they had seen nothing. Other teams did report seeing and hearing something. Mills said one of the officers who told the truth had a splendid record but was later passed over for a promotion he deserved. Another team that reported seeing something was shipped off the base within twenty-four hours.

Mills and his partner continued their Air Force careers. Mills garnered exceptional performance reviews and regular promotions over the course of his career, working at a number of different bases. His partner became a full colonel. As Mills said,

> We kept our mouths shut. We made it, the other teams didn't.[53]

Mills also mentioned another UFO sighting at Ellsworth AFB, which he thought occurred in May 1980. Several thousand people, both military and civilian, were gathered to watch the take-off of the SR-71 or "Blackbird" surveillance aircraft, which visited Ellsworth regularly to refuel. (This Strategic Reconnaissance Aircraft was an early stealth jet developed as a black project by Lockheed Skunk Works in the 1960s. It was used from 1964 until 1998, and it still holds the speed record for an air-breathing jet of 2,393 mph. It could fly at altitudes exceeding 80,000 feet.[54]) Mills and others were watching from the roof of their barracks and had a clear daytime view of a dark, triangular UFO that came over the runway, made a right turn toward them, and suddenly disappeared. For unexplained reasons, the SR-71 did not take off that day.

Mills was certain many people had seen the UFO; the base buzzed with talk about it. Later that day an official "Flash" message came out, which Mills believed originated at a high level in the Pentagon. It prohibited anyone from discussing the "incident" but avoided actually naming it. The following day another Flash message was sent to all Strategic Air Command (SAC) bases saying, in effect, that the event never happened. Use of a Flash message was only for immediate distribution of high-priority information. Mills was relatively certain the base's high command kept "the incident" out of the local newspapers.[55] Again, all words (UFO, flying object, etc.) that researchers might use in a Freedom of Information Act request were carefully avoided in the messages.

In early 1993, Mills was stationed at Malmstrom AFB and sighted a strange light while returning to the base from an assignment. Though he was not sure it was a UFO, other sightings that same night seemed to confirm that possibility. When he arrived at the base, he heard stories of balls of light over the runway. Two tankers coming in for a landing had to reroute and land elsewhere. According to several witnesses who actually saw the balls, some were quite small and others up to three feet in diameter. One witness thought someone had thrown a softball at him, but this was not your ordinary softball. After flying into the vehicle barn and flying around inside it, the ball flew back out. One of the witnesses thought there were about six balls of light, but another thought there were hundreds. Mills heard that at least two of the men were asked to write up reports and had not been "banished." Mills speculated that so many people had seen the balls of light that base commanders could not transfer all of them to other bases.[56]

In 2002, Staff Sergeant Joseph M. Brown published an account online of his and others' 1992 sightings of UFOs over Alpha Flight Launch Facility, located near Sluice Box Canyon and Monarch, Montana:

> This light was doing some wild things in the sky, sudden direction changes, moving very fast, then stopping, then shooting off in another direction. I watched this for about 15 to 20 minutes.[57]

Brown's testimony includes the dilemma he and has team partner felt in reporting to his superior officers. When asked if they saw a UFO, they and the other teams who had seen the object replied circumspectly they didn't know. They saw a light. Their captain threatened them by saying he didn't think they saw anything and they'd better not talk about it. "You guys are under PRP, remember that!" PRP is the Personnel Reliability Program, a Department of Defense directive that dictates conduct of military personnel working with nuclear weapons. If a commanding officer questions his subordinate's reliability, it may lead to psychological examination and possible termination of duty.[58]

## INTO THE 1990S

In 1996 another U.S. Air Force Technical Sergeant, Jeff Goodrich, reported a multiple-witness sighting of triangular UFOs over missile locations in the Great Falls/Malmstrom area. Robert Hastings wondered whether the craft could have been F-117 stealth fighter jets, which have backswept wings that might give them a triangular appearance. However, Goodrich described the craft as white, while the F-117s were black. Furthermore, the objects hovered, an impossible feat for a jet aircraft. Goodrich was Team Chief in Missile Handling and had nineteen years' experience as a missile maintenance technician. Goodrich was also a trained field investigator for MUFON and filled out complete summaries of both events.[59]

*Countdown to Launch*

One astonishing report from the 1990s came not from U.S. military personnel but from former Soviet Union officers. After the collapse of the Soviet Union in 1991, former Soviet military personnel began speaking openly about previously classified UFO encounters. In October 1994, ABC News interviewed retired Army Lt. Colonel Vladamir Plantonev, who described observing a windowless silver disc for several hours near a Soviet ICBM base in the Ukraine in 1982. While the UFO was in the area, the automatic launch sequence in a number of nuclear missiles was turned on, and Soviet launch officers sweated out fifteen horrific seconds of countdown until the launch was aborted and the missiles returned to normal alert status. Another Soviet officer, Colonel Igor Chernovshev, who was the chief investigator of this chilling malfunction, corroborated Plantonev's account.[60]

# The 3rd Millennium: More Witnesses and Documents Undermine Ongoing Secrecy

*National Press Club Conference on UFOs and Nukes, September 27, 2010*

Robert Hastings and Robert Salas organized a second National Press Club Conference on UFO disclosure a little more than nine years after the Disclosure Project held the first event at the club. The press conference featured testimony and reports from Salas and Hastings, and from other highly credentialed witnesses. The conference was video recorded and can be viewed at Robert Salas' website, http://www.spiralgalaxy.org/ As mentioned earlier in this chapter, press coverage was disappointingly poor, though some Montana papers carried a good story on the event.

Researcher Linda Moulton Howe did several radio programs

summarizing the "UFOs & Nukes" conference. After one of these programs, a man whose father had worked on nuclear weapons contacted her with some incredible stories. Alden Stockwell Cole was Boeing's prime troubleshooter for the Minuteman missiles. He told his son Martin Cole about a time he was sent from Warren AFB in Cheyenne, Wyoming, to inspect a missile silo where guards were reporting strange sightings. Massive cement lids cover each missile silo and roll out of the way on a track when the missile is activated. When Alden Cole reached the silo, he found the cement cover had actually been lifted off the silo, something that as far as he knew could only be done with a giant crane. And there were none around. He told his son that the silo's electronics were destroyed and the nuclear material in the warhead had somehow been neutralized.

Martin's father had his own take on the need for secrecy regarding this disarming of our greatest weapons while UFOs were present:

> If you had something like that, would you want to admit it? Would you want to let everybody know that you could not defend yourself? That's pretty much it.

Cole Martin's testimony of his father's account is unique in its report of removed silo covers and essentially the emasculation of the nuclear warhead. This would certainly be a "shock and awe" event, if it were true and became widely known. It significantly raises the bar for the capacities of ET technologies. However, no other such reports have surfaced, and corroboration and additional evidence are needed to verify this single-witness account.[61]

## BACK AT F.E. WARREN AFB

Since 2000, given that so many UFO documents have been declassified and so many witnesses have come forward, it appeared that strict suppression of UFO incidents might be lifting. Recent evidence seems to prove otherwise. Robert Hastings is investigating a failure of 50 Minutemen III missiles at F.E. Warren AFB on October 23, 2010. The timing is curious, so close on the heels of the (widely ignored) National Press Conference on UFOs and Nukes. The problem with the missiles was leaked to *The Atlantic* magazine, which published the story on October 26. Air Force spokespersons admitted it happened but described it as an "engineering failure" when they lost the ability to communicate with five of their flights, Alpha through Echo. However, the article also says the cause of the failure remains unknown.[62]

Hastings began interviewing local police officers and getting some media coverage requesting information on UFO sightings in the area. A retired missile technician found contacts on the base who reported sightings by "numerous [Air Force] teams" of an enormous cigar-shaped craft maneuvering high above the missile field on the day of the disruption, as well as the following day. The huge UFO was described as appearing similar to a World War I German Zeppelin, but it had no passenger gondola or advertising on its hull, as would a commercial blimp. As Hastings writes,

> The confidential Air Force sources further report that the commander of their squadron has sternly warned its members not to talk to journalists or researchers about "the things they may or may not have seen" in the sky near the missiles in recent months and have threatened severe penalties for anyone violating security. Consequently, these persons must remain anonymous at this time.[63]

Take note. Any news of a massive failure of nuclear missiles due to some computer or other technical problem may have other explanations. Check your alternative news sources.

## A SHOT ACROSS THE BOW

What happened in Montana is only a small part of the UFO–nuclear weapons story. I have included some ICBM missile events outside Montana so the reader understands these events are not confined to Montana, or even to the U.S., but I have left much of this international story untold. It is a huge story, and an excellent compendium of the subject is Robert Hastings' book, *UFOs and Nukes*.

Most witnesses and investigators concur that the message of these encounters is to warn us about our journey down the path of nuclear weapons—and perhaps hope that we will abandon that path. There are multiple accounts by those claiming to have contact with extraterrestrials that the ETs express concern over the possible nuclear destruction of our planet.[64] While some of these contactees have long been written off as frauds, publicity seekers, or "kooks," it's not unreasonable to assume they were targeted by disinformation campaigns, and it's hard to sort out truth from attempts at character assassination. Some of their reports include rumors of meetings with political leaders, with the ETs entreating them to abandon nuclear weapons. The 1951 science-fiction film classic, *The Day the Earth Stood Still*, is a dramatization of ET efforts to warn us away from our destructive, warring behavior. Perhaps activities of UFOs at nuclear missile sites could be part of a larger plan to wake up the human race, though for that to happen, the populace as a whole needs to know about these events.

In 2009, Malmstrom Air Force Base deactivated 50 missiles in the 564th Missile Squadron.[65] Those retired silos are in "caretaker" status, monitored for unauthorized entry and flooding.

This effort took 29,000 hours to remove everything in the silos, including the 14,000-pound security doors. Master Sergeant Les Moore, in charge of missile maintenance, said, "Our folks really stayed positive and upbeat throughout the whole deactivation program." Currently, Malmstrom, Minot, and F.E. Warren Air Force Bases maintain 150 Minuteman missiles apiece, comprising the nation's current ICBM program.

Salas' coauthor James Klotz co-manages a website (http://www.cufon.org/) where the full account of the March 1967 events is available, along with links to all the relevant declassified Air Force documents. On the site, Salas and Klotz state:

> There is a great discrepancy between the United States Air Force's public position relative to UFOs and national security, and the established facts of this case. We hope that the Secretary of the Air Force will search for, declassify, and release all information on this case.

From the Computer UFO Network (CUFON) website:

> Our hope is that public knowledge of this now declassified incident will induce those who were among the security policemen and directly witnessed the UFOs over the Minuteman facilities, and others with any pertinent information, to come forward and add their stories to those of the Missile Combat Crew officers. We maintain that the American people have the right to know the truth about this and other UFO incidents which affected national security.

Every new witness helps dismantle the stonewall of suppression and build the solidity of this emerging story. If you are a witness to any UFO-Nuclear Weapons events, please contact Robert Hastings (ufohastings@aol.com), or the Computer UFO Network (CUFON) at mail@cufon.org.

In our interview, Robert Salas stated his conviction that the government does not have the right to keep this information from the public, and I'm sure that every one of the witnesses and researchers and probably most members of the public would agree. Thomas Jefferson said, "Information is the currency of democracy." If information of this significance is deliberately suppressed, which so many witnesses confirm, and for so many years, then we have to ask ourselves the question, how has this impacted our democracy?

## Notes

1. Steven Greer, founder of the Disclosure Project, has done a remarkable job of identifying many of those witnesses, and recording their accounts. On Wednesday, May 9, 2001, over twenty military, intelligence, government, corporate and scientific witnesses came forward at the National Press Club in Washington, D.C., to establish the reality of UFOs or extraterrestrial vehicles, extraterrestrial life forms, and resulting advanced energy and propulsion technologies. Capt. Robert Salas testified about his experiences with UFOs over missile silos in Montana. See http://disclosureproject.org/ to view the 2001 press conference or for more information.
2. Richard Dolan, *UFOs and the National Security State* (Charlottesville, VA: Hampton Roads Publishing, 2002), 21.
3. Jesse Marcel Jr., Linda Marcel and Stanton Friedman, *The Roswell Legacy: The Untold Story of the First Military Officer at the 1947 Crash Site* (Franklin Lakes, NJ: Career Press, 2009), 13, 19-21, 49-68.
4. "Poll finds Montanans believe in UFOs," [Helena, MT] *Independent Record*, November 17, 2007.
5. Robert Hastings, *UFOs and Nukes: Extraordinary Encounters at Nuclear Weapons Sites* (Bloomington, IN: Author House, 2008), 211-12.
6. http://en.wikipedia.org/wiki/Overkill/
7. Hastings, 211-12.
8. Robert Salas and James Klotz, *Faded Giant* (Charleston, SC: BookSurge, 2005), 13-14.
9. Salas & Klotz, 14-15.
10. Salas & Klotz, 16-17.
11. Email communication to author, July 14, 2011.
12. When the first reports of UFOs over Montana missile silos emerged, Robert Salas believed that the Echo and Oscar events happened at the same time. As more witnesses came forward, it became clear that the Echo Flight event preceded the Oscar

Flight event by about a week. In Salas and Klotz's book, *Faded Giant*, this confusion is reflected in some inaccuracies of the dates, but it is cleared up in Robert Hastings' book, *UFOs and Nukes*.

13. Salas & Klotz, 17.
14. Hastings, 241.
15. Author interview with Robert Salas, March 2, 2009.
16. Timothy Good, *Above Top Secret: The Worldwide U.F.O. Cover-Up* (New York: William Morrow & Co., 1988), 300-01; Dolan, *UFOS and the National Security State*, 16.
17. Raymond E. Fowler, *Casebook of a UFO Investigator: A Personal Memoir* (Englewood Cliffs, NJ: Prentice Hall, 1981), 187.
18. Robert Salas, "Back to Montana," 2010, under *The Air Force Cover-up*, http://www.spiralgalaxy.org/
19. Hynek was initially a UFO skeptic, hired as a government consultant to the Air Force because of his credentials and reputation. He was Chair of the Astronomy Department at Northwestern University, and Director of their Lindheimer Astronomical Research Center. After decades of examining cases brought to the various UFO research efforts by the Air Force, Hynek became a believer, and was an outspoken critic of both Project Blue Book and the Condon report. After his government contracts ended, Hynek founded the Center for UFO Studies (CUFOS) and later the International Center for UFO Research (ICUFOR). Stephen Spielberg consulted with Hynek for his film *Close Encounters of the Third Kind*. The movie title is based on the classification system developed by Hynek, whom some refer to as "the father of UFO research."
20. Salas & Klotz, 20-21.
21. Richard Dolan, *UFOs and the National Security State: Chronology of a Cover-up, 1941-1973* (Charlottesville, VA: Hampton Roads Publishing, 2002), 16.
22. Salas & Klotz, 21.
23. Bob Kaminski, *Lying Wonders: Evil Encounters of a Close Kind* (Mulkiteo, WA: WinePress Publishing, 1996).
24. Hastings, 237-73.
25. "1967 Incident Still Mystifies Man," *Great Falls* [MT] *Tribune*, August 13, 1996.
26. Salas & Klotz, 2005, 28-29.
27. "UFO Breaks Monotony of Run," *Great Falls Tribune*, March 26, 1967.
28. "When Is a UFO Not a UFO?" *Great Falls* [MT] *Leader*, March 25, 1967.
29. Author telephone conversation with Dave Krogstad, July 30, 2008.
30. The 1961 Betty and Barney Hill case was the first documented alien abduction account and received widespread press coverage. A number of books cover the event, including Betty Hill, *A Common Sense Approach to UFOs* (Portsmouth, NH: the author, 1995). The most recent and complete account is Stanton T. Friedman and Kathleen Marden, *Captured! The Barney and Betty Hill UFO Experience* (Franklin Lakes, NJ: The Career Press, 2007).
31. Emails to author from Robert Salas, June 29, 30, 2012.
32. Recent information indicates that several Soviet commanding officers in Cuba had the authority to use nuclear weapons if the U.S. had landed on the island, as Kennedy's military advisors wanted him to do. Hastings, 124.
33. http://news.bbc.co.uk/2/hi/uk_news/7892294.stm
34. http://www.theatlantic.com/politics/archive/2010/10/failure-shuts-down-squadron-of-nuclear-missiles/65207/
35. Dr. J. Allen Hynek, *The UFO Experience: A Scientific Inquiry* (Chicago, IL: Henry Regnery Co., 1972), 184-86.

36. Hastings, 215.
37. Salas & Klotz, 11.
38. Kevin Randle, *Project Blue Book Exposed* (New York: Marlowe & Co., 1997).
39. Dr. J. Allen Hynek, "Are Flying Saucers Real?" *Saturday Evening Post*, December 17, 1966, 7-21.
40. Salas & Klotz, 8-11, 120–129.
41. Hastings, 303.
42. Hastings, 303-306.
43. "Air Force Denies UFO Incident," *Christian Science Monitor*, December 5, 1973.
44. Hastings, 232.
45. Hastings, 228-31.
46. Roberta Donovan and Keith Wolverton, *Mystery Stalks the Prairie* (Raynesford, MT: T.H.A.R. Institute, 1976).
47. "UFO Sighted in Sky Early Sunday Morning," *Shelby* [MT] *Times,* October 24, 1975.
48. Lawrence Fawcett and Barry J. Greenwood, *The UFO Cover-Up: What the Government Won't Say* (Old Tappan, NJ: Fireside/Simon & Schuster, 1992), 27-31.
49. Terry Hansen, *The Missing Times: News Media Complicity in the UFO Cover-up* (Bloomington, IN: Xlibris Corp., 2000), 24. Some of the UFOs were described as helicopters, but Hansen argues that there was little information other than general flight characteristics to justify that conclusion.
50. Hansen, 2000.
51. Hansen, 2000, 33.
52. Hastings, 2008, 375-385.
53. Ibid.
54. http://en.wikipedia.org/wiki/SR-71/
55. Hastings, 2008, 385-90.
56. Hastings, 2008, 445-51.
57. Hastings, 2008, 441-45.
58. Ibid.
59. Hastings, 451-55.
60. Hastings, 431-35. A transcript of the ABC interview with the retired Soviet military officers can be seen at http://www.ufoevidence.org/documents/doc459.htm
61. http://www.earthfiles.com. This is Linda Moulton Howe's website and requires a subscription to access the interview. At the time this book was published, the interview could be found on other websites, referenced as "Linda Moulton Howe and Martin Cole."
62. http://www.theatlantic.com/politics/archive/2010/10/failure-shuts-down-squadron-of-nuclear-missiles/65207/
63. http://www.theufochronicles.com/2011/06/huge-ufo-sighted-near-nuclear-missiles_19.html/
64. Leo Dworshak, *UFOs Are With Us: Take My Word* (Pittsburgh, PA: Dorrance Publishing Co., 2004); Timothy Good, *Alien Base: Earth's Encounters with Extraterrestrials* (London: Century/Random House, 1998). See also books from early contactees George Adamski, Daniel Fry, and Frank Stranges.
65. "50 nuclear missiles deactivated," *Independent Record,* October 22, 2009, 9A.

# 3

# CEREAL MYSTERY: CROP CIRCLES IN MONTANA

*Something is trying to tell us something
and we're not even listening.*
Melody Watt
Whitefish, Montana,
Crop Circle Researcher

## EPISODE 1:
## THE FIRST MONTANA CROP CIRCLE (1998)

The caption "Crop Circle" was more attention-grabbing than the actual AP photo. One could make out some downed swaths in a wheat field between Kalispell and Whitefish, but no discernible pattern. A minimal three sentences described the photo. I clipped it from the September 1, 1998, *Independent Record* (Helena) newspaper[1] and put it aside. I was curious, but working two jobs and parenting a ten-year-old, I didn't pursue it. Months later I met a magazine editor interested in an article on Montana crop circles, so I dug out the clipping and set off for the Montana Historical Society Archives.

The *Missoulian* newspaper carried a larger version of the same photo that day with an extensive front page story,[2] but the *Whitefish Pilot* trumped everyone with a color aerial photo.[3] The crop circle was, in fact, an actual circle, split by two perpendicular lines into four equal quadrants. The quadrisecting lines extended beyond the edge of the circle. Shorter parallel lines flanked the extensions on each side, reminiscent of the Zia Pueblo Sun Symbol familiar to many from the New Mexico state flag.

I contacted *Whitefish Pilot* editor Tom Lawrence. He was intrigued by the occurrence, having some experience with crop circle research, but was certain this was a hoax, probably done by college students. Someone slid the small Polaroid photo of the formation under his newspaper office door with no explanation. Lawrence

95th Year / 36th Issue

This crop circle is located in a field between Whitefish and Kalispell.

**Alien signal or just hoax?**

Formation in field has some asking if ET paid a visit

*1998 crop circle article in the* Whitefish *(MT)* Pilot.

noted the formation's close proximity to and easy access from Highway 93, and said he found pegs in the ground while walking through it. He recalled that just prior to the crop circle's appearance, the Discovery television channel aired a documentary about crop circle hoaxers in England, the infamous Doug and

*This AP photo from the September 1, 1998, Helena* Independent Record *was captioned: "Mark Jones and Kelly Cook of Kalispell inspect a crop circle that appeared in Herb Koenig's wheat field between Kalispell and Whitefish Saturday morning. The Koenigs have lived on this land their entire lives and have never seen anything like this. Herb is afraid his land will be overrun by onlookers and believes it may be best to combine it over soon."*

Dave, who demonstrated crop circle construction by strapping boards to their feet and mashing down the plants. The Flathead Valley landowner, Herb Koenig, also believed it was kids playing a prank.[4] *Missoulian* journalist Michael Jamison visited the circle and pointed out it was a mere 200 yards from the local community college, which started classes the following week. The explanation of college kids on a lark seemed to fit.

In the meantime, I went online to investigate the board-mashing theory of crop circle formation. Little did I know what complexity and mystery I was entering. I might as well have been Alice in Wonderland slipping into the rabbit hole.

Crop circles are not a new phenomenon. In 1686, Oxford professor Robert Plot described geometric formations of flattened plants in his book, *A Natural History of Staffordshire*. Plot found designs in both crops and pastures, "obtaining three parts of a circle, others being semicircular, some of them quadrants." Plot also described or drew circles within circles, as many as three concentric circles, spirals

and squares.[5] There is a widely-cited account from 1687 in Hertford-
shire (England) with an accompanying woodcut of "The Mowing
Devil" who "Scorn'd to mow them after the usual manner, and cut
them in round circles and plac't every straw with that exactness that
it would have taken up above an Age for any man to perform what he
did that one night."[6] Around 200 years later, in 1880, the prestigious
scientific journal *Nature* published a letter from British spectrosco-
pist J. Rand Capron who found a number of flattened circular areas
in a wheat field in southern England, though he believed they were
created by a storm.[7] Some farmers and landowners remember their
grandfathers or even great-grandfathers finding circles in crops, and
there are a few reports of more complicated patterns as well as a few
photos of the early circles.[8] Most of these historical reports are from
southern England, where so many recent formations occur, but there
are older reports from Western Europe and North America.[9]

What we have seen unfold in the last thirty years, however, is
unprecedented in recorded history. In the late 1970s and 1980s,
crop circles increased dramatically in both numbers and complexity in England and began appearing in Europe. On September 18,
1989, *Time* magazine carried pictures of some of these large, complex formations in southern England, asking "Who—or what—is
creating those mysterious crop-field rings?[10] Public interest was
high and media around the world were reporting on the phenomenon.

Then in the summer of 1991, the English tabloid newspaper
*Today* reported that Doug Bower and Dave Chorley, septuage-
narians from Southhampton, claimed to be the makers of all the
crop circles.[11] Curiously, their wives were unaware of this noc-
turnal sport, and there were many other pieces of evidence that
did not gibe with their story.[12] In fact, when *Today* held a press
demonstration with cameras on Doug and Dave in action, the
messy results bore little resemblance to the precise crop circles
they claimed to have made. Based on that disastrous exhibition, a

British and a Swiss newspaper reported doubts about Doug and Dave's claims, but to the dismay of serious crop circle researchers, few media were that discerning. As crop circle expert Freddy Silva noted in his history of this event,

> *Time* magazine regurgitated the *Today* article and ABC's Peter Jennings dished out the same to millions of viewers without any question as to the story's authenticity.[13]

The Doug and Dave story effectively snuffed media interest in the subject, even as their outrageous claim was unraveling under closer scrutiny.[14] Many people today still believe that all crop circles are man-made. It certainly makes life simpler to dismiss all crop circles with that explanation. But is it true?

## THE SCIENCE OF CROP CIRCLES

As a scientist, I was most impressed by the numerous biophysical changes found in the plants and soils of crop circles[15] that are not explained by mechanical mashing. These physical and physiological changes do not occur when the crop has been laid down by mechanical rollers or by stepping on boards.

In 1989, William C. Levengood, an American plant biophysicist, was first asked to examine wheat and barley plants from two British crop circles. His initial observations showed a number of anomalous differences in the plant seeds, microscopic changes in cells, and alterations in the growth nodes on the plant stems. Levengood's preliminary findings catalyzed the formation of the BLT Research Team with John Burke and Nancy Talbott. The team organized a multi-country sampling network and a consistent field protocol for more extensive and regulated sampling.

Levengood (1994) and then with Burke (1995) and Talbott (1999) published three peer-reviewed papers summarizing the plant and soil anomalies they found in crop circles. The elongation of the apical (top) plant stem nodes and the presence of expulsion cavities (holes blown out in the lower plant stem nodes) provide some of the strongest evidence of the presence of an intense, but very brief, heating agency at work.[16] Mechanical flattening will break the plant stems (particularly if the crop is mature and drying out) while the heating agency—conjectured to be bursts of microwave radiation—turns the moisture inside the plant stems to steam, softening the stem fibers so they can be bent at the nodes.

The scientific discoveries of the BLT Research Team provided a wealth of consistently replicated physical evidence that some as-yet-unknown form of energy or energy-system was producing many of the crop formations. Following is a brief summary of their most significant findings:[17]

## Plant Abnormalities

*Abnormal enlargement of cell wall pits in the plant tissue surrounding the seed head*—This microscopic analysis was time-consuming and, once determined to be consistent with other testing methods, it was replaced by other equally reliable criteria.

*Elongated and enlarged plant stem nodes*—The most reliable visible plant change indicative of crop circle "authenticity" is the elongation (stretching) and overall enlargement of the apical (top) plant stem nodes. (Nodes look like "joints" in plant stems.) The top nodes in flattened plants inside crop circles—and also in many cases the plants left standing scattered throughout the flattened areas—consistently reveal statistically-significant node-length increase as compared to plants in the same field but outside the circles. This elongation varies, depending on the type of plant and its growth stage. Young green plants have more internal moisture and are more likely to exhibit greater elongation.

*Beer-Lambert relationship*—One of the most persuasive discoveries indicating the involvement of electromagnetic energies in genuine crop circles is the fact that some formations tested by the BLT Team have shown that apical node-length elongation decreases as a precise function of distance. This decrease fits a mathematical prediction of electromagnetic absorption known in physics as the Beer-Lambert Principle. Plants in the center of a crop circle show the greatest node-length elongation, but the elongation decreases linearly in plant samples taken along radii out to the circle perimeters. The best explanation for these results is that electromagnetic energy, or something that behaves very much like it, is causing the elongated nodes.

*Node bending*—Bending at the plant stem nodes was thought to indicate a genuine crop circle, but the situation is more complex. If clear node bending is found on the first or second day after a crop circle has formed in green plants, this bending—particularly if it is to the side or downward— is significant, and an indication the plant stems were heated by the circle-making energy source. If clear node bending is observed in crop circles formed in mature, dry crops—this node bending is also highly significant, though rarely seen.

However, node bending is also found in man-made crop circles. If the formation is in young, green, vigorously-growing plants—two natural plant recovery systems (gravitropism and phototropism) may begin to take effect immediately after the plants have been flattened. All mechanically-flattened young crop (if it is not seriously crushed) will begin to show node-bending up toward the sun and away from gravity within days of being flattened.

*Expulsion cavities*—The second most reliable (and visible to the naked eye) plant abnormality found in "genuine" crop circle plants is the presence of "expulsion cavities," holes literally blown out at the lower plant stem nodes. The external fibers of the lower plant stems are much tougher than the external fibers at the tops of the plants, so when heat turns the moisture at the lower nodes to steam, the nodes sometimes cannot stretch enough to relieve the pressure. The steam pressure bursts a hole in the node, allowing the steam to escape. Again, because of the differences in moisture content, young green crop is more likely to exhibit expulsion cavities than older, dry crop. Not all "genuine" formations exhibit expulsion cavities, since the intensity of the heating component varies from formation to formation.

*Abnormal effects on crop circle seeds and plant growth*—If a circle forms in crop fields before the flowering of the seed heads, seeds may never form at all. If a circle forms while the seeds are embryonic, those seeds may suffer reduced germination rates, produce stunted plants, and in some cases be sterile. Whenever circles form before the seeds are fully formed, the reproductive capacity of those plants will be reduced to some degree. The seeds may have normal germination rates but increased variability in growth rates. Or in some cases involving non-hybridized plants, the seedlings have developed an abnormal synchronized growth.

Finally, if the formation happens when the seed heads are ripe, then "Super Seeds" regularly result. The BLT Team consistently found that seeds germinated from crop circles occurring late in the growing season exhibit growth rates as much as five times that of the controls, produce greater yield overall, and exhibit increased resistance to known plant stressors (lack of water and/or sunlight).

Levengood and John Burke (the "B" in BLT) patented a process (the "MIR" process) producing exactly this same effect by delivering unusual electrical pulses to seeds before planting. It is Levengood's opinion that the MIR process stimulates (as does the circle creation process when it occurs in mature plants) the production of antioxidants in the treated seeds, thus causing their enhanced growth characteristics. This discovery suggests these unusual electrical pulses are another part of the energy system involved in the creation of the real crop circles. The commercial possibilities are obvious and the MIR process is not expensive, but so far, no seed companies contacted about this discovery have expressed any interest. This could be because the process also reduces the need for fertilizers and pesticides—important sources of income for many seed companies.

### Soil Effects

*Magnetic materials in soil*—In the Cherhill crop formation in England in 1993, some of the plants in the center of the circle were found to be coated with an "iron glaze" of hematite and magnetite, thought to be the result of meteoritic material drawn into the plasma field that created the crop circle. This happened during the Perseid meteor shower and turns out to be relatively rare. More common is the presence of tiny magnetic iron spheres found in crop circle soil. Sometimes the spheres are concentrated at the center of the formation, but more often they are at the outer edges of circular components of formations. In some formations they are deposited with the concentration increasing linearly, from the center to the periphery, as if there were some kind of centrifugal force flinging the particles outward. Outside the formations there is often (but not always) some distribution of the magnetic particles, but they are erratic in deposition.

*Clay-mineral crystallization*—In 1996 a crop circle in Logan, Utah, garnered the attention of local geologist Diane Conrad. Conrad's area of special expertise involved the effects of heat on various clay minerals. She was aware of the BLT Team's plasma vortex hypothesis of crop circle formation (and the idea that microwaves might be one of the energies involved in the circle creation process). Conrad decided to take a few soil samples to see if she could find any change in the crystallization structure of the clay minerals. Although she could only afford to submit a few samples for X-ray diffraction testing, the results suggested a change in the crystallization structure of those clays. She also put a few of her control clays into a microwave oven for two minutes and observed what she thought looked like a comparable change. In a conversation with Nancy Talbott (the "T" in BLT Team), Conrad reported this work and her preliminary results.

A few years later New York philanthropist Laurance Rockefeller contacted Talbott and offered to personally finance some additional BLT research. Laurance, who died in 2004, was the fourth child of John D. Rockefeller and brother of Nelson and David Rockefeller. Laurance was unique in the family for his interest in controversial science, such as crop circles, UFOs, and studies of human consciousness. After considering several BLT proposals, he chose to support an in-depth X-ray diffraction study of clay minerals in crop circle soils. In 1999 BLT chose a crop formation of seven circles that appeared near Edmonton, Canada, as the target case, and then carried out a meticulously designed and implemented plant and soil studies.

The plant samples were examined, as usual, by William C. Levengood. BLT provided sampling kits and detailed instruction for the sampling process. All of the scientists involved in the soil work, the statistical evaluation of the data, and the interpretation of these results were chosen not just because of their credentials and expertise but also because of their total ignorance of the crop circle phenomenon. This was done to avoid any possibility of experimenter bias.

The study found changes in the crystalline structure of specific clay minerals that geologists had seen only in sedimentary rock—never in surface soils. Such changes were normally caused by "geologic pressure" (literally the pressure of mountains on sediments over great time) in conjunction with heat from the earth's core. But these specific clay minerals extracted from the Edmonton crop circle showed the same crystalline structure normally produced by "geologic pressure." This finding, in which the scientists expressed a 95 percent level of confidence, was inexplicable in surface soils.

The finding was corroborated by mineralogist/geologist Dr. Robert C. Reynolds Jr., of Dartmouth College's Department of Earth Sciences. Reynolds was past president of the Mineralogy Society of America and a scientist described by his colleagues as the "best known expert in the world" in X-ray diffraction analysis and, specifically, of clay mineralogy.

The other significant result obtained from the Edmonton study was finding (at the 99 percent level of confidence) that the multiple plant changes documented by William C. Levengood occurred at precisely the same sampling locations as the changes in the crystalline structure of the clay minerals—a discovery which is strong evidence that both effects were caused by the same energy source.

According to Dr. Reynolds, the only other possible causation for the changed crystalline structure of the clay minerals might be exposure to intense heat for many hours—the intensity and duration of which would have incinerated the plants. Reynolds concluded that "we must be dealing with an energy unknown to science."[18]

### Other Anomalies

Other odd and unexplainable phenomena within crop circles are consistent with energy anomalies. These include compass deflection, camera and video equipment malfunctions, strange sensations or effects reported by people entering the circles, and avoidance of circles by animals. In addition, there are often odd sightings of balls of light over the fields, or flashes of light in the vicinity of crop circles on the night before they are discovered. The owners of the field in the Edmonton crystallization study reported dramatic aerial light phenomena around the time and area where the crop formation was found, and they also experienced cell phone failure within the formation.

As researchers and observers have increased in number, a growing number of witnesses have actually seen crop circles forming, with no visible agent creating them. However, it is also true that astonishingly complex crop circles can be made by humans.

Laurance Rockefeller, in addition to the BLT clay mineralization study, funded English crop-circle researcher Colin Andrews to determine just how many of the English crop circles were human-made. Andrews hired local detective Roy Compton to assist him in investigations conducted during the 1999 and 2000 crop circle seasons.[19] Andrews is an electrical engineer who began studying crop formations in 1987 and who is credited with coining the term "crop circles."[20] When the investigations were complete, Andrews concluded that 80 percent of the crop circles in those years were human-made. The results stunned the crop circle community, and many did not accept Andrews' conclusions, accusing him of selling out. What they failed to hear, lamented Andrews, was that 20 percent of the crop circles were decisively not of human origin.[21] Although Andrews' study remains controversial, there is no doubt that human circle makers have become increasingly skillful, and that many crop circles are made by humans. However, careful inspection and analysis can distinguish which are made by humans and which remain genuine mysteries.

The stories of the human circle makers are themselves curious, and Andrews asks whether the intelligences behind the "real" crop formations are also interacting with the human circle makers. These human circle makers report various anomalies such as light flashes and balls of amber light in the fields when they are making circles.[22] It's a complex phenomenon, with many unanswered questions. Welcome to the rabbit hole.

## EPISODE 2:
## THE SECOND MONTANA CROP CIRCLE (1999)

Back in Montana, another crop circle appeared in a wheat field on August 6, 1999, near the "Blue Moon" intersection[23] of Highway 2 and 40, about five miles from where the 1998 formation occurred.[24] Whitefish resident Melody Watt spotted it as she drove by. Unable to find anyone who would take an aerial photo, she hired a charter plane to "get 'er done." She also contacted

PHOTO BY MELODY WATT

*The 1999 crop circle.*

the BLT Research Team and collected plant samples as they requested. The new formation was remarkably similar to the 1998 design with some curious differences: the lines projecting beyond the circle did not match up. In the northerly direction there was only one line beyond the circle. In easterly and westerly directions there was a "trident" formation similar to the 1998 circle, the middle line longest as before. In the southerly direction there were no lines beyond the circle's edge.

BLT's plant analysis showed characteristic signs of exposure to an unknown energy, but Nancy Talbott said this formation was the beginning of something new because the alterations of the plants were so dramatic.[25] The numerous expulsion cavities occurred in nearly all nodes, and there were developmental abnormalities: the peduncle or stem at the base of the seed head was twisted and deformed. Levengood saw something like this from a July 29 Avebury crop circle and hypothesized that these crops had been exposed to anomalous energies more than once, probably before the seed head was developing and later when the formation occurred.[26]

Melody Watt found the formation affected her compass; it wouldn't settle on a direction. There was good evidence this was not a man-made crop circle.

Could it have been a response to the 1998 man-made formation? There are a number of examples of crop circles that seem to have been formed in response to human intentions and actions. Colin Andrews came to believe that the intelligence behind the crop formations seemed to respond to thought or speech. Back in the 1980s, Busty Taylor, a pilot and fellow researcher, told Andrews he'd like to see a crop circle made up of all those they'd seen so far. The next day it appeared.[27]

In 1992, Steven Greer, the director of the Disclosure Project,[28] led a group in a crop circle visualization experiment in Wiltshire County, England, where so much English crop circle activity is centered. The group settled on an image of three circles connected by straight lines in an equilateral triangle shape. They meditated on that design and attempted to project it to the "Circlemakers" for about twenty minutes. The next morning, a few miles away, that exact shape appeared below Oliver's Castle, a megalithic hillfort with a commanding view of the surrounding landscape.[29]

One of the clearest responses to a man-made message happened in August 1991, also in Wiltshire. An American tourist etched out these huge letters on the side of a hill, "Talk to Us." According to veteran crop circle researcher Freddy Silva,

> By this time, hoaxing and contamination of evidence was underway to debunk the phenomenon and undermine public confidence in all matters circular. Against this backdrop of deception, the Circlemakers dropped a series of markings upon the formation—fertile field below Milk Hill. So out of character was the scripted pattern that at

first it was dismissed as a hoax, yet closer inspection proved otherwise…Gerald Hawkins felt it was important enough to gather a team of twelve scholars and decipher it. Several months, 18,000 common phrases, and 42 languages later, they arrived at an acceptable solution…Hawkins and his colleagues finally figured the message was in the guise of post-Augustan Latin: The first word, OPPONO, translated as 'I oppose.' The second word provided an object for the verb as ASTOS—"acts of craft and cunning." "I oppose acts of craft and cunning."[30]

Not only was the message in Latin, it was also in an obscure Knights Templar–based script.[31] It was a mere month later, in September 1991, when Doug Bower and Dave Chorley claimed to be the makers of all crop circles.[32] Later, when Colin Andrews questioned them using his database of crop circles, they admitted that, well, there were quite a few circles they hadn't made, after all.[33] No hoaxers ever tried to take credit for the 1991 "OPPONO ASTOS" crop circle. As Gerald Hawkins quipped to Freddy Silva, "Actually if any hoaxers do come forward, then we have a short Latin quiz we would like them to take."[34]

If the 1999 Whitefish crop circle is a response to the 1998 "sun sign" crop circle near Kalispell, how might it be decoded? The Zia Pueblo Sun Symbol is an empty circle with four lines projecting out in each of the four directions. For the Zia Pueblo people, the symbol represents the harmony and balance in the universe. Four is a sacred number for many tribes, referencing the four directions, the four seasons, the sunrise, noon, evening, and night phases of a day, and the four stages of life: childhood, youth, adulthood, and old age. Four is the number associated with the "Giver of all Gifts."[35]

However, unlike the Zia Sun Symbol, the circles in the Montana crop formations are not empty. They contain a cross with equal length arms. Sometimes called a "wheel cross" or sun cross, this is an ancient symbol found in rock art and cultures all over the world.[36] In Native American tradition, it is one form of a medicine wheel. Crop circle researcher Jeffrey Wilson has found that 65 percent of crop circles in the U.S.A. are located close to known Native American burial mounds and ancient archaeological sites, and the formations may point to or possibly even reference those sites in some way.[37]

Considering Native American symbols seems like a reasonable place to begin deciphering the message in the Montana circles. The crop circle lines seem to point in the four directions, based on the single aerial photo. Tribes vary in meanings attributed to the four directions, but in general the medicine wheel is used to portray different aspects of the self, or the greater society. Symmetry signifies balance. The 1999 crop circle differs from the 1998 circle primarily in that it is not symmetric. At the very least we could interpret the 1999 circle to mean something is out of balance. Figuring out what is out of balance is more tricky. The Montana crop circles occurred in Kootenai aboriginal territory. Traditional elders of that tribe may be able to offer a more specific meaning for the symbols, if they are willing to share any insights they may have.

In addition to the 1999 Canadian crop circle in Edmonton, two crop circles appeared in fields belonging to aboriginal peoples near Hagersville, Ontario, that same year. On July 22, Clynt King found a 300-foot, complex pictogram formation in the wheat field behind his home. On the next day his brother Ken found a smaller formation (about 60- to 70-feet long) in an adjacent field. The brothers are Mississaugas of the New Credit First Nation. At the time, Clynt King was Director of the Environmental Department of the Six Nations in Canada. King requested guidance from elders, clan mothers, spiritual leaders, and visionaries, and he used his own traditional knowledge to seek understanding of the two formations.[38] Both were complex "pictogram" formations.[39] He believes they indicate two major events that will affect the entire world. "They are like road signs along the way for us to consider."[40]

## EPISODE 3: A DOUBLE-HEADER IN THE THIRD MILLENNIUM (2000)

On August 15, 2000, while flying north of Kalispell, pilot Gilbert (Gil) Johnson spotted a strange formation in a wheat field and snapped a picture of it. On August 28, a second formation was discovered in the same field about 600 feet south of the first formation. The field was near the intersection of U.S. Highway 93 and Church Drive, about seven miles north of Kalispell. These circles were about five miles north of the 1998 Kalispell crop circle, and on the west side rather than the east side of Highway 93. All these wheat fields belonged to Herb Koenig, who farmed about 500 acres in the Flathead Valley. He harvested the fields not long after the crop circles were discovered.[41]

Gil Johnson reported that his airplane's compass was deflected 10 to 15 degrees each time he flew over the crop circles, at an altitude of about 500 feet. Someone alerted Melody Watt about the new circles, and she set out to document them. She reported that her fully charged camcorder went dead twenty minutes after entering the August 15 crop circle.[42]

*"Mercedes Spins" formation.* PHOTO BY GIL JOHNSON

Johnson and Watt each said they saw no signs of footprints or paths from the edge of the field, and Melody found no sign of broken plant stems in the formation.[43]

Melody named the first crop circle "Mercedes Spins," a poetic description of the formation's design. In its triple-armed symmetry, it is similar to a 2003 formation in a soybean field in Ross County, Ohio. One of the three curved arms in the Ohio formation ends with a small circle inside a ring, much like all three arms in the Montana circle.

Dutch crop circle researcher Bert Janssen specializes in finding underlying geometries in crop formations. Janssen found a strikingly complex "hidden" geometry in the Ohio formation,[44] and told Jeffrey Wilson it incorporated all of the messages he ever learned from crop circles in a single design.[45] Circle researchers widely agree that the mathematical language of the crop circles is an important component of their communication. Gerald Hawkins, an astronomer and mathematician, discovered that a number of crop circles embodied geometric theorems, displaying precise mathematical relationships.[46] In fact, using Euclidean geometry, Hawkins found the crop circles proved five new geometric theorems.[47] He also found that when he compared the measurements of diameters of multiple circles or rings in many of the early formations he found exact numerical ratios (e.g. 3:2, 5:3, 4:3.) These numeric relationships are also found in the frequencies of musical notes in the diatonic (Do-Re-Mi) scale, revealing a connection between crop circles and music. Hawkins calculated that the chance of this happening by accident was 1:400,000.[48] To my knowledge, no one yet has attempted to study underlying geometries or mathematical rela-

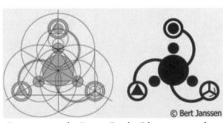

*Geometry in the Paint Creek, Ohio, crop circle.*

© Bert Janssen

tionships in the Montana crop circles. Who knows what secrets might be revealed by a curious mind or a bright geometry class?

The Ohio circle occurred on an island in Paint Creek, at least one-half mile from the nearest road and surrounded on all sides by a belt of trees so it could not be seen from any road. Half the

PHOTO BY JEFFREY WILSON

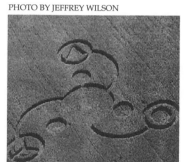

*Paint Creek crop circle in Ohio*

formation was under water when it was found. The 2000 Montana circles were located within a mile of the Stillwater River. This area of the Flathead Valley has a deep, confined aquifer 75 to 300 feet below the surface and typically has high ground water that feeds the surface rivers and streams.[49]

Researcher Jeffrey Wilson found that 95 percent of all crop circles he studied occurred near water (creek, ponds, drainage ditches, or underground aquifers), or on the downslope or bottom of a hill, or the lowest point in a field. Many British researchers have noted the extensive underground aquifers that underlie much of Wiltshire, where so many crop circles have appeared.[50] Wilson also found that 95 percent of crop circles appear near power lines, with a transformer box on the closest pole.[51] Melody Watt noted there were power lines next to the Flathead crop circle fields.[52]

Watt referred to the August 2000 crop circle as the "pendulum arrow." The image suggests to me a radiating sun and a reflecting moon with the earth and its axis positioned between them. The smaller curved lines connecting the axis with the earth could be the mathematical symbol used to indicate angle. Remote viewer and trainer Ed Dames believed this crop formation was telling us something about a polar shift.[53]

Jeffrey Wilson found surprising straight-line connections between U.S. crop circles. In fact, he discovered unreported crop

*"Pendulum arrow" formation*

circles by flying straight lines between known formations. Wilson mapped 160 crop circles in the U.S. and found that every one of the genuine circles had a straight-line component that aligned with another crop circle, though they may not have been present in the same year. Hoaxed circles did not appear to align with anything. According to a an extensive report, the "pendulum arrow" Kalispell crop circle of 2000 aligned with the 2007 Madisonville, Tennessee, crop circle, which in turn aligned with eight other U.S. crop circles.[54] This Independent Crop Circle Researchers Association (ICCRA) report provides an excellent guide to crop-circle research methodology and some of the "landscape" analyses that Wilson has pioneered in North American formations.

## HOW ARE THEY MADE?

Early on, investigators believed crop circles were caused by some kind of natural meteorological event, such as whirlwinds or storms. As the complexity of crop circles increased, that hypothesis became embarrassingly inadequate. In early 2000, Nancy Talbott and the BLT research team hypothesized that some sort of plasma vortex that generated microwave electromagnetic energies formed the crop circles. Many researchers generally agreed that some kind of electromagnetic force was involved. Most recently, evidence is accumulating that the force may be a type of sound wave, either ultrasound (beyond the upper range of human hearing) or infrasound (below the lower range of our hearing). Infrasound produces a short burst of heat, so that could explain node elongation, expulsion cavities, occasional scorching of plant stems, and the mineral crystallization in the soil. Freddy Silva suggested that ultrasound could be used, noting that ultrasound's high frequencies can be precisely directed, like laser light, to rearrange molecules and levitate objects, and that ultrasound is used medically to accelerate healing in muscles and bones.[55]

Specific kinds of sounds are often associated with crop formations. Colin Andrews describes a trilling grasshopper or warbling bird sound, with a frequency range similar to dolphin communications. In one incident while hearing the sound, he observed a strange force pulling on his colleague Pat Delgado, which terrified them both.[56] The landowner and another witness of the Paint Creek Island Crop Circle in Ohio (mentioned above) described hearing a low mechanical sound that was consistent over a several-hour period the night before they discovered the formation.[57]

Veteran crop circle researchers Andrews and Silva reference the science of cymatics to further support the hypothesis that sound might be the energetic source for crop circle formation. The Swiss scientist Hans Jenny, considered the father of cymatics, was able to demonstrate the effect of sound on fluids and on sand spread across a black drum membrane.[58] Amazingly, when sound vibrates the membrane, it creates distinct geometric patterns. Some of these patterns are displayed on Andrews' website under "Crop Circle Research."[59] Acoustics engineer John Stuart Reid has invented and patented a scientific instrument called a CymaGlyph that projects these patterns onto a screen where an observer can watch how patterns change with frequency. Higher frequencies generate more complex patterns, some of which are strikingly similar to some crop formations. The effect of sound vibrations on matter actually has a long and fascinating history,[60] but the actual creation of formations with sound is an intriguing new frontier for science.

## AND WHO IS MAKING THEM?

At the time I was investigating the Montana crop circles, very few crop circle researchers were saying anything about UFOs or aliens. Since the Montana crop circles occurred in 1998-2000, much more evidence has emerged connecting crop circles and UFOs.

Balls of light are often photographed around crop circles, either before or after they form. Usually around softball size, these white- or amber-colored orbs have been seen both day and night, and in every country where crop circles occur.[61] While not spacecraft in any conventional sense, they are definitely "unidentified flying objects." In Holland, a reliable eyewitness reported watching a crop circle form while a disc-shaped light hovered overhead. Melody Watt captured a daytime picture with a disc of light over the 1999 Montana crop circle. Night photos of the 2000 Montana crop circles revealed translucent orbs and a curious image resembling a translucent face.

In the 1999 Edmonton formation, the farmer and his wife, and a couple driving to work on a nearby road, all reported strange aerial phenomena over the site a few days before the crop circle was found. The couple driving to work reported seeing two small brilliant bluish lights that looked like they were playing tag with each other over the field where the formation appeared.[62] The BLT website describes five cases where either disc-shaped UFOs or balls of light are found in association with crop circles in England, the Netherlands, and Poland.[63]

Certainly one of the most blatant connections between aliens and crop circles is the August 15, 2002, crop formation at Crabwood Farm in Hampshire County, just east of Wiltshire. Depicting an alien face on the left, and a disc on the bottom right, crop circle investigators found the disc held a message in ASCII binary code. Several veteran crop circle researchers, including Paul Vigay, worked on deciphering the code, and came to agreement, for the most part, about it's meaning.

> Beware the bearers of FALSE gifts & their BROKEN PROMISES. Much PAIN but still time. (Damaged Word). There is GOOD out there. We OPpose DECEPTION. Conduit CLOSING (*bell sound*). (The damaged word is widely thought to be "Believe.")[64]

While some veteran researchers question the authenticity of the Crabwood formation, very few dismiss it entirely. The decoded message is portentous. Most people who have gotten beyond the tricksters Doug and Dave agree that crop circles are a form of communication from one or possibly more intelligent sources. Are they extraterrestrial? Extradimensional? Unknown human remote-controlled technologies? Advanced classified military technologies? All of the above? At this time there is no consensus, but very few researchers rule out the possibility that at least some crop circles are communications from advanced extraterrestrial civilizations.

## SERIES DISCONTINUED

There have been no more crop circles in the Flathead Valley of northwestern Montana since the year 2000. Perhaps the circle makers decided to take their circles where more people were paying attention. While several Montana papers reported the 1998 crop circle, to the best of my knowledge, the only newspaper reporting the 1999 and 2000 Kalispell crop circles was the weekly *Whitefish Pilot*. The ICCRA website lists additional Montana crop circles in 2002 and 2003 at the USDA Fort Keogh Livestock and Range Research Facility in Miles City, but they are poorly documented and lacking photos.[65] In other places in the U.S. and the world, crop circles continue to appear.

Despite the apparent lack of an interested audience, or at least interested media, it's entirely possible that crop circles have occurred in Montana without being reported, or that they may occur in the future. Should they return, I hope their discoverers will report them so the circles may be documented and investigated, and their message, whatever it is, more widely received. Following are the two primary research sites collecting crop circle reports as of 2012:

ICCRA (Independent Crop Circles Research Association) maintains a state-by-state database. To download a report form: http://www.iccra.org/science.htm/; to contact the director: http://www.iccra.org/contactus.htm/

BLT Research is at http://www.bltresearch.com/contactform/contact.php/ A report form is provided on the website, or call Nancy Talbott at 697-492-0415.

### Notes

1. "Crop Circle," [Helena, MT] *Independent Record*, September 1, 1998, A2.
2. Michael Jamison, "Crop Circle: Inexplicable marks appear in Kalispell farmers' wheat field," [Missoula, MT] *Missoulian*, September 1, 1998, A1, A3.
3. Tom Lawrence, "Alien Signal or Just Hoax?" *Whitefish* [MT] *Pilot*, September 3, 1998, 1.
4. Author telephone conversation with Herb Koenig, February 24, 2000.
5. Robert Plot, *A Natural History of Staffordshire* (repr. 2009, Stoke-on-Trent, England: Malthouse Press), viewed at BLT Research website, http://www.bltresearch.com/otherfacts.php#newplantab/
6. Eltjo H. Haselhoff, Ph.D., *The Deepening Complexity of Crop Circles: Scientific Research and Urban Legends* (Berkeley, CA: Frog, Ltd., 2001), 3-4.
7. J. Rand Capron, "Storm Effects," *Nature* 22 (July 29, 1880): 290-91.
8. http://www.bltresearch.com/otherfacts.php#nongeom/
9. For early reports of North American crop circles, see http://www.iccra.org/usaformations.htm/

10. Sally B. Donnelly and Lisa Distelheim, "Britain Around and Around in Circles," *Time*, September 18, 1989.
11. "The Men Who Conned the World," [London, UK] *Today*, September 9, 1991. This tabloid was published from 1986 to 1995.
12. Lucy Pringle, *Crop Circles: The Greatest Mystery of Modern Time* (London: Thorsons/ HarperCollins Publishers, 1999), 13.
13. Freddy Silva, *Secrets in the Fields* (Charlottesville, VA: Hampton Roads Publishing, 2002), 37.
14. Silva, 37-40.
15. My sincere gratitude to Nancy Talbott, of the BLT Research Team for editing and writing much of this section. Most of what is written here can also be found at the BLT Website, http://www.bltresearch.com/index.php/
16. W.C. Levengood, "Anatomical Anomalies in Crop Formation Plants," *Physiologica Plantarum* 92 (1994): 356-63; W.C. Levengood and J. A. Burke, "Semi-Molten Meteoric Iron Associated with a Crop Formation," *Journal of Scientific Exploration*, Vol. 9, No. 2 (1995), 191; W.C. Levengood and N.P. Talbott, "Dispersion of energies in Worldwide Crop Formations," *Physiologia Plantarum* 105 (1999): 615-24.
17. http://www.bltresearch.com/plantab.php/
18. BLT Research Team, "Clay-Mineral Crystallization Case Study: 1999 Edmonton, Alberta, Canada Crop Formation," March 2004, http://www.bltresearch.com/xrd.php/
19. According to Wikipedia, Laurance Rockefeller in his later life had a high degree of interest in UFOs and related phenomena. He attempted (unsuccessfully) to get the Clinton Administration to declassify and release all UFO documents, and supported Steven Greer's Disclosure Project with the same goal. Until the end of his life he funded some of the most highly credentialed researchers in the field, including this project with Colin Andrews and the clay mineralization study with the BLT Research Team mentioned earlier in this chapter. He died July 11, 2004.
20. http://www.colinandrews.net/
21. Colin Andrews, "Crop-Circles: Mirror Image of World Events and Human Behavior, with One Difference," 2012 International UFO Congress. DVD available at http:// www.ufocongress.com. See also Andrews' website, http://www.colinandrews.net/
22. http://www.circlemakers.org/weird_shit.html/
23. The "Blue Moon" is a western bar, restaurant and more recently casino and event center in continuous operation at this Flathead Valley, MT, intersection since it was built in 1940.
24. To the best of my knowledge, the only press coverage this crop circle received was in the *Whitefish* [MT] *Pilot*, February 3, 2000, A-7.
25. Author telephone conversation with Nancy Talbott, February 18, 2000.
26. Linda Moulton Howe, *Mysterious Lights and Crop Circles* (New Orleans: Paper Chase Press, 2000), 260-66. Also, see http://www.bltresearch.com/otherfacts.php/
27. Colin Andrews, "Crop-Circles: Mirror Image…"
28. The Disclosure Project is a nonprofit research project that work to fully disclose facts about UFOs, extraterrestrial intelligence, and classified advanced energy-and-propulsion systems. http://www.disclosureproject.org
29. Silva, 266.
30. Silva, 170-71. See also Silva's website, http://www.cropcirclesecrets.org/hawkins.html/
31. Gerald Hawkins delivered the results of his decoding project to Freddy Silva by personal communication, per Silva, 171.

32. "The Men Who Conned the World."

33. Silva, 37-39.

34. Silva, 170-71.

35. Donald T. Healy and Peter J. Orenski, "Zia Pubelo" in *Native American Flags* (Norman: University of Oklahoma Press, 2003), in the website http://www.tmealf.com/DH/zia.html/

36. "The wheel cross, sun cross, Odin's cross or Woden's cross," 29.1, *Online Encyclopedia of Western Signs and Ideograms*, http://www.symbols.com/encyclopedia/29/291.html/

37. Jeffrey Wilson in "Crop Circles as a Portal to Personal and Planetary Transformation," August 20, 2011 teleseminar, available at http://evolverintensives.com/archives/personal-planetary-transformation.html/ See also Wilson's website: http://www.iccra.org/

38. First Nations Environmental Network Website (See "Sacred Message" link near bottom of page), http://www.fnen.org/?q=node/30/

39. "First 1999 Crop Circles in Canada," http://netowne.com/strange/cropcircles/canada.htm/

40. Joanna Emery, "Crop Circles: The Canadian Connection," in *UFO Magazine*, 17:6 (December-January 2003), 30-34.

41. Independent Crop Circle Researchers' Association website: http://www.iccra.org/bystate/usaformations-bystate.htm/, "Montana," "Kalispell/Whitefish, Flathead County, August 14, 2000 and August 25, 2000."

42. Tom Lawrence, "Whitefish woman researching crop circles in area," *Whitefish* [MT] *Pilot*, September 7, 2000, B-7.

43. Linda Moulton Howe, "08/27/2000—Crop Circle Reports from Whitefish, Montana—Updated Photos" and "08/30/2000—Second Wheat Formation in Whitefish, Montana," http://www.earthfiles.com/

44. Independent Crop Circle Researchers' Association website, http://www.iccra.org/bystate/usaformations-bystate.htm, "Ohio," "Paint Creek Island, Bainbridge, Ross County (September 25, 2003)."

45. Wilson, "Crop Circles as a Portal."

46. *Science News*, February 1, 1992, 76.

47. *Mathematics Teacher: The Magazine of the National Council of Teachers of Mathematics*, Vol. 91, No. 5 (May 1998), 441.

48. Silva, 193-200.

49. Craig N. Kendall, "Hydrology of the Watershed," in *Flathead Watershed Sourcebook: Guide to an Extraordinary Place*, by Lori S. Curtis (Kalispell, MT: Thomas Printing Co., 2010). Also see website http://www.flatheadwatershed.org/index.shtml/; K.J. Hascall, "Drinking, bathing come with a price," *Hungry Horse* [MT] *News*, March 2, 2011, http://www.flatheadnewsgroup.com/hungryhorsenews/news/article_8edc49be-4510-11e0-ac96-001cc4c002e0.html/

50. See #7, "The Aquifer Connection," at http://www.bltresearch.com/otherfacts.php/

51. Wilson, "Crop Circles as a Portal."

52. Author telephone conversation with Melody Watt, July 15, 2012.

53. Author telephone conversation with Melody Watt, February 5, 2008.

54. Jeffrey Wilson, "Madisonville, Monroe County, Tennessee: Crop Circle Formations analysis 2007-08" (2009; updated 6/18/2011), ICCRA website, http://www.iccra.org/reports.htm/, 38-39.

55. Silva, 216-217.

56. Colin Andrews' presentation at the 2012 International UFO Congress, www.ufocon-

gress.com (UFO Store; Andrews website, http://www.colinandrews.net/

57. "Paint Creek Island, Bainbridge, Ross County (September 25, 2003)."

58. http://en.wikipedia.org/wiki/Hans_Jenny_%28cymatics%29

59. http://www.colinandrews.net/Crop_Circle_Research.html/ A number of informative videos of Colin Andrews' presentations can be accessed at this site.

60. http://www.cymascope.com/cyma_research/history.html/

61. See #8, Light Phenomena under "Other Facts," http://www.bltresearch.com/other-facts.php/

62. BLT Lab Report #122, http://www.bltresearch.com/labreports/edmonton.php/

63. http://www.bltresearch.com/eyewitness.php/

64. http://www.cropcircleresearch.com/articles/alienface.html/ Passage taken from Paul Vigay's website; Vigay died in February 2009, so his website may not continue. Information about this crop circle is widely available elsewhere on the Internet, referenced as "Crabwood crop circle" or "alien face crop circle."

65. http://www.iccra.org/bystate/

# 4

# THE CANYON FERRY SIGHTING —OR SOCORRO COPYCAT?

*[The Air Force officer] told newsmen, "We are not at liberty to say
anything at this point." After chuckling, he added, "I'm not sure
we will make a positive statement about this anytime."*
Independent Record, April 30, 1964

Giant headlines hovered over the masthead of the April 30, 1964, edition of the *Independent Record*: "Spaceship (?) Lands Near Helena." The front page of the Helena newspaper followed with the article, "Children Report Sighting of Strange Craft," along with a photo of the five witnesses, aged eleven to sixteen years, pointing out the site.

About 9:30 P.M. on Wednesday, April 29, eleven-year-old Linda Davis said she saw a glow on her bedroom curtains and ran outside, where her brother and some friends had been playing. The witnesses all reported seeing a glowing oval- or egg-shaped craft about the size of an automobile land and then take off when four of the youngsters approached it.[1] It left behind four shallow holes in the ground and a small patch of singed earth.

Later that night, seventeen-year-old Bill Bahny, a friend of the witnesses, called the sheriff's office. When I interviewed Bahny in 2012, he told me he wouldn't have called if he'd thought it was a prank. "They seemed genuinely scared."[2] Lewis and Clark County Sheriff Dave Middlemas was more suspicious and wanted an adult to check out the story and call back, since his people "frequently get calls from teenagers who are playing pranks."

Every first Friday in May, Helena high school students participate in the Vigilante Day Parade; students have off the day before, Thursday, to build floats and costumes. Though justified as a hands-on way to teach Montana history, this tradition may also be a nod to end-of-school-year attention deficit disorder. The timing of the UFO call, on the eve of the school holiday, certainly raised the possibility of young pranksters.

However, a parent did call back the sheriff and confirmed Bahny's concern. Two deputies were dispatched to investigate. They took measurements of the holes and inspected the burned area. The next morning the sheriff's office continued the investigation, and Chief Deputy Larry Lytle had a long talk with fifteen-year-old Thom Davis, one of the witnesses. That morning, Sheriff Middlemas called the Air Force, and a five-man investigation team from Malmstrom Air Force Base in Great Falls flew in about noon. The team, headed by Lt. Col. Harold L. Neufeld, interviewed five witnesses, according to the Air Force report. Those interviewed were Thom Davis, his sister Linda Davis (eleven), Linda Flittner (sixteen), Diane Flittner (fifteen) and Pete Rust (fourteen). (The Project Blue Book report on the case alleges there were six witnesses, one of whom was not interviewed at his father's request. The names of the witnesses are redacted in the Blue Book report, but the ages match the witnesses named in the front-page photo of the newspaper.[3])

The Air Force team inspected and measured the "landing site" and took eleven photos. Neufeld told newsmen, "We are not at liberty to say anything at this point." After chuckling, he added, "I'm not sure we will make a positive statement about this anytime."[4] This last statement probably reflects the military's regulations against any communication with anyone regarding UFO incidents and its strict security classification of reports involving "unexplained" incidents.[5] Neufeld prepared a detailed report and

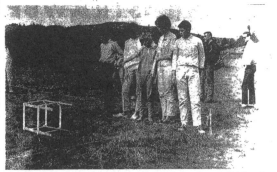

# Spaceship (?) Lands Near

## Children Report Sighting of Strange Craft

### The Independent

Vol. XXI—No. 133      Helena, Montana, Thursday, April 30, 1964      28 Pages, Th

**By George Martin**

Air Force investigators and dozens of curiosity-seekers today invaded a barren slope on the outskirts of Canyon Ferry Village that supposedly was invaded late Wednesday by an unidentified flying object.

This object "whooshed" away when approached, according to four brave village youngsters who attempted to do just that.

Whatever it was, most authorities and newsmen are skeptical. However, the description of the object match those reported from New Mexico. Those descriptions have been printed and broadcast for almost a week.

The Canyon Ferry object apparently was first sighted by Linda Davis, 11, a daughter of Mr. and Mrs. Bert Davis, who live about 100 yards from the scene.

The Davis girl rounded up three neighborhood friends and attempted to approach the object. It took off into the sky and disappeared, they said.

Bill Beheny called this information into the county sheriff's office and was told to have an adult investigate and return the call.

The reason for this, according to Sheriff Dave Middleman is that they "frequently get calls from teenagers who are playing pranks." However, he did not call this particular incident a prank.

Close to Vigilante Day

"Since it is so close to Vigilante Day, the deputy advised the 17-year-old boy (Beheny) to have an adult examine the area after which an investigation would be made. About an hour

☆ ☆ ☆

## Most Flying Phenomenon Not Validated

Washington - - UPI -- The Air Force has investigated more than 8,000 reported unidentified flying

**IT LANDED THERE**—Canyon Ferry Village children who allegedly saw the unidentified flying object take off and disappear point out the area. Left to right: Pete Rust, 13; Diane Flittner, 15; Linda Davis, 11; Linda Flittner, 16; and Tom Davis, 15. (Staff photo!)

[HELENA, MT] INDEPENDENT RECORD, APRIL 30, 1964

sent it to Captain Hector Quintanilla, director of Project Blue Book, where it was received on May 14. The Canyon Ferry Case is part of the Blue Book archives.[6]

For many years the public generally believed that all UFO reports went to Project Blue Book because it was the Air Force's official department for UFO investigations. This may have been more true early in Project Blue Book's formation. Beginning in 1954, Air Defense Command assumed primary responsibility for UFO investigations and became the clearinghouse for all UFO reports. After this, Project Blue Book did not receive all the reports and became more of a false front for presenting the impression to the public that all UFO cases could be easily explained.[7]

The Air Force did issue a statement about the Canyon Ferry Case, presumably because they believed they had satisfactorily explained the event. Headlines in the May 5 edition of the *Independent Record* said, "Helena Saucer Called Prank By Air Force."[8] While the Air Force "hoax" conclusion appeared in a small article on the front page, a much longer article covering the parents' skepticism of the Air Force statement appeared on the back page of the front section.[9] This probably reflected a general suspicion of Air Force conclusions regarding UFOs, as well as an indication of the level of trust the parents had in their children. In 2012, as I was investigating this case, I still found people divided about whether the Canyon Ferry UFO case was real, including classmates of the witnesses. It was reported by highly respected UFO researchers, Coral and Jim Lorenzen, founders of the Aerial Phenomena Research Organization (APRO) in several of their books.[10] They definitely believed the Air Force explanation was a cover-up.

Pete Rust, one of the witnesses, is deceased but his sister Barbara told me she believed it was a prank, although she said she didn't really know for sure. Her brother never told her it was a prank.

Following leads from people who attended Helena High in the 1960s, I was able to find Thom Davis, who still lives in the Helena area. According to Thom, it was a hoax. The "witnesses" dug the holes, poured a little gas on the ground, and lit it. They colluded in the story of the glowing white object and its take-off over Canyon Ferry.[11] Davis also reiterated what was said in the Blue Book report that the youths had been listening to KOMA radio out of Oklahoma City[12] and heard about a UFO sighting in Socorro, New Mexico. This sighting was referred to in some of the newspaper stories about the Canyon Ferry event.

So it seems that Sheriff Middlemas's original instincts were right and so was the Air Force. The Canyon Ferry Sighting probably was a hoax, but it was also, at the very least, a copycat of one of the more significant cases in UFO history.

## THE SOCORRO CASE: CLOSE ENCOUNTER OF THE THIRD KIND

The UFO incident in Socorro, New Mexico, happened on April 24, 1964, five days before the Canyon Ferry event, and was widely reported around the country. It was briefly mentioned in a dismissive AP article picked up by the Helena paper ("Most Flying Phenomenon [sic] Not Validated") and placed next to the first front-page report of the Canyon Ferry incident on April 30. In the second paragraph, the AP article says,

> …(P)robes of such sightings back to 1947 have failed to turn up any evidence that UFOs are alien interplanetary space vehicles under some form of intelligent control.

The debunking article was based on an Air Force press release responding to "a new epidemic of strange sightings in the skies over New Mexico and Montana."[13] It continued:

> One of the Air Force's leading civilian consultants on UFOs has gone to Socorro, N.M., to investigate the latest reports. He is Dr. J. Allen Hynek, director of the Dearborn Observatory at Northwestern University.

The article concludes with the odd sentence, "Air Force sleuths decided that one woman who turned in a UFO report actually had seen spots before her eye."

The *Great Falls Tribune* reported the Socorro Incident on April 29: "Host of UFO Sightings has New Mexico in a Spin." This United Press International article stated that Socorro policeman

Lonnie Zamora reported an egg-shaped object which roared up from the ground, leaving deep impressions and burned patches. It also mentioned how this sighting touched off many more reports from "drunks, obvious quacks, publicity hunters and well meaning information seekers."[14]

Dr. Hynek did visit Socorro and interviewed Lonnie Zamora. Hynek reported:

> My original investigations, directed toward breaking apart Zamora's account by seeking mutual contradictions in it and also by seeking to establish Zamora as an unreliable witness, were fruitless. I was impressed by the high regard in which Zamora was held by his colleagues, and I personally am willing today to accept his testimony as genuine, particularly since it does fit a global pattern.[15]

In another place, Hynek wrote,

> I think this case may be the "Rosetta stone." There's never been a strong case with so unimpeachable a witness.[16]

Hynek referred to the Socorro incident as "one of the classics of UFO literature." Given his illustrious background as a scientist, and his many years of researching UFO cases, this is a particularly meaningful statement.

Hynek obtained his Ph.D. in astrophysics from the University of Chicago in 1935. He established his scientific reputation in stellar spectroscopy at Ohio State University, where he became director of their McMillan Observatory. In 1948, he began his work as a government consultant when Project Grudge asked him to review their UFO reports for misidentifications due to astronomical phenomena. In 1960 he accepted a position with Northwestern University as professor of astronomy and department chair. Later he became director of the university's Dearborn Observatory and the Lindheimer Astronomical Research Center.

Hynek started out as a UFO skeptic, and it took many years before he began to admit that some cases defied conventional explanation. The Socorro case was one of those and marked a significant turning point in his career. By 1964, Hynek had been investigating UFO reports for sixteen years and was becoming increasingly disturbed by the Air Force's insistence at latching on to a conventional explanation, no matter how untenable or ridiculous. Even before his

*Lonnie Zamora*

humiliating "Swamp Gas" blunder (mentioned in Chapter 1) in March 1966, Hynek was beginning to show signs of switching sides.[17] He concluded his first book with the following words:

> When the long awaited solution to the UFO problem comes, I believe that it will prove to be not merely the next small step in the march of science but a mighty and totally unexpected quantum jump.[18]

Although the Socorro incident was widely reported, the most astounding aspect of the sighting was largely kept from the public. Lonnie Zamora was chasing a speeding car south of Socorro when he thought he heard an explosion followed by a roaring sound, and he saw a blue flame south-southwest of his location, near where he knew there was a dynamite shack. He veered off on a gravel road as the flame sank below a hill and the roaring diminished. When he reached the top of the hill, the roaring had stopped and the flame had disappeared.

Peering over the landscape, Zamora noticed what looked like a white car in a ravine about 150 yards away. Next to it, *two small figures in what looked like white overalls, maybe the size of boys*, seemed to be inspecting the vehicle. Thinking they needed help, Zamora started driving toward them and radioed headquarters he was investigating a possible accident. The terrain dipped and he lost sight of the vehicle and the two figures for a few moments. He stopped again about fifty feet from the white object and got out of his car. He saw a symbol on the side of the object and heard loud thumps like closing doors, followed by a crescendoing roar. He saw a blue flame under the white object as it lifted into the air. Fearing an explosion, Zamora hit the dirt. The roar continued and he felt heat, but no explosion, and the object continued to rise. Zamora was now running away and glancing back as the object rose and moved off towards the southwest. Zamora then called the radio operator at the police office in Socorro and asked if they could see anything, and he asked that Sgt. M.S. Chavez be sent to the scene. When Chavez arrived he was struck by Zamora's expression and told him he looked like he'd seen the devil. Zamora replied, "Maybe I have."

Zamora wanted Chavez to see what he had seen: burning brush where the craft had taken off. When they walked toward it, they found four wedge-shaped depressions in the ground in a quadrangle shape, each about four to six inches deep. Where the figures had stood they found four small footprints, each with a small crescent shape in the middle of the print. Zamora's entire sighting from his first glimpse of blue flame to the disappearance of the white craft had lasted less than two minutes.[19]

Hynek arrived on the scene on Tuesday, April 28. He was met by Maj. William Conner from Kirtland Air Force Base. On the way to Socorro, the Air Force vehicle had a flat tire and Hynek had to hitchhike the rest of the way. As UFO historian Jerome Clark commented, the symbolism was too perfect, given Hynek's growing

*Artist's conception of Lonnie Zamora witnessing the UFO near Socorro, New Mexico.*

dissatisfaction with the Air Force's research of UFO reports.[20] Hynek was able to interview Zamora and Chavez that evening and visit the site the following morning, where he had Zamora reenact the event for him. But many other investigators had preceded Hynek.

FBI agent Arthur Byrnes Jr. heard about the incident over police radio and was waiting for Zamora when he returned to the police station. Byrnes called White Sands Missile Range in southern New Mexico, and they sent out Army Captain Richard T. Holder. The two of them interviewed Zamora shortly after the sighting and visited the site that same night. Holder asked Zamora to not describe the symbol he had seen on the object (and later made a drawing of) to anyone except official investigators. Holder then drew a symbol for Zamora to use instead, explaining it would be a way to identify copycat hoaxers. Holder had Zamora sign the drawing as if it were Zamora's original drawing.

Early the next morning, Holder received a call from a colonel who said he was calling from the war room of the Joint Chiefs of Staff at the Pentagon. The colonel wanted him to read the report into the "scrambler," a coding device for classified communications. Obviously, the highest levels of the military took this case very seriously from the get-go. The massive media coverage began hours later, the day after the event happened.

Some of the first newspaper accounts were quite detailed, carrying drawings of the actual symbol and describing the occupants. According to Ray Stanford, who authored a comprehensive and highly regarded book on the Socorro event, FBI agent Byrnes asked Zamora not to "publicly mention seeing the two beings in white," and the Air Force also did not want that information released. At the time, Hynek complied with the Air Force's directive to suppress that information, and according to Stanford, made ridiculous attempts to conceal it.[21] Hynek may have been dealing with his own resistance to that information. In his first book on UFOS, he summarizes the general attitude in those days towards reports of aliens:

> We balk at reports about occupants even though we
> might be willing to listen attentively to accounts of other
> UFO encounters…why should a report of a car stopped on
> the highway by a blinding light from an unknown craft be
> any different in essential strangeness or absurdity from one
> of a craft from which two or three little animate creatures
> descend?…There is no logical reason, yet I confess to
> sharing a prejudice that is hard to explain.[22]

Hynek struggled to resolve what he calls "the most bizarre and seemingly incredible aspect of the entire UFO phenomenon."

> Our common sense recoils at the very idea of
> humanoids and leads to much banter and ridicule and
> jokes about little green men. They tend to throw the whole
> UFO concept into disrepute.[23]

Nevertheless, because he found it so convincing, the Socorro incident forced Hynek to wrestle with his disbelief, and he began to look more closely at reports from all over the world of encounters with various humanoid forms.

> Clearly, it is not only kooks who report humanoids.
> Indeed, I do not know of a report of this kind to have
> come from a person of demonstrated mental imbalance.[24]

Hynek referred to such cases as "Close Encounters of the Third Kind," or "CE-III" in the classification scheme that he originated. (The title for the blockbuster Hollywood film, *Close Encounters of the Third Kind*, was based on Hynek's nomenclature. Hynek acted as a consultant for the film, bringing to bear his years of experience with UFO reports, and director Steven Spielberg gave him a cameo appearance in the movie.[25])

The Socorro event was really the stage entrance for non-human aliens in many UFO research circles, including government investigations of UFOs. It is still considered to be one of the best-documented extraterrestrial (ET) cases on record.

However, as in any famous UFO case, there is always a debunking side. Early on, renowned UFO debunker Philip Klass explained the Socorro incident as a scheme hatched by Zamora and the Socorro mayor to generate tourism.[26] His story was based on numerous fictions, including his claim that the mayor owned the landing site.[27] In 2009, a UFO blogger named Anthony Bragalia made waves in the UFO world by claiming the Socorro case was a hoax perpetrated by students at the New Mexico Institute of

Technology, according to Stirling Colgate, president of the New Mexico Institute of Mining and Technology at the time.[28]

Bragalia's debunking story was hotly debated on the Internet, and experienced UFO researchers found too many facts unaccounted for in his explanation. (For example, Bragalia/Colgate claimed the UFO was a balloon lit by a candle, yet it took off and flew at speeds estimated to be at least 3,000 mph into the wind.) Ray Stanford, author of the book on the Socorro case, characterizes Colgate as a "desperate disbeliever."[29] Kevin Randle, a long-time UFO investigator with many books to his credit, says the hoax story based on Colgate's second-hand accounts first came out in 1968, but since that time no actual hoaxers or first-hand witnesses to the purported hoax have ever come forward to corroborate Colgate's story. Randle fairly states that if hoax witnesses come forward, they could provide important corroborating evidence. As it stands, the Colgate/Bragalia hoax story is completely based on hearsay, and it's nothing new.[30]

Even the best-documented UFO cases—maybe *especially* the best-documented UFO cases—come under attack, and it's important to understand that there is a tremendous amount of noise to sort through in searching for the truth.

So while the Air Force may have been right in declaring the Canyon Ferry case a hoax, those spring-fevered teenagers may have been inspired by a watermark UFO case, one that was the beginning of acceptance by serious UFO researchers that extraterrestrials do visit Earth.

This "ice-breaking" case opened the way for more reports of alien encounters. Over time, and especially after esteemed Harvard psychiatrist John Mack began researching the phenomenon in the 1990s, the subject has become more tenable.[31]

The next two chapters cover remarkable, detailed accounts of ET contact in Montana. The two case histories are not as well documented as the Socorro case. However, the credibility of the witnesses, and the similarity of their encounters to that of other accounts from around the world, make the Montana stories worth pondering in understanding a complex and, to some, frightening subject.

## Notes

1. George Martin, "Children Report Sighting of Strange Craft," [Helena, MT] *Independent Record*, April 30, 1964; Ken Payton, "'Saucer' Sighting Has Canyon Ferry Buzzin'," *Great Falls Tribune*, May 1, 1964, 1.
2. Author communication with Bill Bahny, May 11, 2012.
3. "Blue Book File—30 April 1964—Canyon Ferry Case," accessed at Fold3 website, http://www.fold3.com/imge/#8699462/ Blue Book files were declassified under the Freedom of Information Act, and are located at the National Archives in Washington, D.C. Files may be accessed in the reading room, or purchased at http://www.archives.gov/foia/ufos.html/ Some files are available at other Internet sites.
4. "Air Force Probe: Canyon Ferry Mystery Flying Objects Still Unsolved," *Independent Record*, May 1, 1964.
5. Navy pilot Frederick M. Fox reported in 2012 that he saw a domed saucer-shaped object over the South China Sea in 1964. He told no one, because of military regulations saying he could be fined $10,000 and put in jail for 10 years. He also feared he could be discharged "for a Section 8," as mentally unfit. Fox flew thirty years with American Airlines and had more sightings, but never reported any of them for fear of losing his job, which had happened to other pilots. (Lee Speigel, "UFO Encounters with Airplanes: Pilots, Officials Discuss Potential Safety Hazards," *Huffington Post*, April 13, 2012, http://www.huffingtonpost.com/2012/04/12/ufo-aircraft-safety-hazards_n_1422206.html/
6. Blue Book file, Project 10073 Record Card, 30 April 1964, Canyon Ferry Reservoir, Montana. Accessed at Fold3 website.
7. If sightings or encounters were considered a potential security threat, Blue Book may never have seen them. During the investigation of the April 24, 1964, Socorro encounter, Blue Book's Sergeant Moody told private UFO investigators, "you get lots of cases that we don't." See Richard Dolan, *UFOs and the National Security State* (Charlottesville, VA: Hampton Roads Publishing Co., 2002), 156, 274.
8. Associated Press, "Helena Saucer Called Prank By Air Force," *Independent Record*, May 5, 1964, 1.
9. "On Flying Object: Parents Resent Air Force Calling Report 'Prank'," *Independent Record*, May 5, 1964, 12.
10. Coral E. Lorenzen, 1966. *Flying Saucers: The Startling Evidence of the Invasion from Outer Space* (New York: New American Library), 223-224; Coral and Jim Lorenzen, *Flying Saucer Occupants* (New York: New American Library, 1967), 151; Coral and Jim Lorenzen, *UFOs: The Whole Story* (New York: New American Library, 1969), 241.
11. Author telephone conversation with Thom Davis, June 20, 2012.
12. Throughout the 1960s and '70s, KOMA was a teen favorite, blasting its 50,000-watt signal across the plains after sunset. There were few rock-n-roll radio stations at the time. http://www.komaradio.com/komainfo.aspx/
13. "Most Flying Phenomenon [sic] Not Validated," *Independent Record*, April 30, 1964.

14. United Press International, "Host of UFO Sightings has New Mexico in a Spin," *Great Falls Tribune,* April 29, 1964, 7.
15  J. Allen Hynek, *The UFO Experience: A Scientific Inquiry* (Chicago: Henry Regnery Company, 1972), 144.
16. Jerome Clark, *The UFO Book: Encyclopedia of the Extraterrestrial* (Detroit: Visible Ink Press, 1998), 553.
17. "Hynek, Josef Allen (1910-1986)" in Clark, 304-308.
18. Hynek, 234.
19. "Socorro CE2/CE3," in Clark, 545-58.
20. Clark, 552.
21. Ray Stanford, *Socorro "Saucer" in a Pentagon Pantry* (Austin, TX: Blueapple Books, 1976), 64-72.
22. Hynek, 138.
23. Hynek, 139.
24. Hynek, 143.
25. Clark, 307.
26. Philip Klass, *UFOs Explained* (New York: Vintage Books, 1976).
27. Kevin Randle, "Lonnie Zamora, Socorro UFO, and New Theories, October 7, 2009," The UFO Chronicles website, http://www.theufochronicles.com/2009/10/lonnie-zamora-socorro-ufo-and-new.html/
28. "The Ultimate Secret of Socorro Told: New Details on World-Famous 1964 UFO Hoax," http://www.bragalia.blogspot.com/2012/08/the-ultimate-secret-of socorro-finally.html/
29. Ray Stanford, "Lonnie Zamora (1933-2009): Eulogy, to a Man of His Word, and The Finest Witness One Could Ever Interview," November 7, 2009, The UFO Chronicles Website, http://www.theufochronicles.com/2009/11/lonnie-zamora-1933-2009-eulogy-to-man.html/; Ray Stanford, "Veteran Ufologist & Expert on the Socorro UFO Case: Ray Stanford Challenges Newcomer & Hoax Pronouncer, Anthony Bragalia To a Live Debate on C2C!! [Coast-to-Coast radio program]," http://www.theufochronicles.com/2009/10/veteran-ufologist-expert-on-socorro-ufo.html/
30. Randle, "Lonnie Zamora."
31. John Mack, *Abduction* (New York: Macmillan Publishing Company, 1994); John Mack, *Passport to the Cosmos* (New York: Crown Publishers, 1999).

# 5

# THE LEO DWORSHAK CONTACT CASE

*They seemed to have something about them that other people*
*we had met before didn't have…perhaps it is the other way around…*
*I am certain that hatred and violence are not a part of their behavior;*
*it does not seem to exist with them.*

Leo Dworshak

This story begins just over the Montana border on a little farm near Killdeer, North Dakota. The Dworshak family were German/Bohemian immigrants eking out a living during the dust bowl days of the Great Depression. Egnats Dworshak owned a steam-powered threshing rig and traveled around North Dakota and into Canada doing what is now called "custom combining." His oldest boy, Leo, even at a very young age, helped his dad on nearby jobs, but most of the time Leo was needed at home. The family depended on their two oldest boys, Leo and Mike, to pull their own weight with a long list of daily chores. When chores were finished, the two brothers would take off, sometimes carrying a shotgun for birds, but mostly exploring and looking for some kind of excitement in the plains and hills near their farm.[1]

One dusty afternoon in the summer of 1932, the boys' explorations yielded an unimaginable surprise. From the top of a hill, Leo, twelve, and Mike, seven, looked into a remote valley and saw "a huge round thing, as big as our barn at least." At first the brothers thought it was a giant building or machine, though it didn't look like anything they had ever seen. Leo felt it must be a machine because it was "rotating in a complicated way." Flashing colored lights on the perimeter were turning one way while the inner core was either stationary or turning the other way.

As the boys tried to approach this strange object, they found their way blocked by an invisible shield. It would not let them get closer. This was mystifying and, try as they might, there was no way they could get around or through this unseen wall.

Resigned to watching from a distance, the boys saw the object stop rotating, its lights stop blinking, and a door suddenly appear in its smooth side. Leo later wrote that a ramp "sprouted" out of it and three "people" in identical coveralls walked out of the machine and onto the ground.

The boys watched the three people walk around, though they were too far away to see much detail. According to Leo, "They would look up at the sky, as if they were thankful and pleased with the weather." Eventually they went back into the strange structure. The boys had to hightail it home in time for dinner. They didn't want to get into trouble because they wanted to come back as soon as they could.

So began the otherworldly adventures of the Dworshak brothers later logged in Leo's engaging book, *UFOs Are With Us: Take My Word*.

When the boys returned the next day, they were disappointed that the "machine" was gone. Day after day they came back, not willing to give up hope of seeing the strange structure again. About two weeks after their initial sighting, they returned to the valley and this time they were astonished to see the machine flying above them! It was an airship. They hid as the silver craft descended to its landing spot. Again they were unable to approach very closely because of the invisible shield, but they saw six men emerge from the ship. Instead of coveralls the men wore slacks and shirts that the impoverished boys admired, and they seemed to be picking up things from the ground.

After this encounter, the boys decided to tell their parents what they had seen. To their dismay, their parents told them to forget all about it.

The boys then approached Mr. Brooks, a "man of the world" who worked at the grain elevator in Killdeer and one of the few adults in their lives who had time for kids. The boys wondered if the airship might be part of a government plan to spray pesticides, the new answer for saving crops from grasshoppers. Their confidant told them he did not think they were crazy. In fact, he had seen the same machine flying through the air one evening, though he told no one since he thought no one would believe him. He assured the boys it wasn't an airplane or Zeppelin because it was quiet. By the time the boys arrived home after this discussion, they had decided the machine was a spaceship, and they began imagining getting on board. The boys had no fear of the ship or its occupants. They even allowed themselves to fantasize that the visitors could in some way make their harsh lives a little better.

The boys kept returning to the site and studying it. They looked in vain for holes in the ground from the landing prongs, assuming such a large machine must be very heavy. One day, lucky enough to find the spacecraft in the accustomed spot, they watched in amazement as it took off with a slight hum and flashing colored lights. When it reached about fifteen feet off the ground, it accelerated so fast they couldn't even tell which way it went.

The boys tried to entice friends to come with them. The town boys were put off by the long odds of actually seeing the ship after trudging miles on hot dusty afternoons. Only Mr. Brooks at the grain elevator believed and encouraged them.

During one visit, the ship descended while the brothers were inside the usual perimeter of the landing site. Suddenly the boys found themselves immobilized by the invisible shield. As they watched the craft, they began to receive peaceful and friendly impressions in their minds. Leo began to think the visitors might be here because of the crop failures and pests brought on by the drought. After a couple of hours of entranced observation, Leo realized it was late, and they were going to be in trouble at home. As he voiced his fears to his brother, the force that imprisoned them gave way, and they hurried home.

The boys visited the special valley whenever they could and found they were allowed to come closer. The men began to look at them and even wave. The brothers were excited by the unfolding events and began thinking obsessively about their encounters and the possibility of getting on board the ship. Leo noticed that his mind seemed to be affected in some way he could not describe. Sometimes as they walked out to look for the ship, he got a feeling about whether or not it would be there. He did not quite trust these impressions, and many days he and Mike made fruitless trips to the valley.

The boys were changed by their experiences. They became fascinated with astronomy, and their mother noticed they were learning things she had never talked about. One evening as the possibility of going on the spacecraft began to loom in their minds, they tried again to talk to their parents about it. Their father left after a few minutes to do chores, but their mother heard them out and believed them. She even prophesied that one day, after she was gone, other people would believe them. Her support bolstered their courage and determination to get onto the spacecraft, and it gave them a sense of peace they had not had before.

One afternoon they felt the urge to go look for the ship even though they had made an unrewarded trip that morning. They found the ship in the usual place, and the men were moving about apparently aimlessly, as though they were exercising. Leo had the thought that these activities did not just happen here, but in other spots around the world. And he had a strange feeling that this thought was put in his head by the visitors.

This time, to the boys' amazement, they were able to walk unimpeded to the landing site. They found the men smiling and seemingly unbothered by their presence. They hesitantly approached to within ten feet of the nearest man and stopped to watch.

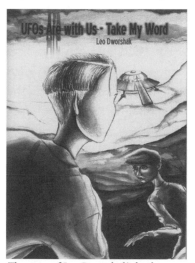

*The cover of Leo Dworshak's book.*

In his book, Leo described the men as healthier and better dressed than anyone he knew, but in some ways quite ordinary looking. They had light brown hair, "tanned" complexions, blue eyes with dark pupils, and were a little bigger and huskier than Leo's father, whom Leo said never weighed more than 130 pounds. This day, instead of coveralls, they wore uniforms of tops and slacks with a subtle pattern visible only when the light was just right. There were no insignias or markings on their uniforms, but the subtle pattern was different on each man's uniform. Other than this difference, the men looked "as alike as peas in a pod." Leo was especially drawn to their unusual smiles, "probably more gentle and relaxed than ours, maybe more gentle than any smile I have ever seen."

Leo's little brother Mike mustered the courage to speak to the visitors in an excited mixture of German and English. Two men walked into the ship and another one came out. Speaking in German, he told them he could speak their language, and then in English, that they spoke all the languages on the planet. This is Leo's recollection of what was said:

> We are very real and we are from another galaxy. We have traveled to your planet for over five thousand years. We are from a place far beyond your world by millions of years in time. We continue traveling to your planet because it is part of our responsibility.[2]

The man told the boys that if they tried to tell others about what they had seen, they would not be believed, until they were old men. But they would always know the truth in their own minds. Though the boys were yearning to see inside the ship, the visitors basically told them that was enough for now and they needed to go home and rest, "because your minds are not big enough to learn everything as quickly as you would like." The visitors promised the boys would see them again before long.

After this first conversation, Leo felt he knew many things that were unspoken. The visitors felt unusually wise and gentle, different from humans and our warring ways. They seemed to have a great deal of respect for the Earth, never leaving garbage lying about like everyone else he knew. Though appearing young and fit, Leo felt they were far older than anyone he had ever met, because of their eyes:

> … [Their eyes] had that long, deep, tunnel-like appearance I only associated with the very old…Somehow I knew they were the eyes of people who had seen and understood a large amount of life over a very long time.

Leo's suspicion that the spacemen could read his mind was confirmed because they responded to his unspoken questions.

Even more surprising, the answers sometimes popped into Leo's head without being spoken. This communication was hard to get used to and made it difficult for the boys to speak, knowing that whatever they would say was already known. Leo tellingly wrote, "It was like opening a window to another world we could only dimly understand."

During the three days following that first conversation, the boys developed the sense they would be welcomed when they returned. When they were next able to get away—Leo gives the date as September 19—the boys arrived at the valley just after sundown. They passed through the force field as if the visitors knew they were coming and had somehow "tuned" it to allow their passage. Although they were not giving up on eventually getting inside the ship, their goal for the night was to touch it or at least shake hands with one of the "people" on it.

Leo had great difficulty describing the ship because it was like nothing they had ever seen. It did not reflect light, and it seemed to produce its own light in a spectrum of colors. The last time he had seen it, the ship had looked blue and blended into the sky. This time the ship changed its colors as if putting on a show. At first it blended with the sunset, then in succession it looked like oily water, a reflective mirror, and a dark nonreflective surface.

Leo wondered whether the colors were coming from the other side of the ship and just passing through it. In recent years, the development of optical camouflage, or "invisibility technology," validates Leo's conjectures so many years ago. This technology uses cameras to project what is behind an object to its front surface, making it appear invisible.[3]

Mesmerized by the changing colors of the ship, the boys were surprised to see two of the visitors standing near the landing supports. One of the visitors told the other they needed to make sure the ship was well-grounded because the boys wanted to touch it, and it may have picked up some electricity in its travels.

There are other UFO accounts supporting electrical danger in close proximity to spacecraft. In 1975, near Snowflake, Arizona, a young man named Travis Walton was headed home with his logging crew after a day's work in the woods. The entire crew saw a bright light in the woods and drove toward it. They were amazed to find a large silvery disc hovering above a clearing. Walton got out of the vehicle and ran toward it, to the horror of his fellow crew members. He was knocked unconscious by an energy beam from the craft. This scene was reenacted in the Hollywood movie, *Fire in the Sky*, based on Walton's book by the same name.[4]

Walton now believes the bolt from the spaceship was actually an accidental static electricity discharge and that the reason he was taken onboard the ship was most likely to treat his injuries. Rather than an abduction, he sees his experience as an "ambulance call." The other logging-crew members saw the bolt hit him and presumed whoever or whatever was in the ship had purposely killed him. Fearing they were next, they fled the scene, later returning to find both Walton and the spaceship gone. Walton was returned five days later to a phone booth and, although in psychological shock, he was without physical injury. (Howard Menger, a contactee from the 1950s, also was cautioned by "visitors" about the dangers of electromagnetic fields around the spacecraft.[5])

When Leo was allowed to touch the ship, he found that effort as perplexing as viewing it. He expected the ship to feel like metal, but it exchanged no heat with his hand and it felt smoother than any metal or polished glass. Leo said it actually felt like he never quite touched it but just got close to it, like trying to push one magnet against the same pole of another magnet. Mike placed both hands and his cheek against the ship and looked as puzzled as Leo felt. While recalling the experience so many years later, Leo still could not explain it to his own satisfaction but said he remembered it sent a chill up his spine.

The boys' next wish was soon granted when one of the men

greeted them with a handshake, and without the gloves they often wore. "It was like shaking hands with the priest," Leo wrote. "The hand was soft and warm, the grip firm." Thrilled as he was, Leo couldn't help thinking about his great desire to get on the ship. To this unspoken plea, the visitor said out loud that he thought that could be arranged, though first the boys would have to go through a process. He assured them the process would not hurt them and compared it to the energy shield they had already experienced. He then told them they would begin to see things that would happen in the next thirty years.

Leo didn't understand. He just wanted to hurry up and get on the ship, but he began to notice they were giving him information in ways other than speaking. He again noticed the warmth he felt in their presence. He wasn't sure if they *had something* that the real people he knew didn't have or that they were *missing something* he was used to in other people. At any rate, Leo felt certain that hatred and violence were not part of their culture. Perhaps this was all the more apparent to these children of a German immigrant as they regularly experienced teasing and taunting from kids in town.

No longer tongue-tied, the boys felt totally comfortable talking with these kind visitors. Though he was only addressing one person, Leo felt the whole crew was listening as if they shared a group mind. He found himself describing how difficult life was for their family and so many of the people they knew, because of the droughts, grasshoppers, and crop failures. The visitors told the boys that the people of Earth had brought many of the current problems upon themselves and would soon bring great wars and suffering upon themselves, and it was up to humans to solve their own problems. The boys were told that government corruption was at the heart of the problems, and that if this could be addressed, much suffering would be avoided.

Leo confessed how strange it was to converse with them since so much of their communication was without spoken words. "Sometimes the meaning of their words did not come to me until days, weeks, or even years later." It was hard for the boys to grasp all they were being told, and much was not good news. The visitors let them know they always tried to help when they visited Earth, but they could not solve our problems. However, Leo believed, in their many activities and contacts around the Earth, they may have left the knowledge to solve the problems.

The boys had taken in about all the information they could, and in his head Leo began to repeat the words, "Go in the ship," and visualize himself and his brother walking up the ramp. At long last, their wish finally came true, and they found themselves entering the ship. When the outer door closed, a mist sprayed across it. The boys were asked to remove their clothes for disinfection, and though hesitant, the prospect of wearing the visitors' fine clothing overcame their embarrassment. Once dressed in the clothing they'd admired, though it was ridiculously large for them, they passed into another chamber where a haze went all over their bodies, evidently completing the decontamination process.

A door finally opened to an inner compartment. Leo was especially struck by the beautiful chairs: "out of this world," he wrote, maybe a little tongue in cheek. The chairs slid under you as you made a motion to sit and then automatically adjusted to your body "from heels to head." Mike ran around trying to outwit the chairs by sitting before they moved under him, to everyone's amusement.

The next thing that caught Leo's attention was a small "movie screen" about four feet by five feet in size, showing images that made no sense to him. When writing the book years later, Leo said he could see the images in his mind but still could not explain what they meant. A machine on the opposite wall that operated continuously was described as a magnetic sensor. Their hosts explained their food and cooking equipment, though it made no sense to the boys. They were also shown sleeping quarters and fully automatic toilet facilities without toilet tissue or towels. Another room, the largest they saw, was full of machines, and the hosts confessed they could not explain their function to the boys. When Mike asked why they kept coming back to this same spot, they said they were studying the life patterns in the valley. Maybe that included the human ones.

To their surprise, the boys could see outside the ship as if looking through a window. They were told it was not glass but another material. Their hosts pointed to a picture of a sunset, which turned out to be a live aerial view of the landscape outside the spacecraft, including the lights of moving vehicles on the nearest highway. The men were monitoring their various machines and equipment and seemed very busy with their tasks. Leo sensed the machines were all of a peaceful nature and posed no threat to humans. While the visit inside the spaceship lasted only a few hours, Leo said it seemed like days.

Many UFO contactees have reported telepathic ability in extraterrestrial beings, but it is particularly interesting to hear it described from the viewpoint of children in the 1930s, when the information received and the method of receiving it was so foreign to the world they knew:

> While they are speaking to you about one thing, at the same time they can fill your mind with thoughts and information about many other things that you hardly even notice…The ideas they gave us came trickling back out of our brains later on and often could not be told from our own.

The most baffling thing that happened was some kind of discontinuity in the boys' experience or memory. Sitting inside the ship in comfortable chairs and listening to one of the hosts talk about their distant galaxy, the boys suddenly found themselves walking on a hillside while the host showed them how grasshoppers laid their eggs under the dirt. Then they were back listening to the galaxy lecture, and then the host was showing them how the magnetic laser beam worked. It could stop a rabbit or bird and then release it. These abrupt changes of locations and topics were disconcerting, almost as if they were happening simultaneously, but the brothers' minds could focus only on one scene at a time.

The magnetic laser beam particularly captured Leo's imagination. The power of this tool to stop all movement convinced Leo there was no way the visitors could be harmed, should any human try. Combined with their mind-reading skills, he felt it impossible for humans to pose any danger to them and fully believed their peaceful ways posed no danger to us.

> We were told that they will continue traveling to our planet, to this very spot, and to many other places as our world gets deeper into trouble....They told us that twelve people from their galaxy live full time on our planet Earth. These people live among us, but we cannot tell that they are different from us. We were also informed that these twelve people have often offered to help our world and were rejected every time. No one was interested in talking with them. These people from another world must be asked and must be made welcome before they will give advice.

At this point in his book, Leo expresses astonishment at human indifference to this opportunity to gain from an exchange with these highly advanced and peaceful visitors. Other contactees have reported similar offers of assistance and similar disinterest on the part of individuals and even government officials.[6]

As an example of how their knowledge could benefit mankind,

the visitors told Leo that humans could extend their life spans to 250 or 300 years by eliminating things that were harmful to our bodies. Leo said we only had to ask for information and it would be given. He also believed they may have already been communicating with humans through brain-wave transmission. Today, many people say that extraterrestrial entities communicate with them through mental telepathy, sometimes called "channeling."

After Leo and I became friends, I asked him if his intergalactic friends still communicated with him. Leo nodded, though his cautious expression intimated he was a little nervous about sharing this particular piece of information, as if it might be the piece that discredits everything else. (After all, many people who "hear voices" inside their heads are deemed mentally ill.) Yet Leo's description of how he gradually became aware of this phenomenon makes it easier to understand and believe.

On the day of their visit aboard, it was late when the boys realized they needed to get home. Their amazing adventure was coming to an end. Their hosts made it a little easier by assuring the boys they would see them again, though that was the last time they saw the ship that year.

> No matter how many people I could talk to, five hundred or five thousand, I could not receive the amount of knowledge and feeling that I received from them in only a few hours. Again it is hard to explain why I have these feelings about them. They just gave me the feeling I could trust them and that I could confide in them. All they seemed to have toward me was trust. That made me feel very welcome.

Leo saw the ship land several times over the next few years in the vicinity of Dunn Center, North Dakota, a little south and east of Killdeer. It was sometime in these years that his mother died giving birth to his sister, Mary. The new baby was cared for by an aunt, and Leo's father kept Leo, Mike, and little brother Henry (Hank).

These must have been hard times for the whole family. Leo turned sixteen on July 16, 1936, and joined the Civilian Conservation Corps that year. According to his obituary, he worked in Roosevelt Park, not far from Killdeer or Dunn Center, South Dakota.[7]

In his book, Leo says he saw the ship land again, four years later, at the end of August 1936. He walked toward it. Three of the men he had met before were there and invited him onboard. "I found them most welcoming—the feeling was very good, like going to visit my grandparents for Thanksgiving or Christmas." They told him the same thing that his mother had said before she died and what turned out to be true: that he would be the last survivor of the four siblings. They also told him he would see the world in a lot of trouble before the year 2000. They assured him that planet Earth would continue to exist, but they could not assure "that man would exist on it, if he did not learn to take better care of his most valuable possession."

In 1938 Leo saw the ship land near Watford City, about sixty miles northwest of Killdeer in North Dakota, near the bridge over the Missouri (Author's note: maybe Leo meant the Little Missouri, as Watson City is some distance from the main-stem Missouri.) About this meeting Leo said,

> Each visit with them was like going home to a family that loved me…Every word they said to me, I believe was true, and gained more meaning for me as I was able to reflect upon the ideas over time.

In the summer of 1939, Leo was working in Sidney, Montana. Returning home at about 9:30 P.M. on September 15, he saw a spacecraft above the highway. Something told him to turn onto the next dirt road, which he did, following that track until he saw the ship in a field. As he walked toward it, two men emerged and raised their hands toward him. He hoped they were the men he knew. They approached him, each in turn putting their hand on his shoulder, and said, "It is good to see you again." Leo said his heart jumped in his throat when he realized they were his friends. They commented on how much he had changed, while Leo detected no change at all in them. "We are several thousand years ahead of you in time. We are germ-free and our life expectancy is quite different from yours." They reiterated their conviction that humans could significantly increase their life spans if scientists would work on it.[8]

Leo again went through the misting process to go onboard the ship and found six men sitting in the "miraculous" chairs watching the large screen with the inscrutable images. They told him the images were from their galaxy many millions of miles away and were somehow meaningful to them in their work here. Leo was puzzled by the lighting both outside and inside the ship. It was a shadowless glow that seemed to have no source. He was told the lighting system was in the metal and that the power for their machines was also generated in the metal.

> The ideas behind these systems are unknown to your scientists at the time. You have seen all these things with your own eyes, but you know by now that no one will believe any of it, no matter how you try to tell them.

When Leo departed, one of the men again placed a hand on his shoulder. This time Leo mirrored the gesture of affection and repeated this ritual with all six men. Though it was late, Leo's path back to his car was lit with the shadowless light. Once he got in his car, there was only darkness in the direction of the ship.

In 1941, Leo joined the U.S. Navy where he served on board the USS *Skirmish* (hull number AM-303), an amphibious unit minesweeper. He participated in the invasions of Okinawa and Iwo Jima, and he was in the occupying force in Japan. The visitors had told him the war would be violent and inhumane, but it went far beyond anything Leo had imagined from their conversations. His brothers Mike and Hank also served in the war. Leo had no contact with the extraterrestrial visitors during the war or for some time after. Although his war experiences were horrific, Leo did not know what else could have been done and hoped the visitors understood.

Leo was discharged in 1946 and returned to Killdeer. He would occasionally spot the ship, but for some reason, contact just did not happen. In 1948 he moved to Bozeman, Montana, and took a job as a salesman traveling around the area. He often returned home late at night. One evening in 1950, he finally saw a ship along Highway 287 between Norris and Sappington Junction. It landed in the hills a few miles off the road. Remembering that they returned again and again to the same locations, he began choosing that route to return home in the evenings and saw the ship several times in that place, though he did not see how he could get to the landing site over the rough terrain.

In July 1950, Leo's brother Mike was killed in the Korean War. The death devastated the family and must have been particularly hard on Leo because of the "otherworldly experiences" they shared. It was Mike's death that pushed Leo to put his memories on paper. He was now the only one who could record their incredible experiences.

Over the years Leo intermittently saw ships along Highway 287 between Norris and Sappington Junction. In 1962, Leo was driving a carload of little girls, three of his daughters and two of their friends, when he spotted a ship near the highway. He pulled over so the girls could see it hovering about 200 feet away and 20 feet off the ground, flashing its full spectrum of brilliant color. To

*The Dworshak family during World War II, Egnats seated in front and, from left, Leo, Mike, Hank, and Mary.*

Leo's disappointment, the girls were too frightened to watch.

Leo longed to share his experiences with someone who would understand these incredible events. He hoped his children would be able to meet the visitors, though he realized they would be cursed with the same problem he'd had: trying to get anyone to believe him. "It is quite a thing that a person faces, being certain inside, but unable to prove it."

On a summer evening in 1963, Leo was driving from Ennis to Sappington Junction when he saw a spacecraft descending toward the foothills about six or seven miles west of the highway. He pulled over as it dropped in front of the setting sun. A car pulled up behind him and a couple got out. The woman excitedly confirmed what Leo saw. Hoping at last to have companion witnesses, Leo asked if they would follow him on a dirt road to get closer. The man, obviously afraid, adamantly refused to follow and even refused to give his name and address so Leo could let him know what he found. The man said, "I don't want to be involved in this in any way." He then told Leo of another sighting he had in California and said he'd never told anyone else. "I hoped and prayed

I'd never see another one again." Leo was disgusted and sat in his car, musing about human fear and denial:

> Many times I have asked myself why people are not interested. After all, this is their life, their country, their world, and they have the responsibility of paying attention to what's happening...Mankind will eventually have to recognize the visitors are here with us and we will have to learn to live with it.

Leo passed the same spot on October 21, 1963, and this time decided he would make whatever effort it took to get to the ship. "Maybe I had grown lonely for them, for I felt they were friends of mine, and I longed for their company and that remembered warmth of their presence." After driving as far as he could, Leo hiked about three miles to the top of a ridge where he could see that yes, they were there. Though he still had to go another mile through rough country in the dark to reach them, he felt no fear, only joy and anticipation. It had been a long time. As he approached, the area around the ship was lighted and he could see about six people moving around, two coming his way. They greeted each other warmly, with the hand-to-shoulder greeting. "I could feel him pressing my shoulder with his fingers, giving me the feeling he was more than just happy to see me." When they approached the ship the remaining crew greeted him. He felt they made this statement to him in unison,

> It is the most welcome sight to see you again. We regret that your brother cannot be here with us. We enjoyed him very much.

The visitors had monitored his encounter with the frightened couple and expressed their bafflement at the man's level of fear.

Why people continue to fear us, we do not know.
Throughout the years we have walked on this planet
without harming anyone. Always, we have been willing to
help, but no one seems to want our help.

Leo boarded the ship with the usual protocol. Inside, he remembered Mike trying to sit before a chair could slide underneath him, and he saw that his friends were smiling as they "read" his memory.

Their communications were full of warnings. "Your science and technology have advanced enough to pose a threat to our ships, as well as to the entire planet." The image of an atomic mushroom cloud filled his mind as they spoke. They knew that military leaders were making efforts to detect and capture one of their ships, and they said they would defend themselves if necessary.[9]

Our laws allow us only the right to return anything that
is thrown at us. We are allowed to return it to the same
place it came from, back to the source.

Even though it was clear they were deeply concerned about the direction humans were headed, Leo felt the ease and comfort of being with old friends. After several hours, Leo knew he must leave. They read his mind and told him they hoped to see him again, though it might be a long time since they were headed back to their own galaxy. Another ship like theirs would be traveling around the Earth but making fewer landings since their interests were changing to what we were doing in outer space. They also told Leo a far larger ship would be landing in this area in 1971, 1972, and 1973, and thought he would have many opportunities to see it. They told him to always believe and to work to understand what he had seen. They reminded him not to forget they were always willing to help if asked. Leo told them he "would always be concerned about their activities and would take every opportunity to see them again." The difficult hike back to his car was not only lighted as before, but the temperature seemed curiously warm although Leo knew it had grown quite cold. When he arrived at his car, it was already running and warm.

This was the final visit onboard the ship that Leo reports in the book. I don't know if he ever saw the larger ship mentioned by the visitors. I am still looking for accounts or witnesses that might verify the visitors' prediction of the landing of this larger ship.

It was hard for Leo to process all the things he had witnessed. He used this metaphor:

> How do you explain to a bright kindergarten student the meaning of the information displayed on the screen of a computerized automobile engine analyzer, a gas chromatograph, or a CAT scan system?

There were many things Leo just was not able to understand. Leo did come to believe the visitors were analyzing grasshoppers and other insects to monitor environmental toxins. He only saw the ships in the summer or fall, and always in the afternoons or evenings when the bugs were out. He also knew they were "very concerned about our nuclear and chemical weapons, and our war-like nature. What a problem we must be for them, always threatening the health and safety of this beautiful planet, which is their responsibility to protect." Leo felt one of the visitors' most important messages was that "Mankind must grow up and mature to be entitled to possess their knowledge and abilities."

Over the years, Leo tried to tell his story and was usually mocked or ignored. He became frustrated with the world's disbelief and posed some thoughtful questions in his book: "Man has now succeeded in traveling into space and has walked on the moon. Why do we feel that people from another galaxy cannot travel to our planet? Is it our pride?" He asks what might have happened if we had taken all the money and resources that have been used throughout history for wars and instead put it to productive use addressing the needs of humanity. He feels we could have eliminated so much suffering and extended our life spans. He suggests an educational system working for the greater benefit of our people and better care of the planet's resources.

I first met Leo in 2001. A friend who shared my interest in UFOs heard of a man in Helena who was writing a book about his encounters with aliens. I called to see if he would be willing to meet with us. We met Leo and his wife Ryniene for breakfast at a local establishment with regular clientele and cheap, decent food. He was eighty-one years old, a small man, balding, with large, owlish, black-rimmed glasses. He was suspicious, crusty, and freely expressed his strong opinions about politics and other subjects.

In that first meeting, Leo shared a little of his remarkable experiences and his commitment to finishing and publishing his book. I offered to help him with publicity after the book came out and that offer seemed to soften his demeanor.

Leo was adamant that any contactees who described visitors as different than those he had seen could not be believed. I found it curious that someone who had undoubtedly suffered with people's disbelief would be so skeptical of others' accounts. This insistence may have been tied to the abduction stories and more negative experiences with small grey aliens that have been described from the 1950s to the present. Leo's experiences were entirely positive, and as far as he was concerned, his experience was the only true contact experience and all ETs look like us. Perhaps he felt loyal to his friends and took offense at any reports maligning the kind, benevolent beings he had known.

After another visit at the restaurant, Leo began to warm up to me and eventually invited me to his home, where we had longer talks over coffee. He gradually shared more about his experiences and kept me posted on the progress of his book.

Leo's book came out in 2003. I arranged a public presentation featuring Jesse Marcel of Roswell fame (see Chapter 2) at the United Methodist Church in Helena. The *Independent Record* announced the presentation with front-page coverage and a large photo of Leo.[10] One-hundred and fifty people attended the presentation, swamping the meeting space. After that event, Leo and I stayed in touch and I visited him a couple of times at his home.

Leo expressed concern that if we did not help the visitors care for the Earth by addressing some of our environmental issues, we might have some problems with them. I found this a puzzling remark because of his many statements about the visitors' peaceful, gentle nature. Perhaps this was his own projection of what he felt humans deserved, and his memory of the visitors' warning that humans might not continue to exist on the planet unless we learned to take better care of it. My own sense is that the visitors were warning that the natural consequences of environmental disregard could be human extinction, rather than warning of punishing actions on their part.

During these visits, Leo hinted there were things he was unable to talk about, and it seemed he may have been under security constraints. Leo was very patriotic and unwilling to divulge much about his military career. He told me he was working on a second book to be published posthumously. I had not heard from him in some time when I learned he was in hospice care. He died soon after, on April 28, 2007.

My experience of Leo was that he was not a warm, welcoming person like the visitors he so admired. Who knows to what extent he was changed by his experiences in World War II and after? When I read his book, I was surprised by his clarity about the futility of war because the Leo I knew staunchly supported the ongoing war in Iraq, even though many others felt it was a waste of lives and resources. Leo, like so many of us, was not always consistent. Though he did not come across as a sensitive person, Leo repeatedly emphasized the quality of his feelings in the presence of the visitors:

> I think it is as important to concentrate on the feelings and emotions they gave us as it is to try to understand their precise thoughts or learn their knowledge...Nothing about them gave us any hint of evil or trickery. They were wise, kind, and clean and never made us feel like stupid kids, as so many adults do without thinking...They are perfect role models, the kind of people each of us would like to be when we grow up.

Leo repeated this message again and again: feelings he experienced in their presence told him more about who they were than any of the amazing technologies they showed him or the things they told him. Leo's crustiness in person makes his recurring emphasis on this aspect of his experiences all the more compelling. It raises the question: if we were to encounter advanced spiritual consciousness in an alien species, would we know? Leo felt strongly that he knew.

> We did not experience discrimination, suspicion, greed, and hatred when we were with these people from the stars. That is the most important thing I can tell you about them. They are kind and understanding and love us in spite of our dangerous behavior. I know they will do everything they can to help us learn from our mistakes and improve our lives as we grow into more mature and responsible behavior. Because of their concern for us, they will not give us dangerous tools or abilities we are not mature enough

to handle and use, to lessen their burden of maintaining the planet. Think what it must cost them in terms of their own economy to build and send these ships to our world. Think what an individual sacrifice these men make by leaving behind the benefits and conveniences of their world to spend years of their lives analyzing grasshoppers on our world. These great men willingly took the time to speak to two grubby little farm kids in North Dakota and changed our lives forever.

Leo's story, beginning in 1932, is one of the earliest accounts of contact with extraterrestrials. It has caught the attention of some of the most highly regarded UFO researchers in the world. In 2004, British UFO authority Timothy Good visited Helena to interview Leo, and told newspaper reporter Martin Kidston, "I find this one of the most compelling contact stories I've investigated."[11]

Leo's book ends after that last encounter in 1963, when Leo was forty-three years old. When I asked about ongoing communication with the visitors, he acknowledged it was happening but wouldn't elaborate. He did mention continuing communication with some kind of government entity connected with his experiences. There are cases of contactees being recruited for government intelligence work,[12] and perhaps that was the case with Leo.

At his funeral, I learned that Leo left the notes for a second book with the Helena writer who helped him with his first book. His daughter has additional photos and materials for the second book, which Leo titled *UFOs and What's To Come*.[13] I am hopeful that Leo's second book will be published sometime in the near future, as many of us are eager to hear the rest of this man's remarkable story.

Whether another Dworshak book coalesces remains to be seen, but I predict his first book will become a classic. During the early years of serious government and private UFO investigation in the late 1940s and early 1950s, anyone who claimed actual contact with ETs was automatically labeled a "crackpot." As these accounts have accumulated over the years, the reality of alien contact has gradually become better documented and more established.[14] What is unique about Leo's account is its early date, preceding by twenty years the many contactees of the 1950s, not to mention the rash of abductions and examinations since the 1960s by beings commonly referred to as "greys."

Leo's book is also unusual in its benevolent and even reverent account of the visitors. There are many accounts of negative experiences with aliens, as well as experiences with negative aliens (not necessarily the same thing). Some in ufology believe that the positive alien encounters are the ones most severely suppressed.

Leo's somewhat isolated circumstance and innocent age at first encounter allowed him a rare openness, curiosity, and receptivity. The continued contacts over a thirty-year period fostered ongoing relationships. From Leo's view, the friendships were deeper and more profound than any he experienced with humans. Though simply written, his book is full of information, much of which has been validated over time. I believe it is also brimming with wisdom and with keys to discernment that will also be validated with time.

### Notes

1. Quotations about Leo Dworshak's childhood and visits with extraterrestrials are from Leo Dworshak, *UFOs Are With Us: Take My Word* (Pittsburgh, PA: Dorrance Publishing Co., 2003).
2. It's not uncommon for people to confuse the terms "galaxy" and "star system," especially those unfamiliar with astronomy. Given Leo's age and lack of education at the time, it could be that the visitors were referring to star systems, rather than galaxies.
3. http://www.howstuffworks.com/invisibility-cloak.htm/
4. Travis Walton, presentations to the International UFO Congress, February 26, 2010, and February 23, 2012. See www.ufocongress.com/

5. Howard Menger, *From Outer Space* (1959; repr. New York: Pyramid Books, 1967).
6. See Frank E. Stranges, *The Stranger at the Pentagon* (Van Nuys, CA: 1967; the author, 3rd printing, 1972); Stefano Breccia, *Mass Contact* (Bloomington, IN: AuthorHouse, 2009).
7. "Leo Dworshak," *Independent Record*, May 1, 2007, 8A.
8. According to Leo's friend in later life, Barry Potter, Leo was very interested in extension of the human life span.
9. In 1949, rumors were circulating that the U.S. military was determined to capture a flying saucer. U.S. Air Force Captain Edward Stone told Donald Keyhoe that the Air Force was ordered to get a flying saucer "by any possible means"; see Richard Dolan, *UFOs and the National Security State* (Charlottesville, VA: Hampton Roads Publishing, 2002), 66. Timothy Good, in *Need To Know: UFOs, the Military and Intelligence* (New York: Pegasus Books, 2007) provides evidence that the U.S. shot down several flying discs in the late 1940s.
10. Martin Kidston, "Eyes on the Skies: Helena Man a True Believer in UFOs," *Independent Record*, April 25, 2003.
11. Martin Kidston, "Author Researches Stories of Alien Encounters," *Independent Record*, June 20, 2004, 7A.
12. Dan Sherman, *Beyond Black: Project Preserve Destiny* (Kearney, NE: Morris Publishing, 2006).
13. Author communication with Barry Potter, August 12, 2012.
14. See: John Mack, *Abduction* (New York: Macmillan Publishing Company, 1994); John Mack, *Passport to the Cosmos* (New York: Crown Publishers, 1999); Budd Hopkins, *Intruders: The Incredible Visitations at Copley Woods* (New York: Random House, 1997) or any of his other books; Mary Rodwell, *Awakening* (Agnes Water, Queensland, Australia: New Mind Publishers, 2010).

# 6

# THE UDO WARTENA
# CONTACT CASE

*At this particular time, any help that can be given in respect
to the energy crises should be welcomed…If and when
we will be able to develop these ships, our mode of transportation will
change greatly. Not to go to different planets but here and now.*

—Udo Wartena, 1981

about thirty miles east of Helena, as the crow flies, a county road curves up Confederate Gulch from Canyon Ferry Reservoir into the Big Belt Mountains. If you follow that road just past Boulder Creek, you come to what was the site of Diamond City, home of the richest gold strike in Montana history.

Since the 1860s, many people have made a living on the minerals in the Confederate Gulch drainage. In 1940, a Dutch immigrant named Udo Wartena was prospecting near Boulder Creek, not far from former Diamond City, when he heard a noise, "like that of a high-flying plane." The humming sound continued, so he believed a car must have driven up a nearby road. Walking uphill toward the sound, he discovered not a car, but a large "ship" that was hovering over a pond Wartena had made to hold water for sluice mining.

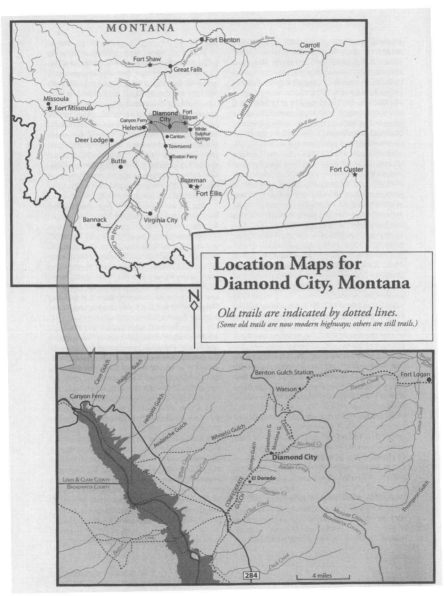

*Diamond City maps used courtesy of Kelly Flynn, from his book* Goldpans, Guns & Grit: Diamond City, Territorial Gold Rush Montana Ghost Town

This remarkable event happened before the infamous 1947 Roswell Crash, and before Kenneth Arnold's attention-grabbing sighting of "flying saucers" near Mount Rainier in 1947. (Many ufologists consider Arnold's sighting on June 24, 1947, to be the official beginning of the "flying saucer age."[1] Arnold told newsmen in Pendleton, Oregon, that he'd seen a fleet of strange aircraft while flying his private plane west of the Cascade Mountains in Washington earlier that day. He described the aircraft "flying like a saucer would if you skipped it over the water." A reporter coined the term "flying saucer," and the story about the sighting exploded on national and international news wires.)[2]

Wartena's encounter also happened before atomic weapons had ever been tested or used on Earth.[3] One UFO theory is that the testing and use of atomic weapons in World War II attracted the attention of extraterrestrials, resulting in a surge of UFO visits immediately following the U.S. bombing of Hiroshima and Nagasaki.

Udo's case was brought to light in a presentation at the 1997 International MUFON (Mutual UFO Network) Symposium in Grand Rapids, Michigan, by Australian UFO researcher Warren Aston.[4] Later that year, a copy of Aston's paper about the case landed on the desk of Mary Alice Tupton, mayor of Townsend, Montana, the community nearest the area of Udo's encounter.[5] On December 24, 1997, the local weekly newspaper featured a lengthy front-page article about Udo Wartena,[6] and that article was reprinted in Helena's *Independent Record* in early January,[7] announcing this historical event to Montana audiences.

Aston considers it a "landmark case in Ufology." Not only is Udo a highly credible witness, as attested to by friends, family members, and church members, but also it is an apparently "accidental" contact with beings that look like us. The case includes an astounding description of a conversation with the occupants and a description of the exterior and interior of the spacecraft. This is unusual in that it is not an abduction case, nor is there any telepathic communication as is commonly reported in contact cases. Aston believes this account offers significant insight into the origin of some UFOs and why they visit Earth.

## UDO WARTENA'S LETTER TO JOHN GLENN

In 1976 Udo described his encounter in a letter to U.S. Senator and former astronaut John Glenn. Udo thought the ship he saw might help future air and space travel. He wrote:

In the forepart of May 1940, I had gone upon the mountain and found a glacier deposit. And from all indications had every possibility of carrying values.

As I was working part-time for the Northwest Mining Co., I could only prospect on my days off. So it was into the summer before I could prove the ground. There were a lot of large boulders to move but when I got to bedrock, I found some fine gold.

As I would need water for washing the material, I figured it was wise to bring the water down to where I could use it.

The early day miners had dug a ditch around the mountain side (this was over sixty years before my time), so after clearing the logs and large trash out of it, I diverted the water out of the creek, into the ditch. As the ditch had not been used these many years, it was quite a mess.

The ditch was practically level for the first quarter of a mile, so it was late in the afternoon by the time it would flow freely. The next morning I cleaned the main ditch to where I put in a dam. Then, dug a ditch to where I could use the water.

As the work for the Northwest Mining Co. had picked up, I wasn't able to work the prospect too much. Though every spare day I had was used there.

2)
fall, so it was late in the afternoon to where
the water would move freely, I then cleaned
till late. The next morning I finished the
cleaning of the ditch to where I wanted to
divert the water, then by putting a dam
in the main ditch I turned the water in a
lateral I dug to where I would need the water
I then started opening up the ground
in earnest, and ~~white~~ while working on a
large boulder, trying to roll it down the
mountain, I heard a noice somewhat like
that of a high flying plane. As army planes
would occasionally pass over, flying from
Great Falls south. At first I didn't take
too much note, but as the noice continued
I thought a car had driven up, so I got upon
the higher ground. I saw "where I had put
the dam in the main ditch" a large (I will
call it a ship) it looked like a blimp, from
where I stood, only it wasn't as thick and
more pointed.
    As I stood there a stairway was led
down and a man came down this and
started walking towards me. As I was

*A page from Udo Wartena's handwritten Account B
of his contact with extraterrestrials.*

I still had some large boulders to move and while doing this
one morning I heard a noise. Like that of a high flying plane, as
Army planes flying over, from Great Falls.[8] At first I didn't take
much note, but as the noise continued, I thought a car had driven
up. So I got upon higher ground.

I saw, where I had put the dam in the main ditch, a
large (I will call it a ship). It looked like a blimp, only more

pointed on each end, and not as thick through the middle. About 35' thick better than 100' long.

As I stood there, a stairway was let down and a man came down this and started walking towards me. As I was somewhat more than interested, I went to meet him. He stopped when we were about ten or twelve feet apart.

He was a nice looking man, seemingly about my age, 35 or more. He wore a light gray pair of coveralls, a tam of the same material on his head, and on his feet were slippers or moccasins.

He asked me if it would be alright [sic] if they took some of the water. I could not see why not, I said sure. He then gave a signal and a hose or pipe was let down.

His English was like mine, but he spoke slowly, as if he was a linguist. He asked me what I was doing. I explained this to him. He asked me if I would be interested to come aboard. As he seemed an intelligent and pleasant person, I figured it would be interesting.

As we got closer to the ship, I noticed that it was round, like two dinner plates, one inverted over the other. It seemed to be made of metal. As I look back and compare, it seemed like stainless steel, though not bright or shiny.

The ship appeared to be about 35' thick and well over a hundred feet in diameter. When we got into the ship, we entered into a room about twelve by sixteen feet, with a close fitting door on the farther end. Indirect lighting near the ceiling, and nice upholstered benches around the sides.

There was an older man in the room, plainly dressed and with white hair. It was then that I noticed that the younger man also had white hair. Some how I believe they knew who I was, but they did not introduce themselves. Perhaps if they had, I may have been a bit upset.

The younger man asked me what I would be interested in. So I first asked why they wanted this particular water. He said the water is good, as if they had gotten the same before, and it was convenient.

After we had entered the ship, I had noticed that the sound I had heard outside, was hardly noticeable, except what came up the stairwell. So I asked him what caused the noise or humming. He said this would be a bit complicated, but he would try to explain so I could understand.

He said as you noticed we are floating above the ground, and though the ground slopes, the ship is level.

There are in the outside rim of the ship two flywheels one turning one way and the other the opposite direction. He explained that this gives the ship its own gravitation, or rather overcomes the gravitational pull of the earth, other planets or the sun or stars. And though this pull is light, we use this gravitational pull of the stars and planets to ride on.

He went into somewhat greater detail on the power development by these two flywheels. He mentioned something about them developing an electromagnetic force. As this was quite new to me and he realized that, but he saw I had gotten the picture, so he stopped.

I asked him where he got the energy to run the ship. He said from the sun and stars, and he would store this in batteries, though this was for emergency use.

I also asked him what their object was or purpose in coming here. Well, he said, as you have noticed, we look pretty much as you do, so we mingle with you people, gather information, leave instructions, or give help where needed. I would have liked to ask him more about that, but didn't feel this proper, so let it ride at that.

While we had been talking, a light had come on

apparently signaling that the water had been taken care of.

When I felt it was time for me to leave, I mentioned this. He asked me if I would be interested in going with them. I said that I thought it would be interesting to go with them but it would inconvenience too many people. Later I wondered why I had said that.

As I started to leave, they suggested that I tell no one, as no one would believe me at that time, but in years to come I could tell about this experience.

When I walked away from the ship, they raised the stairway, and when I got a couple of hundred feet away from the ship, I turned around.

A number more portholes had opened up and though I could see no one, I felt sure they saw me. Anyway, I waved at them.

The ship then rose straight up, then while circling slightly it continued going straight and in a very short while was completely out of sight.

As I didn't have a watch, I did not know how long I had been with them. It was around noon so it must have been about two hours from the time I first saw the ship.

This whole experience was so overwhelming that I did not go back to work. I kept going over in my mind all that had happened. I went back to where the stairway had been and though it hadn't gone into the soil, the grass was crushed down.

I wondered at the time, why I hadn't accepted the invitation to go with them but instead had said "that it would inconvenience too many people." I then recollected an incident which happened a few years before I came to this district.

A young man was staying with an old prospector, and early one morning before eating he put on a light jacket and told the man he would be gone for a while. When the young man did not show up all that next day or the next, the old prospector notified the Sheriff, and he with his deputies and about forty C.C.C. boys looked all over for him, but no trace was found.

I have wondered if he might have accepted an invitation to board a ship similar to mine.

I have wondered at times if this could have all been in my imagination. But then again I saw the impression of the ship in the grass.

Then over the years a number of things have come to mind. The explanation of how this ship moved, seemingly not affected by earths gravitational pull.

From what the man told me at the time and what has come to me since, I believe I am not too far from an answer to this.

It is for this reason I am writing to you. No doubt with the help of some other minds, the answer will be forthcoming.

We have just about reached the stage where we need a different type of air transportation and this is the answer.

I feel confident that you could put me in touch with some people who could help to this end.

*Udo Wartena*
West Linn, Oregon
[Account A]

Queries to the Ohio Congressional Archives and personal letters to Senator John Glenn were unsuccessful in determining whether John Glenn ever received Udo's letter.[9] Because Udo was not a constituent of Ohio, his letter may have been discarded.

Aston first learned of the Wartena case in a 1993 book by James Thompson analyzing UFOs and the contact/abduction experience from a Mormon perspective.[10] Thompson's short summary of Udo's encounter is based entirely on his communications with Tim Grossnickle, a family friend of Udo's. Although Udo was no longer living when Aston first learned of his encounter, Aston was able to speak with a number of Udo's friends and family members, including Tim Grossnickle and his father, Robert Grossnickle. The older man had been a close friend of Udo's and was the Lake Oswego LDS Stake Patriarch, a position held in great respect in the Mormon church.[11] According to Tim Grossnickle, his father was the first person Udo told about his encounter, in 1967 or 1968, nearly thirty years after the fact. Tim also told Thompson he heard the account firsthand on a bus trip to the Oakland Mormon Temple with Udo in 1979.[12]

We don't know when Udo first wrote about his experience. There are two handwritten accounts by Udo and one of these (Tim Grossnickle calls it "A") is identical to the John Glenn letter, so it could have been written as late as November 1976. However, Tim Grossnickle thought that handwritten account could have predated Udo's first verbal account to Robert Grossnickle in 1967 or 1968.[13]

Tom Cottle, one of Udo's closest friends, thought the first handwritten account, A, may have been written when Udo was younger, perhaps as early as the late 1950s or early 1960s, because Udo's handwriting is so steady. Account "B" was apparently written for UFO Researcher Stanton Friedman and differs only slightly from A. Tim Grossnickle believes Udo penned account B in late 1980.

It is possible that Udo never recorded his experiences until he thought they might be of use to others. Based on comments Udo made in his writings, he may have been motivated to write the letters to John Glenn and Stanton Friedman because of the 1970s energy crisis:

Mr. Stanton T. Friedman
Dear Sir,
~~On page~~ I read an article by you in the magazine U.F.O. report on page 26.
As I had an experience in 1940 which gave me some insight into a U.F.I. as far as I was concerned, and of which I had since not found, and may shed some light on the workings of these ships I felt that through you and some others

As the need for this ship _Typed_ increases by the day. It seemed to me that if I could explain, (what I discovered over the years to one like you, It would be practicaly impossible to do by myself.

I have made three copies of this idea so we could somehow, reach some group who would be able to build it.

At the time I first had this experience I felt it wa some how for my personal benefit but not till in reasant years the value of this type of vibicle

*Udo Wartena's cover letter to Stan Friedman.*

At the time I first had this experience I felt it was somehow for my personal benefit but till in reasant [sic] years the value of this type of vihicle [sic].… The ability to develop a cheaper and more practical energy source, is of utmost importance.[14]

Udo's grammar and spelling are imperfect, perhaps reflecting the fact that he was thirteen when his family arrived in the U.S. from Holland, and English was not his first language. Udo evidently had little formal education, but this did not detract from his many areas of competence. His daughter shared a relevant story from his youth. A teacher in Great Falls told Udo's father that his son was so smart that the teacher wanted to advance him two years, and his father responded by taking Udo out of school.[15] Nevertheless, Udo learned many trades—farmer, miner, logger, and carpenter—and was known as a resourceful and practical man.

After his encounter, to the best of our knowledge, Udo continued working for a mining company and prospecting on his own through 1940 and part of 1941, until the Northwest Mining Syndicate ceased operations in August of 1941.[16] That same year Udo met Donna Stoddard and they were married in Butte, Montana, on August 17. The newlyweds stayed in Butte at least a short while, based on local newspaper accounts of Udo as a church vocalist and on an official notice in April 1942.[17] They lived a number of places after that, moving to Oregon in 1946 and eventually settling down in the Portland area where they raised their four children.[18]

Udo earned his livelihood as a carpenter in Oregon but returned regularly to Confederate Gulch by himself or with his family, ostensibly to prospect, but perhaps for other reasons as well. Udo's son Scott said the whole family went back to Montana every summer for a week's vacation, either camping or staying in a cabin. He recalls

*Udo and Donna Wartena's wedding portrait.*

that these trips began in the 1950s and continued until 1985 or 1987. Udo was born in 1903, so he would have been in his early eighties during this last trip.

Dana Thelin, Udo's second child and eldest daughter, was the only one of the four children who heard the account directly from Udo. She recalls driving with her father from Provo to Ogden, Utah, sometime when she was in her forties. Her father began by saying there was something he wanted to tell her. After hearing his fantastic account, she told him sincerely she believed him, because in all her life he had never lied to her.[19]

When conducting a teen drug and alcohol prevention program in the Provo schools, Dana used this story as an object lesson on the value of honesty. If you have a sterling reputation for honesty and integrity, people will believe you even when you say things that are difficult to believe. She reports that thousands of teens heard the account. She said it was particularly useful when they were bored and distracted, and it never failed to gather their attention. She has also passed on her father's story to all of her children, never doubting its truth.

Udo told very few people about his experience, and Dana had a poignant anecdote to relate in this regard. A friend of Udo's died, and Udo took this man's son under his wing, inviting him on a trip to Montana and even sharing the story of his encounter. Upon their return, the young man made so much fun of Udo that Udo became even more reluctant to speak of the event.

Who knows how many encounters are never shared because of the great human fear of ridicule and its power to shape our behavior? We tend to underestimate the impact of social pain on human behavior. Ridicule is a form of social rejection, which surprisingly affects the brain in the same way as physical pain.[20] British and U.S. military and intelligence agencies purposefully employed ridicule as a psychological weapon for discrediting witnesses, diverting public attention, discouraging scrutiny, and generally suppressing information-sharing.[21] Part of its success is due to the fact that the population becomes self-policing; ridicule is passed on. As social animals, we are highly susceptible to ridicule as a "disciplinary" measure, and social scientists maintain it's been used deliberately throughout history to shape conduct and enforce specific worldviews.[22]

Dana thinks Udo would probably have preferred to make his living as a miner rather than a carpenter ("He loved to dig."), but he was a devoted family man and wanted to provide more stability for his wife and children. Dana clearly enjoyed reminiscing about her father, whom she described as an amazing man. Her final comment was, "He loved his children." Udo died December 15, 1989, in West Linn, Oregon. He had been battling cancer but died from complications resulting from a fall.[23] He was eighty-six years old.

## CORROBORATIVE EVIDENCE

There are still landowners in Confederate Gulch and people in the nearby town of Townsend who remember Udo. Emma Doig Morrison of Townsend said that Udo leased their family's mining claim in the 1950s and 1960s, and she remembers his coming to their house. She said they did not own the claim in 1940 when Udo's encounter took place, but that he told them their claim was close to one he knew.[24] Presumably, it was near the site of his encounter. She suggested that some of the Flynn family might remember Udo, as they were among the original landowners in the area. Indeed, Joel Flynn remembered Udo well.

> My dad [Frank] really liked Udo, and that's saying something because some of the other miners he didn't care for. He would take me up to Udo's claim to visit with him, and I can still picture him up there. Dad really enjoyed his conversations with Udo, and we had him to the house for dinner a time or two.

Joel remembers finding a mining claim in a "Band-Aid" tin nailed to a tree on the bench above Boulder Creek. The claim

*Remains of the Doig/Morrison cabin.* PHOTO BY JOAN BIRD

had Udo's name and a 1962 date on it. I asked Joel if he knew what Udo and his father talked about, but he had no recollection; he was about twelve or fourteen at the time. He did remember his father always looked forward to Udo's visits and thought him a very interesting person.[25] One can only wonder if, in all those years of visiting, Frank Flynn might have heard Udo's amazing story.

In 2008, I was able to get permission to access the Doig/Morrison cabin site along Boulder Creek, one of the places Udo stayed while prospecting in Montana. The cabin is now collapsed, but the site, next to the burbling creek, is picturesque and peaceful.

In July 2012, Warren Aston visited Montana with the hope of finding the site where the encounter took place. Joel Flynn again granted permission to access the area and then graciously offered to show us around the relevant parts of the Flynn ranch. Joel took us to where he had found Udo's claim in the bandage tin, to where the Boulder Ditch originated out of Boulder Creek, and to his best guess at where the encounter took place, based on Udo's description.

*Warren Aston in the meadow where Wartena likely met the UFO crew, with Boulder Peak on the horizon.* PHOTO BY JOAN BIRD

The Broadwater County Courthouse recorded a mining lease signed March 15, 1970, between Frank and Rose Flynn, and Udo Wartena and Thomas D. Cottle, Udo's close friend from Oregon. The 1970 mining lease required $80 per month rent of the property from June 1 through the end of October, and 10 percent of any gold taken from the property. This lease seems to indicate Udo's confidence in his mining, to plan that far in advance and invest that much time and money.

Both Warren Aston and I were able to interview Tom Cottle at different times. Tom recalled two trips to Montana with Udo in the late 1960s and early 1970s. He found a journal entry he had made from August 1970 during the term of the lease with the Flynns.[26] That year, Tom Cottle, his son Mike, and a young man named Gordon Zimmerman all joined Udo, and the four of them were able to hand dig a 39-foot shaft, moving boulders as wide as four feet. Their accomplishments made quite an impression on Tom. He reported that they all worked very hard and he learned a lot, but what gold they found was not enough to make it worth their time and effort. There is no record the lease was renewed.

On one of Tom's trips to Montana, Udo showed him the landing site and made drawings of the spacecraft, which unfortunately have been lost. Tom Cottle noted that the site where the ship landed was about three miles away up on a bench toward Boulder Peak above the cabin.[27] Tom held Udo in the highest regard:

> Udo was one of my Idols, one of the few men of complete integrity. He would rather take a beating than tell an untruth. He would work his fingers raw helping someone that really needed it and who could not do it themselves…He taught me so much about life. There is nothing a human can not do if he is so determined. He proved it on three or four occasions by accomplishing the impossible. He is a very talented man of the Kingdom.[28]

In my conversations with Tom in 2010, he fondly recalled his friend and reiterated his belief in Udo's integrity and the truth of Udo's encounter.[29] He said Udo was one of the hardest-working men he had ever met. Cottle was the first president of the LDS Stake in Lake Oswego, Oregon, so was himself highly regarded by his peers. Cottle was also able to solve the mystery of John Dell, a person to whom Udo copied the letter to John Glenn. It turns out that Cottle and Dell are close friends, and I was able to interview another friend of Udo's who knew of his encounter.

Dell was cordial and more than happy to provide information

about Udo.[30] He said the Dutchman called one day and wanted
to talk to him because he "was a forest ranger and knew a lot
about the outdoors." In fact, Dell was the Regional Fire Specialist for the Pacific Northwest Region of the USDA Forest Service.
Dell described Udo as a very fine person, and perfectly sane. He
remembers Udo as interested in mechanical things and as being
a "do-it-all person." After hearing the account, Dell told Udo, "I
feel really good that you told me this." As Dell related, "We'd had
some things going on in the '70s," at fire lookouts and around
Yakima, Washington, and at Bureau of Indian Affairs sites, so
Dell was aware of other UFO reports. (Author's note: I happened to be working in fire control on the Gifford Pinchot National Forest in southwestern Washington during the summers
of 1972 and 1973 and can vouch for UFO activity in the area.[31])
Historically this has been an active area for UFOs. Kenneth Arnold first sighted the formation of nine "flying saucers" in 1947
near Mount Rainier, just north of the Gifford Pinchot National
Forest. Lookout Jim Doerter had two sightings from Flat Top
Lookout over the southern part of the Gifford Pinchot in 1959.
Doerter has collected ninety-six reports of UFO sightings from
many different lookouts, mostly in the Pacific Northwest.[32]

John Dell had recommended that Udo contact J. Allen
Hynek. Dr. Hynek was an astronomer/astrophysicist and a consultant to government UFO investigations during the 1950s and
1960s. Originally a skeptic, Hynek eventually became convinced
we were being visited by extraterrestrial craft and founded the
private research organization, the Center for UFO Studies (CU-
FOS). We have no record that Udo followed up on Dell's suggestion.

Dell passed on Udo's account to a cousin, who used it as a
source for a science fiction book on a benign alien presence on
Earth.[33] It's not surprising how often contactee accounts find their
way into science fiction, though Hollywood seems to fixate on

predatory or imperialistic aliens that are relatively rare in the UFO contact literature.

In 1979, on a U.S. Forest Service mining permit application, Ray Doig of Townsend wrote that he was "drawing up a lease with a person that has mined on the claim off and on for the past 5 years." In 1980, Udo filled out his own "Notice of Intent to Conduct Mining Operations on Forest Service Lands," on the claim owned by Ray Doig and Emma Ringer,[34] complete with a hand drawn map of the intended excavation area near the cabin where he stayed.[35]

Kelly Flynn, Joel's younger brother, wrote a book on the history of gold mining and settlement in Confederate Gulch. It includes maps of the 1860s ditches that were helpful in locating the approximate area of Udo's encounter, and it brings alive the history of one of the earliest gold mining strikes in Montana.[36] It is eye-opening to learn how many people were poring over this country in the 1860s, and how mining operations have continued, even to this day. If you drive up Confederate Gulch you will still see prospectors and mining claims and plenty of "No Trespassing" signs. As people find it safer to share, perhaps more UFO reports will emerge from this area.

Udo Wartena's encounter, according to Warren Aston, was unique because it was a physical ship and because there was spoken communication. Aston reports that every other contact case previous to 1952 relies on astral-travel or some type of teleportation or psychic device to meet those of other worlds.[37] However, Aston was unaware of Leo Dworshak's encounter because Leo's book was not published until 2003. Since Aston's presentation in 1997, British UFO researcher Timothy Good has documented other early reports of encounters with physical beings and ships, including an extraordinary 1920 encounter in Ontario followed by ongoing contact, also with human-appearing extraterrestrials.[38]

## COMPARING THE DWORSHAK AND WARTENA ACCOUNTS

### *The Visitors, Appearance and Knowledge*

It's interesting that Montana claims two of the best early descriptions of benevolent alien encounters, and they are remarkably similar. Both describe the human appearance of the spacecraft occupants and similar "coverall" type clothing that they wore. Udo's visitors spoke perfect English and told him they could speak five hundred languages, while Leo's visitors spoke perfect English and German, and said they spoke all the languages on our planet. Leo describes a decontamination process required for entry onto the ship. Udo's contacts invited him to be examined for impurities by an X-ray–like machine that passed over him.[39] When Leo met his contacts seven years after his first encounter, he commented on how little they had changed. They responded:

> We are several thousand years ahead of your time. We are germ-free and our life expectancy is quite different from yours[;]…if your scientists would devote their time to increasing your life span, people on Earth would be capable of living in good health much longer than you do now.[40]

Perhaps the scanning or decontamination processes are part of the knowledge that keeps the aliens germ free and long-lived. Udo's visitors told him they were 600 and 900 years old, a human life expectancy unheard of except in the Book of Genesis.[41]

### Propulsion and Energy Systems

Both Leo and Udo describe a humming sound coming from the spaceship. Udo says in one of his handwritten accounts that, when he was under the ship, "the noise was not loud, and seemed to go through you." Both describe some kind of counter-rotation-al movement in the outer rim of the craft,[42] and Tom Cottle reported that Udo's lost drawings showed a circular tube around the outside of the dish, which spun to cause the force.[43] Udo's hosts told him the two counter-rotating flywheels produced an electromagnetic force that gave the ship its own gravitation, overcoming the gravitational pull of the Earth, as well as those of other planets, the sun and stars. Tim Grossnickle remembered Udo saying,

> They focused on a distant star and used its energy to draw them through space at speeds greater than the speed of light. My host specifically mentioned, "skipping upon the light waves."[44]

(This description is reminiscent of Kenneth Arnold's 1947 account of the "skipping across water motion" of his flying saucers.)

Udo's visitors also told him they used energy from the sun and the stars and could store it in batteries, though this was for emergency use. In one account, Udo wrote they said there was another energy source, which they did not explain. "As time goes on these things will become clear to you…they will become known to you as you go on." Years later, Udo told his daughter Dana he believed the fuel source for the craft was hydrogen, extracted from water.[45]

These prescient comments about understanding more in the future seemed to take root in Udo and perhaps gave him a sense of purpose in wanting to share information he felt would be beneficial to mankind. Tim Grossnickle wrote that Udo's wife, Donna, described him as an imaginative "tinkerer."[46] Udo was fascinated by the extraterrestrial technology and believed it could be a solution to Earth's energy needs and to our transportation problems.[47] The letters he wrote to John Glenn in 1976 and to UFO researcher Stanton Friedman in 1981 both request help in relaying information about these technologies to those who could develop them. Counter-rotating wheels are often described in UFO literature and in documentation about anti-gravity technology currently being tested on Earth.[48] Leo described watching the outer shell of the ship rotating faster and faster just before the craft lifted off the ground, and both he and Udo described the amazingly rapid disappearance of the ship after take-off.[49]

While Udo did not experience the force field that originally kept Leo and his brother from approaching that ship, he did have a similar experience after leaving the ship:

> An energy had permeated the area and I lost all my strength for some hours. I was unable to walk. When my strength finally returned I walked back to the [mining company] base camp.[50]

### Purpose and Character of the Visitors

Curiously, Udo and Leo were both instructed not to tell anyone about their experiences, as no one would believe them at the time, but in years to come they would be able to talk and would be believed. This implies some understanding of the state of human awareness in the 1930s and 1940s, and perhaps some ability to see into the future.

When Udo asked about their purpose in coming, they replied:

> ...[A]s you have noticed, we look pretty much as you do, so we mingle with you people, gather information, leave instructions, or give help where needed.[51]

Leo's visitors had similar comments. In his last boarding on the ship in 1963, they expressed their concern for the future of humans on earth:

> Throughout the years we have walked this planet
> without harming anyone. Always, we have been willing to
> help, but not one seems to want our help.[52]

One of the most striking similarities between the two accounts is the emotional responses both Leo and Udo had to their visitors. They both speak wistfully, and even reverentially, of them. According to Warren 's account, Udo stressed his impression that they were men, "just like us, and very nice chaps." He felt remarkable "love, or comfort" in their presence and did not want to leave them.[53] Leo wrote at length about their kindness and loving, helpful nature.

According to the verbal account provided by Robert Grossnickle's son Tim, and perhaps by his father as well, Udo asked the visitors "if they knew of Jesus Christ and if they held the Priesthood?" They replied, "We would like to speak of these things, but are unable. We cannot interfere in any way."[54] This statement suggests an allegiance to some kind of cosmic ethical code and deference to human free will on this planet.

Udo's and Leo's accounts of their contact experiences are not unusual in being so positive. While there are troubling and frightful reports of abductions by "grays," reptilian, and even human-appearing visitors,[55] there are many reports of encounters with benevolent, wise, and kind beings from other planets who urge humans to end the development of nuclear weapons and offer technologies and information to end poverty and illness on Earth.[56]

Although Udo never saw the ship or its crew again, he never stopped hoping for their return.[57] In one of his handwritten accounts, he says, "everything was so clear, and still is...[O]ne time when I was in Portland, Ore. I thought I saw a man like the younger man, but by the time I had gone around the block he had gone. Then this summer when I was in Hawaii, I saw a man that looked just like him, tho it wasn't him."[58] Udo was clearly deeply affected by his encounter throughout his entire life.

I have heard tales of other sightings and even possible encounters in the Townsend area and nearby Elkhorn Mountains, but nothing with the detail that Udo recorded. Out of his desire to assist humankind by alerting it to these advanced technologies, Udo left us a remarkable legacy. Sadly, his attempts to pass on this valuable information were seemingly as futile as the assistance offered from these cosmic travelers. However, efforts towards the development of these technologies have been continued by others who recognize their value. Perhaps someday, in the not too distant future, these technologies will become available on earth.

### *Notes*

1. Jerome Clark, *The UFO Book: Encyclopedia of the Extraterrestrial* (Detroit: Visible Ink Press, 1998), 58-62.
2. Bruce S. Maccabee, "June 24, 1947: How It All Began; The Story of the Arnold Sighting," in MUFON 1997 International UFO Symposium Proceedings (Seguin, TX: Mutual UFO Network, Inc., 1997).
3. At least in historical times. There is evidence suggesting that atomic weaponry may have been used in ancient times. Ancient Hindu texts describe a terrible weapon, "a gigantic messenger of death," and there are ash-covered ruins of an ancient site near Jodhpur, India, with high levels of radiation, http://veda.wikidot.com/ancient-city-found-in-india-irradiated-from-atomic-blast/. Ancient-astronaut theorists have speculated about other possible sites of ancient nuclear blasts.
4. Warren P. Aston, "An Analysis of the 1940 Udo Wartena Case: Discovering the Alien Agenda," in *MUFON 1997 International Symposium Proceedings* (Seguin, TX: Mutual UFO Network, Inc., 1997). Also available in Warren P. Aston, *The Alien Files* (digital book only), (www.amazon.com: Amazon Digital Services, Inc.: 2012).
5. Linda Kent letter to Warren Aston, December 15, 1997.
6. Linda Kent, "The Udo Wartena Encounter," *Townsend* [Montana] *Star*, December 24, 1997: 1, 9.
7. "Alien Encounter," [Helena, MT] *Independent Record*, January 7, 1998, 6A.
8. The Great Falls Army Air Base (later Malmstrom Air Force Base) was not built until 1942; the municipal airport (Gore Field), however, was leased to the military during World War II and may have had an Army Air Corps Squadron in 1940. See http://flygtf.com/?p=History/

9. Archivist Jeffrey W. Thomas at the Ohio Congressional Archives searched Senator Glenn's records unsuccessfully for Udo's letter. "The lack of the letter in the collection does not mean the letter was never sent to Senator Glenn, but rather that the letter, and any reply sent to Mr. Wartena, were not kept as part of Senator Glenn's permanent papers." Udo was not an Ohio constituent so his letter may have been culled. Senator Glenn did not respond to my personal letters asking if he remembered receiving Udo's letter about his encounter.

10. James L. Thompson, *Aliens & UFOs; Messengers or Deceivers?* (Bountiful, UT: Horizon Publishers, 1993), 142-43. Thompson's book has a number of inaccuracies, some of which were later corrected by Tim Grossnickle in communications with Aston. Where there are contradictions in the sources, Aston and the author have deferred to Udo's handwritten accounts.

11. In the Mormon Church, also known as The Church of Jesus Christ of Latter-day Saints (or LDS Church), the Stake is an administrative division, which may include five or more wards and branches, or congregations. Usually there is only one Stake Patriarch in service at a time, whose responsibility is to give patriarchal blessings. See http://www.mormonwiki.com/Stake_patriarch/

12. Thompson, 142-43.

13. Margin notes from Tim Grossnickle to Warren Aston, written on a copy of one of the handwritten manuscripts.

14. Udo Wartena to Stanton Friedman, ca. January 1981.

15. Author telephone conversation with Dana Thelin, December 5, 2010.

16. Kent, "The Udo Wartena Encounter."

17. *Montana Standard*, September 7, 1941; January 18, 1942; April, 16, 1942.

18. Author telephone conversation with Scott Wartena, April 14, 2009.

19. Author telephone conversation with Dana Thelin, December 5, 2010.

20. "Rejection Really Hurts, UCLA Psychologists Find," *ScienceDaily*, October 10, 2003, http://www.sciencedaily.com/releases/2003/10/031010074045.htm/

21. Lee Speigel, "As U.K. Releases UFO Files, Former UFO Project Chief Admits 'Spin and Dirty Tricks' (Exclusive)," *Huffington Post*, August 17, 2011. See also Richard Dolan, *UFOs and the National Security State* (Charlottesville, VA: Hampton Roads Publishing, 2002), 129. The Robertson Panel recommended enlisting scientists, psychologists, mass media and celebrities in their debunking campaign. From all appearances, it's been highly effective.

22. Michael Billig, *Laughter and Ridicule: Towards a Social Critique of Humor* (Thousand Oaks, CA: Sage Publications, 2005).

23. Author telephone conversation with Scott Wartena.

24. Author telephone conversation with Emma Doig Morrison, August 9, 2008. BLM Mining Claim Geographic Reports, in an online database, indicate the West Boulder #1 and #2 claims were first recorded on October 13, 1950, with Ray Doig, Emma Morrison's father, and continued through the time period of Udo's return visits.

25. Author telephone conversation with Joel Flynn, August 11, 2008.

26. Tom Cottle letter to Warren Aston, May 1997.

27. Ibid.

28. Tom Cottle letter to Warren Aston, March 28, 1996. Tom Cottle asked the author to change the word "great" to "talented" during a telephone conversation, December 17, 2010.

29. Author telephone conversations with Tom Cottle, December 7 and 17, 2010.

30. Author telephone conversation with John Dell, December 15, 2010.

31. During July or August, 1973, the author was driving around on fire patrol and heard the pilot of the observation plane say to the lookout, "Did you see that?" The lookout replied, "10-4. Switch to channel 2." Neither one of them used their call numbers to identify themselves, which I believe is an FCC violation. It happens rarely, so I knew something was up. The next time I saw the lookout in person, she told me they both saw a cigar-shaped object that the observation plane felt he had to swerve to avoid, though it was moving so fast that ended up being unnecessary. They both saw the unidentified aircraft clearly. The Forest Service issued a press release saying many people had seen a meteorite that day.

32. Jim Doerter's presentation at the 1997 UFO Congress, "Fire in the Night," available at http://www.ufocongressstore.com. Doerter e-mail to author, June 29, 2012, stated that his book about lookouts and UFOs, *Out of Nowhere* was scheduled for late-2012 publication by Galde Press of Lakeville, Minnesota.

33. S. Gill Williamson, *The Observers* (Bloomington, IN: iUniverse Publishing, 2006).

34. Emma Ringer's maiden name was Doig. When the author spoke with her in 2008, she was Emma Morrison.

35. "Notice of Intent to Conduct Mining Operations On National Forest Lands," July 13, 1979, and May 22, 1980, Mining Permits File #2810, USFS Helena National Forest, Townsend Ranger District, Townsend, Montana 59644.

36. Kelly Flynn, *Goldpans, Guns & Grit: Diamond City from Territorial Gold Rush to Montana Ghost Town* (Townsend, MT: Hidden Hollow Hideaway Cattle & Guest Ranch, 2006).

37. J. Gordon Melton, ed. by James R. Lewis, *The Gods Have Landed* (Albany: State University of New York Press, 1995), 5-8.

38. Timothy Good, *Alien Base: Earth's Encounters with Extraterrestrials* (London: Century Random House UK Limited, 1998), 30-39.

39. Aston, 126.

40. See Leo Dworshak, *UFOs Are With Us: Take My Word* (Pittsburgh, PA: Dorrance Publishing Co., 2003), 60.

41. Aston, 125.

42. Dworshak, 4; Aston, 125-26.

43. Author telephone conversation with Tom Cottle, December 6, 2010. Udo drew the pictures for Cottle, who was unable to find them after returning from a mission trip.

44. Thompson, 143.

45. Author telephone conversation with Dana Thelin, December 5, 2010.

46. Margin notes on the first handwritten account (labeled "A") provided by Tim Grossnickle to Warren Aston in 1997.

47. Second handwritten account ("B") provided by Tim Grossnickle to Warren Aston.

48. See http://www.esotericscience.com/Antigravity.aspx/

49. Dworshak, 13; Aston, 126.

50. Thompson, 143.

51. Aston, 126.

52. Dworshak, 67.

53. Aston, 128.

54. Thompson, 143.

55. John Mack, *Abduction* (New York: Macmillan Publishing Co., 1994); Budd Hopkins, *Missing Time: A Documented Study of UFO Abduction* (New York: Richard Marek Publishers, 1981).

56. Many examples appear in Good, *Alien Base*; Howard Menger, *From Outer Space*

(1959; repr. New York: Pyramid Books, 1967); Bryant and Helen Reeve, *Flying Saucer Pilgrimage* (Amherst, WI: Amherst Press, 1957).

57. Thompson, 143.

58. Second handwritten account (B).

# AFTERWORD

## Now What?

One of the most common reactions to the evidence of UFOs and extraterrestrial encounters is the question, "So what do I do with it?" This is a huge dilemma.

UFO information is not easy to integrate into the prevailing views of academia, the government, or the media, and therefore into one's own internal files. For this reason, many who have witnessed UFOs choose to discard or ignore the event, a decision that makes life simpler. Yet for serious truth seekers, whether scientists or philosophers, theologians, historians, or just the curious human soul wanting to learn and grow, the evidence cannot be dismissed.

One of my UFO mentors suggested creating a mental "Hold" basket for stashing everything that challenged our credulity while continuing to gather more information. In other words, suspend judgment, neither believing nor disbelieving, until you learn more. He believes this practice produces the fastest learning curve.

In my own experience, it took some time for all this new information to settle in. There was a lot of rearranging of "mental furniture" as I tried to process and accept new information, and for many years I waffled back and forth between belief and doubt. We cannot help but be influenced by the thoughts and beliefs of "consensus reality."

My humble suggestion is to go easy, especially if this is all new, but not to walk away. Maybe there is a particular aspect of the subject that you feel drawn to explore in more detail. One of the reasons for my diligence in citing references was to leave you a trail for further exploration.

## THE COVER-UP

Many people new to the subject have trouble understanding why UFO information is suppressed; others don't believe in UFOs because they doubt the government could keep a secret of such magnitude. These issues have been addressed throughout the book, but I will summarize my response to them here.

The U.S. government and military have demonstrated their ability to keep secrets of great significance. One example was the supreme secrecy of the Manhattan Project. Even within the project itself, compartmentalization of the necessary work and "need to know" restrictions meant that most project members did not really know what they were working on. "Screen stories"— fictional disinformation disseminated to cover what was really going on—were highly effective in concealing the birth of atomic weaponry even from those involved in the project.

In the history of ufology, the sophisticated use of disinformation, ridicule, and other tactics developed by intelligence agencies for keeping secrets have been remarkably effective in convincing large numbers of people that the idea of extraterrestrial craft and visitors is silly. It is interesting that pressure to keep this information from the public (at least in recent history) does not seem to be coming from our top elected officials. In fact, some U.S. presidents have had difficulty accessing classified UFO documents.[1] Perhaps President Eisenhower's oft-quoted warning about the military-industrial complex in his 1961 farewell address may be relevant to UFO secrecy:

> In the councils of government, we must guard against the acquisition of unwarranted influence, whether sought or unsought, by the military-industrial complex. The potential for the disastrous rise of misplaced power exists and will persist.

Many ufologists point out that advanced extraterrestrial technologies could make current technologies obsolete, a change that would greatly upset current global power structures, especially those associated with fossil fuels. But, as I and others have pointed out, much government information about UFOs has been declassified and is available to those willing to look. I believe simple human fear and resistance to discomforting information is as much of a factor in the suppression of UFO evidence as any government or quasi-government policy.

## DEBUNKERS

I hope I have presented enough evidence to give you some immunity to the debunkers. There are many books debunking and dismissing UFOs and ETs. There are many more books presenting evidence of UFOs, ET encounters, and the long-term cover-up, but for some reason libraries feel they need equal numbers of both. For those looking for a vehicle to help dispel inconvenient and disturbing information, the books by the debunkers provide that. The Internet also abounds with debunking websites and bloggers who ridicule those reporting UFOs or ET encounters. Keep in mind that, over the years, some of the most influential debunkers had ties to government intelligence agencies.

Harvard astronomy professor Dr. D.H. Menzel was one of the most credentialed and famous UFO debunkers from the early 1950s until his death in 1976. After his death UFO researcher Stanton Friedman discovered that Menzel held one of the highest U.S. military security clearances, Top Secret Ultra, had a long association with the highly secret National Security Agency, and also worked for the CIA. Menzel authored or co-authored three books debunking UFOs that convinced a generation of physicists in both the U.S. and the U.S.S.R. that the subject of UFOs had no scientific legitimacy, and he personally attacked those who thought otherwise. He was clearly passionate in his crusade.

Now we know he led a double life, which helps explain how he summarily ignored all witness testimony and concocted fantastical explanations to dismiss well-documented UFO sightings.[2] Although clearly a very intelligent man, he was not infallible; he flatly declared that "black holes" at the center of galaxies were a myth.[3]

Knowledge of the history of UFO debunking should alert us that there may be paid debunkers out there. The study of ufology is cluttered with disinformation "noise," honed and perfected by intelligence agencies. This makes the study of UFOs an advanced course in truth seeking and discernment. These are skills worth developing. And not all naysayers are professional debunkers.

## AUTHORITATIVE PERSUASION AND SCIENCE

We cannot all be experts on everything, so we end up accepting the judgments and opinions of those we presume to be experts. Some scientists have come to the conclusion that humans, including many scientists themselves, are more influenced by "authoritative persuasion" (what the "experts" say) than trust their own examination of the evidence, especially on topics that question dominant paradigms.[4] In the eighteenth century, the French Academy of Science stubbornly denied the mounting evidence that meteorites fell from the sky. In deference to the French "authorities," museum curators all over Europe actually ridded their collections of meteorites.[5] The scientists of the day did not yet have a satisfying scientific explanation for rocks falling from the sky and were affronted by popular superstition about heavenly interventions. In their defense, intractable religious belief was (and still is) a problem for science. When presented with inconvenient evidence, dogmatic science and religion both say, "This doesn't fit with what we already know, therefore it can't be true."[6]

Those of us who believe in UFOs face a similar kind of resistance from many quarters of the scientific community. The problem is compounded by the confiscation of or tampering with the physical evidence of UFOs (such as the disappearance of the "hovering" footage from the Mariana film). However, scientific discovery—not to mention invention and innovation of all kinds—are dependent on people willing to think beyond accepted norms and understanding. In the unfettered thinking space outside the current box (that extraterrestrial spacecraft are scientifically impossible and therefore do not exist), there are many extremely bright and highly educated people working on understanding and integrating this complex and challenging phenomenon. You can be assured they are not receiving grants from the National Science Foundation, NASA, the military, or the aerospace or petroleum industry. They pursue their understanding on their own, out of their own love of truth and their concerns about the implications of the evidence. Many believe this study may offer hope for mankind and the planet.

## The Question of Human Readiness

Public awareness of the UFO and extraterrestrial phenomenon may depend on the extraterrestrials themselves. Witness accounts, including that of Udo Wartena (Chapter 6), report that at least some ET visitors try to avoid being seen and that the encounters are accidental. Why don't ETs make themselves obvious? Some contactees say the ETs have told them that humans are not yet ready for entry into the greater galactic community of more evolved civilizations. It may be that human civilization needs to reach a higher level of cooperation and moral development before "graduating" to peaceful galactic relations. Or perhaps a critical mass of the earth's population needs to be mentally and psychologically prepared for ETs so as not to react in panic and violence when ETs publicly "arrive."

Contact with aliens is a fearful proposition to many people, especially if we project on extraterrestrials our own human history of ruthless conquerors and brutal subjugation. But many accounts, such as those of Leo Dworshak and Udo Wartena, suggest that at least some of the visitors are as morally and spiritually advanced as their superior technologies, and that they could be allies of humanity at a crucial time in our future.

What we as humans most fear is the unknown. It may be up to us individually to educate and prepare ourselves for contact before the extraterrestrials are willing to make themselves known. To face this situation with as much knowledge and collective wisdom as possible, I hope I can convince others that educating yourselves on the subject is a worthwhile investment of your time. At times it can be a wild ride, but it's actually been an incredibly wide-ranging and gratifying education.

The deeper I delve into ufology, the more I see how it impinges on so many other topics. Along the way, I've increased my understanding of astronomy, physics and quantum physics, military and political history, government secrecy, advanced energy technologies, multi-dimensional and time-travel theory, psychology, hypnotherapy, mind control, consciousness studies, altered states of consciousness, extended human capacities (such as telepathy and remote viewing), geometry and sacred geometry, Native American teachings, pictographs and petroglyphs, art history, archaeology, world geography, anthropology, mythology and folklore, ancient texts and civilizations, religious history, the Bible and ancient texts of other religions, philosophy, epistemology (how we come to know what we know), and critical thinking. I find the subject endlessly fascinating and edifying. In my experience, this field is the most challenging and exhilarating frontier humans face, and I believe it is our future.

It is my hope you will be willing to engage in conversation with friends and family about UFOs. I have been astounded at how often, when I introduce the subject, people tell of their sightings or those of close friends and family. As a result I have heard some amazing stories from highly credible people. It's also not unusual for them to end their accounts by confessing, "I've never told this to anyone before." Everyone who shares their stories of sightings or encounters creates a little more space for public discourse and the sharing of information.

In general, I find the topic is getting less taboo as more people encounter the evidence. Even mainstream astronomers are considering the idea of intelligent life on the many newly discovered planets. Conferences and scientific articles in the "hot" new field of astrobiology are popping up all over. Mainstream academic science is at least considering the possibility that other forms of intelligent life could be "out there, somewhere," if not here and now. Some day, as more and more people who have had sightings and experiences feel free to share them, the lid will come off.

## LOOK UP!

Once my science-mind was convinced that UFOs were a real phenomenon, I began watching the skies and learning the stars and constellations, especially those identified by visitors in the contactee literature as home-star systems. Initially, I made the same mistakes many people make when skywatching. My advice is to learn to identify the appearance of satellites, the International Space Station, and conventional aircraft, especially at night. Bright stars and planets are often reported as UFOs. They can look quite bright, multicolored and twinkly, but they don't move. Balloons and lighted Chinese lanterns are often confused with UFOs, so notice the wind direction and consider these objects when you see something moving with the wind. UFOs that fly on a straight or curvilinear trajectory at a consistent speed are more difficult to separate from conventional aircraft, balloons, and meteorites. Erratic flight, sharp turns, rapid starts and stops, sudden appearance or disappearance, and dramatic changes in brightness are all more typical of nighttime UFO sightings. Certain shapes are consistently reported in daytime sightings, including disc-shaped, egg-shaped, bell- or hat-shaped, cigar-shaped, spherical, and amorphous balls of exceptionally bright light. Familiarity with both conventional flying objects and witness accounts of UFOs will increase your chances of actual sightings.

I am aware of several credible Montana residents who are currently getting videos and photos of UFOs in both the Helena and Great Falls areas. At some point I hope to study those cases more closely and potentially share that information. In the meantime, you might want to keep your camera (or cellphone) ready.

There are two major organizations that accept UFO reports on their websites and maintain long-term databases:

NUFORC, http://www.nuforc.org/—The National UFO Reporting Center has been maintained by Peter Davenport for many years. Reports can be entered online or with their telephone hotline (206) 722-3000 for sightings within the last week. Since June 2012, they have experienced a tripling of monthly UFO reports, and caution that they are not able to screen reports as carefully as in the past. They advise discretion in use of the database, as many of the reports may be conventionally explainable.

MUFON, http://www.mufon.com/—The Mutual UFO Network is currently the largest and oldest UFO organization in the world that publishes a monthly journal, holds an annual symposium, has a structured field investigator training program, and maintains a computerized and standardized UFO database. Their reporting form can be found at http://www.mufon.com/reportufo.html.

The "Best UFO Resources" website, http://www.hyper.net/ufo.htmlwebsite/, offers tips on what to pay attention to in a sighting and how to maximize the scientific value of a UFO report. They also offer professional suggestions on maximizing the credibility of UFO video footage to distinguish it from computer-generated images. It's also a good general information website for those beginning UFO research on the web, with links to the most reputable UFO websites. For someone new to the subject, there is a dizzying array of choices, and Internet search engines do not distinguish trustworthy sites.

## To Be Continued

When I began work on this book, I was astounded at the vast literature on this subject, even when I narrowed my scope to Montana. Much more deserves documentation in the annals of Montana history, including such subjects as Native American UFO and ET stories, a catalog of well documented multiple-witness accounts, historical sightings from around the state, an update on what we know about cattle mutilations, and the presentation of more recent evidence. The journey will continue.

If you have experiences of sightings or contact, especially multiple-witness events and/or photos or films taking place in Montana, I would be interested in receiving your reports or copies of your NUFORC or MUFON reports at this email: joanbird@mt.net, or by a letter in care of Riverbend Publishing, P.O. Box 5833, Helena, MT 59604.

### Notes

1. UFO Researcher Grant Cameron has researched documents shedding light on what each president from Franklin D. Roosevelt to Barack Obama knew about UFOs. http://www.presidentialufo.com/
2. Jerome Clark, *The UFO Book: Encyclopedia of the Extraterrestrial* (Detroit: Visible Ink Press, 1998), 386-396.
3. http://en.wikipedia.org/wiki/Donald_Howard_Menzel/
4. Dean Radin, *Entangled Minds: Extrasensory Experiences in a Quantum Reality* (New York: Paraview Pocket Books, 2006), 278-79.
5. Michael Polanyi, *Personal Knowledge: Towards a Post-Critical Philosophy* (Chicago: University of Chicago Press, 1974), 138.
6. Elizabeth Lloyd Mayer, *Extraordinary Knowing* (New York: Bantam Dell, 2007), 103-104.

# BIBLIOGRAPHY

Andrews, Colin. *Circular Evidence.* London: Bloomsbury, 1991.

————. *The Andrews Catalog: 2011 Special Edition.* New York: Archive House Media, 2011.

————. *The Assessment: A Two-Year Investigation into Human-made Crop Circles in England During 1999-2000.* New York: Archive House Media, 2011.

Aston, Warren P. "An Analysis of the Udo Wartena Case: Discovering the Alien Agenda," in *MUFON 1997 International UFO Symposium Proceedings.* Seguin, TX: Mutual UFO Network, Inc., 1997.

————. *Alien Files.* Amazon Digital Services, 2012. Kindle e-book.

Axline, Jon. "Montana's Flying Saucer Film (Or How the Great Falls Baseball Team Got its Name). *Montana Magazine,* May/June 2008, 29-30.

Baker, Robert M.L. Jr., "Observational Evidence of Anomalistic Phenomena," in *Journal of the Astronautical Sciences* 15 (January/February 1968): 31-36.

————. *Photogrammetric Analysis of the 'Montana Film' Tracking Two UFOs.* Santa Monica, CA: Douglas Aircraft Company, 1956.

Barrow, Robert. "UFO Revisited" in *Official UFO Magazine,* February 1977. Also available on the NICAP website http://www.nicap.org/ufochop1.htm

Billig, Michael. *Laughter and Ridicule: Towards a Social Critique of Humor.* Thousand Oaks, CA: Sage Publications, 2005.

Breccia, Stefano. *Mass Contact.* Bloomington, IN: AuthorHouse, 2009.

Carey, Thomas J., et al. *Witness to Roswell: Unmasking the Government's Biggest Cover-up.* Rev. and exp. ed. Pompton Plains, NJ: New Page Books, 2009.

Clark, Jerome. *The UFO Book: Encyclopedia of the Extraterrestrial.* Detroit: Visible Ink Press, 1998.

Condon, Edward U. *Final Report of the Scientific Study of Unidentified Flying Objects Conducted by the University of Colorado Under Contract to the United States Air Force.* New York: Bantam Books, 1969.

Corso, Col. Philip J. (Ret.). *The Day After Roswell.* New York: Pocket Books, 1997.

Craig, Roy. *UFOs: An Insider's View of the Official Quest for Evidence.* North Denton, TX: University of North Texas Press, 1995.

Doerter, Jim. *Out of Nowhere*. Lakeville, MN: Galde Press, 2012.

Dolan, Richard, Bryce Zabel and Jim Marrs. *A.D.—After Disclosure: When the Government Finally Reveals the Truth About Alien Contact*. Pompton Plains, NJ: New Page Books, 2012.

_____. *UFOs and the National Security State: Chronology of a Cover-Up*. Charlottesville, VA: Hampton Roads Publishing, 2002.

_____. *UFOs and the National Security State: The Cover-Up Exposed*. Rochester, NY: Keyhole Publishing Co. , 2009.

Donovan, Roberta & Keith Wolverton. *Mystery Stalks the Prairie*. Raynesford, MT: T.H.A.R. Institute, 1976.

Dworshak, Leo. *UFOs Are With Us: Take My Word*. Pittsburgh, PA: Dorrance Publishing Co., 2003.

Fawcett, Lawrence and Barry J. Greenwood, *The UFO Cover-Up: What the Government Won't Say*. Old Tappan, NJ: Fireside/Simon & Schuster, 1992.

Flynn, Kelly. *Goldpans, Guns & Grit: Diamond City: from Territorial Gold Rush to Montana Ghost Town*. Townsend, MT: Hidden Hollow Hideaway Cattle and Guest Ranch, 2006.

Fowler, Raymond E. *Casebook of a UFO Investigator: A Personal Memoir*. Englewood Cliffs, NJ: Prentice Hall, 1981.

Friedman, Stanton T. and Kathleen Marden. *Captured! The Barney and Betty Hill UFO Experience*. Franklin Lakes, NJ: The Career Press, 2007.

Friedman, Stanton T., Dr. Edgar Mitchell and Dr. Bruce Maccabbee. *Flying Saucers and Science: A Scientist Investigates the Mysteries of UFOs: Interstellar Travel, Crashes and Government Cover-Ups*. Pompton Plains, NJ: New Page Books, 2008.

Good, Timothy. *Above Top Secret: The Worldwide U.F.O. Cover-Up*. New York: William Morrow & Company, 1988.

_____. *Alien Base: Earth's Encounters with Extraterrestrials*. London: Century Random House UK, 1998.

Greenwood, Barry. "On the Question of Tampering with the 1950 Great Falls UFO Film," *U.F.O. Historical Review #7*, September 2000. www.greenwoodufoarchive.com

Greer, Steven M. *Extraterrestrial Contact: The Evidence and Implications*. Afton, VA: Crossing Point Inc., 1999.

Hansen, Terry. *The Missing Times: News Media Complicity in the UFO Cover-up*. Bloomington, IN: Xlibris Corporation, 2000.

Harris, Paola. *Connecting the Dots: Making Sense of the UFO Phenomenon*. Columbus, NC: Granite Publishing, 2005.

_____. *Exopolitics: How Does One Speak to a Ball of Light*. Bloomington, IN: Author House, 2007.

_____. *Exopolitics: All of the Above*. Bloomington, IN: Author House, 2009.

_____. 2012. "An Interview with Kim Arnold: Daughter to the 1947 UFO Wave Witness," *Open Minds Magazine* 13 (April/May 2012.

Hart, John. *Cosmic Commons: Spirit, Science, and Space*. Eugene, OR: Wipf & Stock, 2013.

Haselhoff, Eltjo H., Ph.D. *The Deepening Complexity of Crop Circles: Scientific Research and Urban Legends*. Berkeley, CA: Frog, Ltd., 2001.

Hastings, Robert. *UFOs and Nukes: Extraordinary Encounters at Nuclear Weapons Sites*. Bloomington, IN: Author House, 2008.

Hill, Betty. *A Common Sense Approach to UFOs*. Portsmouth, NH: the author, 1995.

Hopkins, Budd. *Intruders: The Incredible Visitations at Copley Woods*. New York, NY: Random House, 1987.

_____. *Missing Time: A Documented Study of UFO Abduction*. New York: Richard Marek Publishers, 1981.

Howe, Linda Moulton. *Glimpses of Other Realities Volume II: High Strangeness*. Jamison, PA: LMH Productions, 1998.

_____. *Mysterious Lights and Crop Circles*. New Orleans, LA: Paper Chase Press, 2000.

Hynek, J. Allen. *The UFO Experience: A Scientific Inquiry*. Chicago: Henry Regnery Company, 1972.

_____. *The Hynek UFO Report*. New York: Dell Publishing, 1977.

Jacobs, David Michael. *The UFO Controversy in America*. Bloomington, IN: University Press, 1975.

_____. *UFOs and Abductions: Challenging the Borders of Knowledge*. Lawrence, KS: University Press of Kansas, 2000.

Kaminski, Bob. *Lying Wonders, Evil Encounters of a Close Kind*. Mulkilteo, WA: WinePress Publishing, 1996.

Kean, Leslie. *UFOs: Generals, Pilots and Government Officials Go on the Record*. New York: Three Rivers Press, 2011.

Kent, Linda. "The Udo Wartena Encounter," *Townsend* [MT] *Star*, December 24, 1997: 1, 9.

Keyhoe, Maj. Donald. E. (Ret.) "Flying Saucers are Real," *True* (January 1950): 11-13, 83-87.

_____. *The Flying Saucers Are Real*. New York: Fawcett Publications, 1950.

_____. *Flying Saucers from Outer Space*. New York: Henry Holt & Company, 1953.

Kidston, Martin. "A History of Montana's Alien Encounters," [Helena, MT] *Independent Record*, October 29, 2000.

_____. "Eyes on the Skies: Helena man a true believer in UFOs," [Helena, MT] *Independent Record*, April 25, 2003.

_____. "Author researches stories of alien encounters," [Helena, MT] *Independent Record*, June 20, 2004: 7A.

Klass, Philip. *UFOs Explained*. New York: Vintage Books, 1976.

Lorenzen, Coral E. *Flying Saucers: The Startling Evidence of the Invasion from Outer Space*. New York: New American Library, 1996.

_____ and Jim. *Flying Saucer Occupants*. New York: New American Library, 1967.

_____. *UFOs: The Whole Story*. New York: New American Library, 1967.

Maccabee, Bruce. *UFO-FBI Connection: The Secret History of the Government's Cover-Up*. St. Paul, MN: Llewellyn Publications, 2000.

Mack, John. *Abduction*. New York: Macmillan Publishing Company, 1994.

_____. *Passport to the Cosmos*. New York: Crown Publishers, 1999.

Marcel, Jesse Jr. and Linda Marcel. *The Roswell Legacy: The Untold Story of the First Military Officer at the 1947 Crash Site*. Franklin Lakes, NJ: Career Press, 2009.

Mayer, Elizabeth Lloyd. *Extraordinary Knowing*. New York: Bantam Dell, 2007.

Melton, J. Gordon; ed. by James R. Lewis. *The Gods Have Landed*. Albany: State University of New York Press, 1995.

Menger, Howard. *From Outer Space*. Repr. New York: Pyramid Books, 1967.

Menzel, Donald H. *Flying Saucers*. Ann Arbor, MI: University Microfilms International, 1969.

_____ and Lyle G. Boyd. *The World of Flying Saucers: A Scientific Examination of a Major Myth of the Space Age*. New York: Doubleday, 1963.

_____ and Ernest H. Taves. *The UFO Enigma: The Definitive Explanation of the UFO Phenomenon*. New York: Doubleday, 1977.

Pringle, Lucy. *Crop Circles: the Greatest Mystery of Modern Time*. London: Thorsons, An Imprint of HarperCollins Publishers, 1999.

Project Blue Book. PBB files were declassified under the Freedom of Information Act, and are located at the National Archives, Washington, D.C. Files may be accessed in the reading room, or purchased at http://www.archives.gov/foia/ufos.html/. Many files are available on the Internet, for example at: http://www.bluebookarchive.org/

Radin, Dean. *Entangled Minds.* New York: Paraview Pocket Books, 2006.

Randle, Kevin. *Project Blue Book Exposed.* New York: Marlowe & Co., 1967.

Reeve, Bryant and Helen. *Flying Saucer Pilgrimage.* Amherst, WI: Amherst Press, 1957.

Ruppelt, Captain Edward J. *The Report on Unidentified Flying Objects.* 1956; Seattle, WA: Pacific Publishing Studio, 2011.

Salas, Robert, and James Klotz. *Faded Giant.* Charleston, SC: BookSurge, LLC, 2005.

Salla, Michael E. *Exposing U.S. Government Policies on Extraterrestrial Life.* Kealakekua, HI: Exopolitics Institute, 2009.

Saunders and Harkins. *UFOs? Yes: Where the Condon Committee Went Wrong.* New York: Signet Books, New American Library, 1968.

Silva, Freddy. *Secrets in the Fields.* Charlottesville, VA: Hampton Roads Publishing, 2002.

Speigel, Lee. "As U.K. Releases UFO Files, Former UFO Project Chief Admits 'Spin and Dirty Tricks' (Exclusive)," *Huffington Post,* August 17, 2011.

Stanford, Ray. *Socorro "Saucer" in a Pentagon Pantry.* Austin, TX: Blueapple Books, 1967.

Sturrock, Peter A. *Evaluation of the Condon Report on the Colorado UFO Project: SUIPR Report #599,* Stanford, CA: Institute for Plasma Research, Stanford University, 1974.

_____. *The UFO Enigma: A New Review of the Physical Evidence.* New York, NY: Warner Books, Inc, 2000.

Swords, Michael, et al. *UFOs and Government: An Historical Inquiry.* San Antonio, TX: Anomalist Books, LLC, 2012.

Thompson, James L. *Aliens & UFOs: Messengers or Deceivers?* Bountiful, UT: Horizon Publishers, 1993.

Thompson, Keith. *Angels and Aliens: UFOs and the Mythic Imagination.* New York: Addison-Wesley Publishing, 1991.

Vallee, Jacques. *Anatomy of a Phenomenon: UFO's in Space.* New York: Ballantine Books, 1965.

Vallee, Jacques and Janine. 1966. *Challenge to Science: The UFO Enigma.* New York: Ballantine Books, 1966.

# INDEX

Adams, William 58
Air Defense Command (ADC) 45
Air Force, U.S.: Air Force Office of
Special Investigations (AFOSI)
26; Air Intelligence Service
Squadron 45; Air Materiel
Command (AMC) 22, 26; Army
Air Forces 22, 78; Directorate of
Intelligence 29; Directorate of
Intelligence (DI) 26, 29, 58–59.
*See also* Project Blue Book, Project
Sign;
Air Materiel Command. *See* Wright-
Patterson Air Force Base
Aldrich, Jan 23
Andrews, Colin 130, 139
APRO (Aerial Phenomena Research
Organization) 150
Armstrong, Mary Lou 60
Arnold, Kenneth 21, 33, 66, 189,
206–209
Aston, Warren 189–190, 201, 204
Bahny, Bill 148
Baker, Robert M.L. 50, 60
Barrow, Robert 47–53
Bay of Pigs invasion 81–82
Beer-Lambert Principle 125
Bell, Art 92
Blanchard, William 78–79
BLT Research Team 123
Blue Book. *See* Project Blue Book
Boeing Corporation 92–93
Bower, Doug 122–123, 133
Bragalia, Anthony 157–158
Brown, Joseph M. 109
Brynildsen, John P. 26–28, 65
Burke, John 123–145
Byrnes, Arthur Jr. 155–156
Canyon Ferry (MT) UFO incident
147–160
Capron, J. Rand 122
Carlson, Eric 89–90
Cavitt, Sheridan 78

Chavez, M.S. 154–155
Chernovshev, Igor 111
Chop, Albert M. 47–51, 52, 53–54
Chorley, Dave 122–123, 133
CIA (Central Intelligence Agency)
26, 36
Clark, Jerome 60
Close Encounters of the Third Kind
(CE-III) 157
Cole, Alden Stockwell 112
Cole, Martin 112–113
Colgate, Stirling 158–159
Colorado UFO Project. *See* Condon
Committee
Compton, Roy 130
Condon Committee 53–64;
aftermath of 64–65
Condon, Edward U. 54–56, 61–63;
and "trick memo" 59–60
Condon Report 61–64
Congress, U.S.; UFO Symposium
60–64
Conner, William 155
Conrad, Diane 127
Considine, Bob 34–35, 35
Cottle, Mike 202
Cottle, Thomas D. 196, 201, 206
Craig, Roy 56–58, 59, 91
Crawford, Don 92
Crop circles 119–145; scientific
studies of 123–129
CUFON (Computer UFO Network)
115
CUFOS (Center for UFO Studies)
203
CymaGlyph 139
Dalich, Tony 32, 56
Dames, Ed 137
Davis, Linda 147–148
Davis, Thom 148, 150
Delgado, Pat 139
Dell, John 202–203
Disclosure Project 98–99, 132

Doerter, Jim 203
Doig, Ray 204
Donovan, Roberta 105
Dworshak, Leo 161–186, 205–208
Dworshak, Mike 161–165, 176
Echo flight. See Minuteman missiles
    and UFOs (1967)
Edelstein, David N. 35
Eldridge, George 90
Ellsworth Air Force Base UFO
    incident 105, 107–108
Ennis (MT) UFO landings 176–177
F-94 aircraft 42, 50, 64
F-117 aircraft 110
FBI 26, 157–158
Figel, Walt 89–90
Flittner, Diane 148
Flittner, Linda 148
Flynn, Frank 201
Flynn, Joel 200
Flynn, Kelly 204
Flynn, Rose 201
Fournet, Dewey J. Jr. 23, 40, 44,
    51–52
Fowler, Ray 90–91, 105
Friedman, Stanton 79, 196–197
Furlong, E.P. 56, 66
Glenn, John 190, 195, 206
Goodrich, Jeff 110
Good, Timothy 184, 204
Great Falls (MT); Air Force base 19.
    See Malmstrom Air Force Base;
    baseball team 19, 38–39, 68;
    UFO incident 15–76
Greene, Clarence 46–47, 52
Greenwood, Barry 64
Greer, Steven 132
Gregory, George T. 48
Grossnickle, Robert 196–197
Grossnickle, Tim 196–197
Hansen, Terry 106
Harder, James A. 60
Hartmann, William K. 63
Hastings, Robert 102, 111, 113–114,
    116
Hawkins, Gerald 133, 136
Holder, Richard T. 155

Howe, Linda Moulton 111
Hughes, David 105–106
Hynek, J. Allen; and Minuteman
    missile UFOs 102; and Montana
    Movie 43–44, 52–53, 60, 63–64;
    and Socorro incident 151–160;
    and Udo Wartena 203
ICCRA (Independent Crop Circle
    Researchers Association) 138,
    141, 142
Jamison, Michael 121
Janssen, Bert 136
Jenny, Hans 139
Johnson, Gilbert (Gil) 135
Kalispell (MT) crop circles; in
    1998 119–123; Mercedes Spins
    136–138
Kaminski, Bob 92–94
Keyhoe, Donald 24–25, 54, 60
King, Clynt 134–135
King, Ken 134
Klass, Philip J. 61, 67, 157
Klotz, James 92–93, 115
Koenig, Herb 121, 135
Krogstad, Dave 96–97
Lawrence, Tom 120
Levengood, William C. 123–145
Lorenzen, Coral and Jim 150
Low, Robert 54–55, 59–60
Lytle, Larry 148
McDonald, James 55, 56, 59–62
Mack, John 158
Malmstrom Air Force Base 114–115;
    early UFO event 105–106;
    missile/UFO incident of 1967
    84–118
Marcel, Jesse Jr. 78–79
Marcel, Jesse Sr. 78, 182
Mariana, Claretta Dunn 19
Mariana, Michele 68
Mariana, Nick 15–19, 26–28, 30–31,
    35–36, 57; in later years 65–67
Mariana, Nick III 68
Mariana, Nick Jr. 67
Marquez, Peter 37–39
Meiwald, Fred 85–88
Menzel, Donald H. 61

"Mercedes Spins" crop circle 136–137

Middlemas, Dave 148, 150

Mills, John W. III 107–118

Minot Air Force Base UFO incident 103–104

Minuteman missiles and UFOs (1967) 77–118; missile specifications 84–85

Mississaugas of the New Credit First Nation 134

Montana Movie 15–76

Moore, Les 115

Moore, Richard 95

Morrison, Emma Doig 200

MUFON (Mutual UFO Network) 91, 100, 110, 189

Nader, Bud 95

National Press Club 111

Native Americans and crop circles 133–134

Naval Intelligence, Office of (ONI); 29

Neufeld, Harold L. 148–149

Newhouse, Delbert 32. See also Utah Movie

NICAP (National Investigations Committee on Aerial Phenomena) 25, 54–55, 59–60, 91, 94–95

Norris (MT) UFO landings 176–177

O'Connell, James 26

Office of Naval Intelligence 29

Ohio: Paint Creek Island Crop Circle; 136–137, 139

ONI 29

OOAMA (Ogden Air Material Command support facility) 93–94

Oscar flight. See Minuteman missiles and UFOs (1967)

Page, Thornton 43

Paun, Paula 97

"Pendulum arrow" crop circle (2000) 137

Peterson, Don 93–94

Plantonev, Vladamir 111

Project Blue Book 16, 27, 39, 45, 64, 103; statistics 103

Project Grudge 24–25, 26, 30–31, 36, 103, 152; Report 25–26, 29

Project Saucer 22–24

Project Sign 22–24, 29–30, 103

Purdy, Ken 24

Quintanilla, Hector 102, 149

Ramey, Roger M. 79

Randle, Kevin 103–104, 158

Raunig, Virginia 18, 56–57

Reid, John Stuart 139–140

Reynolds, Robert C. Jr. 129

Ringer, Emma 204

Robertson, H.P. 39–46, 43

Robertson Panel 39–46

Rockefeller, Laurance 128, 130

Roswell incident 78–80

Roush, J. Edward 60

Ruppelt, Edward J.; and Montana Movie 16, 22, 25, 32–33, 36, 39–42, 52; on Project Blue Book 45, 46, 52–53, 53; on Project Grudge 24

Rust, Barbara 150

Rust, Pete 148, 150

Sagan, Carl 60

Salas, Robert 85–89, 97–101, 115–116

Samford, John A. 37

Sappington Junction (MT) UFO landings 176–177

Saunders, David R. 56

Schuur, David 104–105

Scientific Advisory Panel on Unidentified Flying Objects. See Robertson Panel

Seitz, Frederick 62

Shallett, Sydney 24

Shelby (MT) UFO incident 106–107

Silva, Freddy 123, 132–133

Sneider, Robert R. 22

Snowflake (AZ) incident 168–169

Socorro (NM) incident 151–160

South Dakota: Killdeer incident 161–186

Stinebaugh, Lloyd 106

Sturrock, Peter 63

Sullivan, Clifton T. 21, 66
Swords, Michael 64
Talbott, Nancy 123–145
Tennessee: Madisonville crop circle (2007); 138
Thelin, Dana Wartena 198–199
Tremonton (UT) incident 32, 41
Tupton, Mary Alice 189
Twining, Nathan F. 22
U.S. Air Force Project Blue Book. See Project Blue Book
Utah Movie 32, 41
Vandenberg, Hoyt 22
Voyagers baseball team 68
Walton, Travis 168–169
Warden, Bob 66
Warden, O.S. 66
Warren AFB UFO incident 102, 113–114
Wartena, Donna Stoddard 197–198
Wartena, Scott 198

Wartena, Udo contact case 187–212
Waterton Lakes National Park UFO sighting 96
Watt, Melody 131–132, 135, 137, 140
Weapons System Evaluation Group 39
Whitefish (MT) crop circle (1999) 133–135
Williams, Kenneth C. 94–95
Wilson, Jeffrey 134
Wiltshire (England) crop circles 132–133, 137–138, 140–141
Wolverton, Keith 105
Wright-Patterson Air Force Base 22, 27, 28–29, 103
Wuerthner, John 56
Zadick, Ed 66
Zamora, Lonnie 152–160
Zimmerman, Gordon 202

# ABOUT THE AUTHOR

Joan Bird moved to Montana in 1973 to pursue graduate studies in zoology at the University of Montana. In 1983, she completed her Ph.D. on inter-island variation in West Indian finches. Joan worked as a conservation biologist for the Montana Environmental Information Center, The Nature Conservancy, and Montana Department of Fish, Wildlife and Parks. She has also worked as a fire lookout in both Washington and Montana. Joan freelanced as a nature interpretation writer and has written numerous articles for scientific and conservation publications. Actively involved in women's empowerment, she is currently a columnist for *Crone Magazine*. A lifelong student of unexplained phenomena and long-time member of the Institute of Noetic Sciences, she has worked as a community educator and change agent.